ASIA'S STAR BRANDS

ASIA'S STAR BRANDS

Paul Temporal

John Wiley & Sons (Asia) Pte Ltd

This publication is designed to provide accurate and authoritative information with regard to the subject matter covered. It is sold with the understanding that the Publisher is not engaged in rendering professional services. If professional advice or other expert assistance is required, the services of a competent professional person should be sought.

Other Wiley Editorial Offices

John Wiley & Sons, Inc., 111 River Street, Hoboken, NJ 07030, USA
John Wiley & Sons Ltd, The Atrium, Southern Gate, Chichester PO19 BSQ, England
John Wiley & Sons (Canada) Ltd, 5353 Dundas Street West, Suite 400, Toronto, Ontario M9B 6H8, Canada
John Wiley & Sons Australia Ltd, 42 McDougall Street, Milton, Queensland 4064, Australia
Wiley-VCH, Boschstrasse 12, D-69469 Weinheim, Germany

Library of Congress Cataloging-in-Publication Data:

ISBN-13 978-0-470-82156-5
ISBN-10 0-470-82156-6

Typeset in 11/13 point, Sabon by KnowledgeWorks Global Ltd.
Printed in Singapore by Markono Print Media Pte Ltd.
10 9 8 7 6 5 4 3 2 1

To my daughter—Maria Anne Temporal
A rising star and a wonderful person

CONTENTS

ACKNOWLEDGMENTS

Many organizations and individuals have helped in the creation of this book as always. My thanks to all the companies featured for the information provided, and special thanks to the following people:

Akshay Singh
Banyong Pongpanich
Chris E. Kidd
Dato'Seri Chew Weng Khak
Dixon Chew
Lee Hwee Meng
Lee Yew Weng
Mohammed Azhar Osman Khairuddin
Mohamed K. Bin Hareb Al Muhairy
Mohammed Reza Abdul Mubin
Premeeta Kour Nijhar
Richard C.M. Wong
Ron Sim
Shirley Poo
Suhaimi Halim
Tan Cheng Cheng
Tony Fernandes
Tunku Siti Raudzoh Tunku Ibrahim
Udaya Indrarathna

I would also like to say a big thank you to those in Temporal Brand Consulting who have been a great source of support, ideas and material, especially

Jamal Mohd. Aris
Ornuma Prayoonrattana
Mazatul Affendy
Rachel Wai Han Shiang
Wong Puei Ee
Shilin Ong
Sue Ann Chew

To Nick Wallwork, Janis Soo and all at John Wiley who have made me feel like a family member over the years, thanks once again for the opportunity and professional assistance. Special thanks to Robyn Flemming, who broke all speed records for editing without compromising quality.

INTRODUCTION

This book is, in its own way, a celebration of Asian branding.

For decades now, Asian companies and institutions have lagged behind their Western counterparts in the creation, development, and management of their brands. The main reasons for this fact, from a corporate standpoint, have been to do with the pursuit of short-term profits at the expense of investment in brand over the longer term. This has been supported by the skepticism of many boards of directors as to the return on brand investment—brand rewards being somewhat difficult to quantify—coupled with a mistaken view that brand building is largely accomplished by advertising, promotion, and logo design. Thankfully, these long-held views of top managers are now changing.

In *Branding in Asia* (Singapore: John Wiley & Sons, 2001), I outlined the fundamentals of branding for companies either Asian or interested in breaking into Asia, and highlighted some Asian brands that were heading in the right direction. I am happy to say that Asian branding has improved in recent years, with more and more companies using brand as a strategic weapon and, importantly, treating their brands as valuable, though intangible, assets.

Unfortunately, it is still true to say that Western brands dominate the global and Asian market landscape in most, if not all, industries. But Asian brands are fighting back, not just by building brands to defend their markets from increased competition due to the deregulatory effects of AFTA (ASEAN Free Trade Area) and WTO (World Trade Organization) legislation, but also in moving out into international markets to attack the competition. Some are moving quickly, others more cautiously, yet the steady rise to prominence of Asian brands continues.

Powerful economic shifts have occurred that have stimulated this behavior. Principally, this has been seen in the rise of China as a global industrial powerhouse, and in the aggressive brand-building activities of other countries such as South Korea. The use of brand as the main weapon of corporate strategy has been fueled by ambition and the deregulation of markets. Indeed, the focal point for investment among the Western countries is Asia, and China in particular. With its 1.3 billion people, an increasing level of consumer disposable income, and an enthusiastic willingness to trade, China is now the world's magnet for business development.

It is my view that we will witness the Asian brand revolution led by China over the next 10–15 years. As a nation, China is branding itself using several massive initiatives such as Formula One, the 2008 Olympic Games, and the World Expo in 2010 to showcase its culture and achievements. The government of China is not just developing its brand image at a national level, either; it has earmarked many companies for assistance in gaining global brand status in the future. Other Asian countries are trying hard to follow the pace, and many are offering educational and financial assistance to help companies in their branding efforts.

Furthermore, Asian companies are no longer hampered in brand development by low levels of quality, with world-class products appearing from most countries. This in itself has been a factor in the lack of brand leadership in the past, as strong brands must have a consistently high quality of product and service. Coupled with this, the costs of production are still favorable in Asia, and many Western brands outsource production to countries such as China, Malaysia, and Vietnam.

But while cost leadership and high quality levels are vital for successful branding, it is the image-building process that is the decisive factor. In this respect, some Asian brands are hampered by their country of origin; for example, the "Made in China" tag on consumer goods still has a debilitating effect, generating perceptions of cheapness and low quality. In the way that Japanese companies have successfully done, some Asian companies will have to work hard to change such perceptions.

THE BRAND CASES AND INDUSTRIES

I have not included some brands that deserve to be in the book, such as Toyota (this brand is now regarded as the world's number one manufacturer of motor vehicles and is a truly giant, global brand) and other Japanese brands such as Canon and Nikon, which have been around for some time and continue to occupy prominent positions. Brands such as Sony are not faring so well. Sony appears to be unfocused and unable to manage its brand properly. But the Japanese big brands are here to stay and much has been written about them.

Rather than write about these brands, I have instead concentrated on those brands that are coming up in the world from positions of difficulty, and/or where their brand images have, in the past, not occupied top positions in people's minds.

Connected with this point, I haven't written *Asia's Star Brands* from a country perspective, despite being tempted to do so; instead, I have focused on looking at examples (regardless of origin) where I feel there has been an attempt at good branding practice. Moreover, it isn't easy to find any brand that gets everything right, even in the West, but the learning comes from seeing what has worked in Asia. I have also included the Arabian Gulf under the broad heading of Asia.

On occasions I have taken the liberty of commenting on aspects of branding that could possibly be improved upon. I would stress that these are only personal opinions and, in the absence of detailed information, are fairly superficial and not necessarily correct.

The strategic brand elements covered by the cases in the book include:

- brand as corporate strategy;
- first mover advantage;
- brand renewal and revitalization;
- brand naming and identity;
- challenger brands;
- brand positioning;
- emotional branding;
- service branding; and
- branding commodities;
- branding conglomerates;
- brand alliances, and mergers and acquisitions; strategic alliances, partnerships, and co-branding.

- destination branding;
- brand management; and
- holistic branding.

There is one more element of branding that is covered in the book, and that is brand architecture. It is worthwhile introducing this now, as it affects every brand.

BRAND ARCHITECTURE

I have not devoted a chapter to brand architecture, as it is an issue faced by all brand builders and all the case studies in the book have made decisions—rightly or wrongly, consciously or in an ad hoc way—on what architecture they should use. For each case, therefore, I have added at the end the main architecture model used so that you can see the range of alternatives and the degree of emphasis placed on both company and product.

Brand architecture is an interesting topic and one that is occupying a great deal of time and thought in modern-day brand strategy and management, as brand owners seek answers to how their brands should, if at all, relate. This is the purpose of brand architecture—to recognize the relative importance of a company's brands and to leverage the equity of each to the full by treating it as a stand-alone brand or linking it to other brands.

What makes brand architecture so interesting is that there are no rules as to how corporate and product brands should be linked to each other. Even close observation of global power brands gives no indication that there is one correct way to do it, as they use various formats. The options are fairly straightforward, though, and I will describe them now so that you can relate them to the cases as you read on.

- *True corporate branding:* This is where the company believes that building up the equity and value of the corporate brand name is of utmost importance. Products are relegated to being branded only in terms of alphanumerics. An example here is Nokia, with all mobile phones assigned only a number.
- *Corporate branding with product descriptor:* Here, the company is basically using a true corporate branding stance but labels its products with descriptors. An example is Heinz Baked Beans.
- *Shared branding:* A departure from the above is where the product is given more recognition in terms of brand status

with its own brand name, but the corporate brand name comes first and is usually visually depicted above and next to the product brand. An example is Intel Centrino.

- *Corporate–product name linkage:* Sometimes, but this is not very common, a company will combine the corporate brand name with the product descriptor to produce a single but recognizable brand name, such as Nescafé, from Nestlé.
- *Endorsed branding:* Under this type of brand architecture, the product gets the spotlight while the corporate brand name appears as an endorser, usually in small print. An example is BAND-AID by Johnson & Johnson.
- *True product branding:* This architecture places each brand as a stand-alone brand without corporate linkage. Few people realize who owns the brand. An example is Hugo Boss, which is owned by Procter & Gamble.

Brand architecture decisions have become part and parcel of the brand manager's job, regardless of what industry the company is in. In this book you will find cases from the following industries:

- air travel;
- asset management and development;
- automotive manufacturing;
- building materials;
- clothing and fashion;
- commodities;
- consumer electronics;
- destinations and tourism;
- food and beverage;
- healthcare;
- hospitality;
- household appliances;
- oil and gas;
- technology;
- telecommunications; and
- travel.

Diverse they may be, but all the cases have a commonality. They are examples of organizations that are trying hard to create, develop, and manage international brands. Most of them are at different stages of development and face different challenges, but all have achieved some degree of success.

I must re-emphasize that the brands mentioned in the book are not the only ones that have done well; there are too many examples to fit into one book. For example, I have not written about Hyflux, a Singapore business-to-business brand that is fast becoming famous under the guidance of Olivia Lum. And there are others. It is a pity to leave out some of these companies.

However, in selecting the case studies I have chosen a cross-section of brands that I feel represent some of the best in Asia. Some have already gained a kind of "star status," while others have not yet made it on to the "big screen." Some of them might never really become global—or even regional—household names, and indeed may fail in their ambitions, but I wish them every success.

You will notice that I have included two destination brands—Shanghai and Dubai. The purpose of this is twofold: first, to demonstrate that nations and destinations are adopting branding principles that traditionally have been the preserve of corporations; and second, to show how powerful public-sector branding can be.

According to world atlases. Asia is the world's largest continent and stretches from the Black Sea in the west to Japan in the east. Hence you will find that West Asia is represented by two cases from Dubai.

By contrast, you may have observed that in the brand-new world of Asia there are few examples of Asian luxury brands. It will take much longer for Asia to compete with the West in the luxury categories; the emotional elements of glamour, prestige, and status are still owned by Western brands. However, companies such as the Beijing Lingerie Company are close to developing some really competitive luxury- and emotionally-based brands with its product brand called "Aimer."

In choosing the brands to profile in the book, a decisive factor has been the intense commitment of the people driving them—those top managers who are determined to make branding happen. This book is really dedicated to them, and demonstrates how the mindset of Asian business and government leaders has changed over the last few years from a business to a branded business perspective.

There is no doubt in my mind that Asia will dominate world trade in the not-too-distant future, and some of the brands in this book are likely to be leading the way.

Paul Temporal
September 2005

CHAPTER 1

Brand as Corporate Strategy

Introduction

Strategy is everything. Brand is everything. Brand strategy is the best vehicle for corporate success. In a world where any competitors can copy your products, services, technology, systems, processes, and everything else your company chooses to employ, the one thing they cannot copy is your brand image. So, in reality, the only route to sustainable competitive advantage—and, for that matter, profitability—is brand image.

While many companies recognize this, few are courageous enough to put all their faith in the brand and to outsource everything else. Consequently, such companies are hard to find. In Asia, I know of only one—OSIM International Ltd.—that truly adopts this philosophy, and so this chapter focuses on one brand only.

Although all the other cases in this book use brand as the primary means to achieve various aspects of their corporate strategy, only OSIM chooses to own and build one strategic asset—its brand. This company is unique and offers a glimpse into the future of Asian brands whose founders and CEOs take the view that the brand drives the business, and not the other way around. OSIM is a brand marketing machine that in just a few years has achieved global reach and gained international brand acclaim.

CASE STUDY 1—OSIM INTERNATIONAL LTD.

The Brand Marketing Machine

★ ★ ★ ★ ★

OSIM is one of the most admired brands in Asia. Probably the most unique aspect of OSIM is the fact that the company doesn't own any physical assets—just the brand name. It even sold its headquarters building and now leases it back, preferring the intangible asset of brand to tangible assets in their many forms.

According to founder Ron Sim, OSIM has been "inspired by the success of global brands like Nike and Starbucks." In fact, he says, "Brand is an important intangible asset that will grow over time and beyond. Give me the largest factory in the world versus the Nike brand and I will take the brand. . . . *That*'s how important."

Knowing the man behind the brand, this statement doesn't surprise me at all. Sim thinks, eats, sleeps, dreams, and acts out the brand. He leads by example; his energy is ceaseless; he is the personification of what the brand stands for.

Sim's brand (and corporate) strategy is to anticipate and exceed customers' wants. OSIM adopts a similar brand and business model to Nike with an emphasis on building the brand while outsourcing the manufacturing of the products. The intention is to reposition OSIM from an original equipment manufacturer (OEM) to an original design manufacturer (ODM).

OSIM is indeed reminiscent of Nike when it was small in its attitude and philosophy, but OSIM has had the benefit of learning from the past mistakes of other brands. No doubt it will make its own mistakes, too, but so far it has done remarkably well in avoiding some of the pitfalls.

THE OSIM BUSINESS

The company had its origins in Singapore in 1980 where it began as R. Sim Trading Co., a business that sold household goods such as knife sharpeners. In 1982, the company started to sell "healthy lifestyle" products, such as handheld massagers and foot reflexology rollers.

In 1994 the name "OSIM" was launched, followed in April 2000 by the new and enhanced OSIM corporate brand logo and identity.

OSIM is innovation driven. It is an IP (intellectual property) developer that uses innovative selling approaches and constantly enhances its innovation capabilities to produce successful products with superior designs, features, and quality. As an IP developer, OSIM controls its brands, designs, technologies, and concepts. It is in the business of marketing, distributing, and franchising a comprehensive range of healthy lifestyle products.

All the group's production needs are outsourced to contract manufacturers in Japan, Taiwan, Spain, Italy, the United States, Australia, and Korea, as it believes in focusing on its strengths in marketing and brand management.

The OSIM business consists of four focuses—health, hygiene, nutrition, and fitness—which together reflect the brand's holistic and integrated approach to healthy lifestyle.

- *Health focus:* is about making the right choices and managing a healthy lifestyle. It is the core business, with products such as ear scans, massage chairs, nerve stimulators, and blood pressure monitors.
- *Hygiene focus:* is about clean air, clean water, and a clean home and office environment, with products such as water-based cleaning systems and water purifiers.
- *Nutrition focus:* is about supplementing daily nutritional needs for a balanced diet, with products covering health supplements and skin collagen repair, and others that promote good health from within.
- *Fitness focus:* is about bringing the convenience of fitness to the comfort of home, and here there is a wide range of home gym equipment products.

EXPERIENCING BRAND OSIM: A HOLISTIC VIEW OF BRANDING

Brand is always foremost in the mind of the company, and it makes sure that everyone gets involved to ensure that customers see and get consistency in the brand experience. It achieves this in several ways; however, two core competencies stand out:

- *People:* The company embraces continuous improvement and life-long learning to keep the skills of its staff up to date through training and development. OSIM understands that skilled staff are an important asset and supports the notion of "Happy staff, happy customers."

- *Internal branding:* Internal branding is the key to OSIM's success. The founder is the brand evangelist. He is known for developing creative initiatives that allow staff to truly "live the brand" internally, and he is the company's most compelling brand spokesperson.

Here is an indication of how these competencies are achieved.

Vision and Values Drive Daily Activities

Like all great brands, the vision and values of the brand dictate not only strategy, but also the daily activities of the business. OSIM's 2003 Annual Report states: "Throughout OSIM, the offices, the conference rooms and the shop floors are buzzing with activity. Decisions are made and actions taken. These daily activities are driven by the vision and values of BRAND OSIM."

OSIM's brand values are neatly described in terms of what the brand beliefs are and how they relate to employees and customers. They are:

- *Intelligent, innovative and interactive:* Our revolutionary products will interest, excite and delight the customer in new ways. We set the standard with everything we do.
- *Uncompromised integrity:* We take pride in whatever we do and stand behind the quality and reliability of our products and services.
- *Holistic well-being:* We believe that good health starts with the right attitude and is achieved physically, mentally, and emotionally.
- *Leading authority:* Our reputation and proven track record help us promote our message to customers—they trust that we are the best in what we do.
- *Positive thinking:* We believe in the power of positive thought. Having an optimistic, can-do attitude will help us overcome all obstacles.

The tagline for the brand, "Health is an attitude to life," summarizes the values and OSIM's philosophy of challenging your spirit to do your best.

People Drive the Brand and the Brand Motivates People

Brands move and motivate people, and OSIM is no exception. OSIM says, "A strong brand is like a magnet, attracting positive people. It unifies our people, providing them with a sense of belonging and purpose that they can work towards collectively." The 2003 Annual Report describes OSIM's fighting spirit: "From a single shop to a leading brand with over 500 outlets in more than 20 countries, this is not a miracle. It is the vision, as well as the sheer hard work by everyone at OSIM who constantly challenges himself to lift the brand further."

Even the independent non-executive directors feel the power of the brand. Mr. Ong Kian Min says, "We focus on attracting and grooming great talent committed to our company's goals. These are our people with so much passion that they make our customers want more products—our OSIM brand of products." When you visit OSIM, you can feel this passion.

BRAND CONSISTENCY

Great brands are built on consistency. Product innovation tends to provide the brand with its relevance to the changing needs, wants, and lifestyles of the customers in its evolution, but the brand name itself provides the security and comfort that consumers also desire. People are uncomfortable with the idea of schizophrenia in brands, just as they are with schizophrenia in people.

OSIM realizes this and innovates constantly, renewing its product line by up to 25% every six months, while declaring that "BRAND OSIM delivers consistent experience for its customers throughout the world. Be it in Dubai or in Hong Kong, customers will enjoy the OSIM brand experience." And a look at its outlets, franchised or not, shows that OSIM delivers on this promise. Currently, plans are under way to improve the design of all retail outlets; this will reinforce the OSIM brand as a recognizable, sophisticated, yet approachable brand.

Talking up the Brand

Whether you read an annual report, a press statement, a media interview, or any quote from any OSIM member of staff, the brand is always placed clearly as the focal point.

Sponsorships, Events, and Endorsements

OSIM is all about developing a positive attitude to life and health, and so it gets involved in many relevant community activities and sponsorships. In addition to giving ongoing support to the Children's Cancer Foundation, the company also sponsored the OSIM Singapore International Triathlon in 2003. It has set up an endowment fund for a Professorship in Branding and Innovation with the National University of Singapore to promote the study of branding and innovation in business. It supported the Healthy City project in Hong Kong and a Healthy Walk event in Taiwan, and sponsored a major cultural event in Malaysia called "Dances of the Dynasties." It involved celebrity Andy Lau during the SARS outbreak in Hong Kong to lift the spirits of the local people. And in 2002, in order to gain more international exposure, OSIM engaged internationally acclaimed actress Gong Li as the celebrity face of the brand.

THE COMPETITION

Competition is getting pretty hot in the healthcare business and OSIM has to keep one step ahead, which isn't easy. While OSIM brought out the first massage chair with built-in music that synchronizes the massage effect to the rhythm of the music, other companies are copying and competing with OSIM by focusing on product features and attributes. OSIM continues to innovate with products such as iSQUEEZ, which was described when launched as "The world's first massager that relieves your calves, ankles and feet, all at once." As usual in a growing category, product competition is fierce and tends to be driven by product positioning based on features and attributes.

On top of this type of competition, OSIM is faced with the companies who wait until a new product is launched and then copy it and sell it at a much lower price. This is especially true of the business in China, and OSIM has to change its product range in this category by 25% every six months!

But OSIM says, "We are not threatened [by] or reacting to what the other brands do. Competition is healthy for us . . . we look forward to the challenges as it'll make us more creative and stronger."

A strong brand will survive heavy competition if it is managed well and all other things, such as product innovation and quality, are equal. OSIM realizes that the only way to survive in such a market is to keep innovating and maintain quality, but more than anything else, to invest in the brand. And they are doing just that.

EXTENDING THE BUSINESS

The "Nutrition Focus" business (compared to OSIM's other three business divisions—Health, Hygiene, and Fitness) poses a problem for the OSIM brand, which doesn't really have any experience in the nutrition sector, and which to date has not performed very well in comparison with the other divisions, despite encouraging results from the Nourish Refine skincare supplements range.

However, the company appears to have tackled that gap by obtaining a major share in the GNC Global Active franchise. GNC is a massive retail chain of stores that sells healthcare supplements and vitamins. Global Active is the sole franchisee for Singapore, Malaysia, Brunei, Guam, and Saipan. This move will add around 90 more outlets to OSIM's 530 or so outlets, giving it more presence and the opportunity to cross-sell its products to an ever-increasing health-conscious market.

The latest acquisition for OSIM is Brookstone Inc., a niche US retail chain that sells an extensive range of lifestyle products. Michael Anthony, president and chief executive officer of Brookstone, says that around a million people walk through its 289 retail outlets every day. Again, cross-selling of OSIM and Brookstone products is a huge opportunity.

THE FUTURE?

Having created the category in which it dominates brand space, OSIM continues to achieve and has an international reach that is increasing with enormous rapidity. The business has set goals of growing annually at 20–30% to reach a turnover of S$1 billion, and to nearly double its outlets to 1,000 by 2008. With the Brookstone acquisition, it now has nearly 1,000 outlets. It is becoming a truly global business that is totally brand-driven.

Brand strengths

- The biggest strength is that for OSIM the brand is everything— the most important and valuable asset and what drives the business.

- OSIM is a leader in innovation.
- OSIM is a niche market leader in healthy lifestyle products, having a first mover advantage in a fast-growing market.
- The values of the brand are lived and brought to life by the staff.
- The founder and chairman has tremendous drive, charisma, and understanding of branding.
- A good management team displays courage in innovation and determination in execution, and possesses the discipline to stay focused on its key strengths.
- Investment is made in R&D to ensure consistency in product quality, design, and innovation.
- There is consistent growth due to strong OSIM brand management throughout the region.

Brand weaknesses

- Strong brand management and tracking is not in evidence as yet. Although the small brand management team has done a remarkable job, there is still an element of gut feel about brand decision-making due to a lack of research.
- Continued expansion through franchisees can weaken the brand if strong brand management is not in place.

Brand architecture

Corporate, and shared product branding (example: OSIM iSQUEEZ).

Sources

- OSIM management.
- *The Edge*, Singapore, April 25, 2005.

CONCLUSION

In the next chapter, you will see how first mover advantage can be gained not by creating a category (which OSIM did), but by reinventing the category.

CHAPTER 2

FIRST MOVER
ADVANTAGE

INTRODUCTION

In the last chapter, you read about the very real advantage a company can gain by putting its brand at the very center of its strategic universe. OSIM saw a gap in the market and filled it with a focused brand strategy that drove its corporate strategy.

In this chapter, you will see a different way of gaining first mover advantage. Where OSIM basically created the category, the brands here gained their competitive advantage by building or reinventing their categories.

Being a leader in a category is an enviable position; if you are not the leader, you continually struggle to become one and have to reach and then defend the number two or three spot. In the book I co-authored with Al Ries and Jack Trout, entitled *The 22 Immutable Laws of Marketing in Asia-Pacific* (Singapore: John Wiley & Sons, 2003), law number 1 is the law of leadership, which says that the basic issue in marketing is creating a category in which you can be first. It's better to be first, than it is to be better! It's much easier to get into the minds of consumers first, than try to convince consumers that you have a better product than the one they are already aware of.

So, being the first mover (the first into a category) puts all the pressure on the competitors following behind. Not many brands manage to attain first mover status, but those that do usually have lengthy and rewarding lives. They often retain their leadership position and market share.

Coke was in before Pepsi; Gillette was the first safety razor; Hewlett-Packard introduced the first desktop laser printer. All are leaders. The case of Red Bull typifies this pioneering spirit. Although it wasn't actually the first in its category of energy drinks, it saw the opportunity and built the category and its leadership position worldwide.

There are always opportunities in markets, even though the category already exists. The most exciting brand in this area at present is AirAsia, an airline that is a charismatic and cheerful brand, and definitely one to watch as it grows and develops. It offers a value proposition of low cost, no frills in what promises to be an extremely competitive market. It was the first serious player in the category and will take some dislodging from its leadership position.

CASE STUDY 2—RED BULL

From Zero to Hero

It all started in 1982, when Dietrich Mateschitz became aware of products called "tonic drinks," which enjoyed wide popularity in Asia. He got the brilliant idea to sell those functional drinks outside Asia.

Two years later, Mateschitz founded the company Red Bull GmbH. He improvised the product, which he adapted from the Thai beverage called *Kratingdaeng,* and approached the local firm TC Pharmaceuticals to manufacture it. They agreed and took a 51% stake in Red Bull Gmbh, while Mateschitz owned 49%. He started selling Red Bull Energy Drink on the Austrian market in 1987. The product took off quickly.

Today, Red Bull is available in over 100 countries around the globe and a billion cans of the drink are consumed each year. The sales have risen from US$920 million in 2001 to US$2 billion in 2004. This amazing success is shared by the company's 1,850 employees, 200 of whom work at Red Bull headquarters in Fuschl am See, Austria.

THE ENIGMATIC BRAND MAN

Little is known about the publicity-shy but highly talented, creative, and determined salesman Dietrich Mateschitz, the man who practically invented the energy drinks category in the beverage world.

Mateschitz is often referred to as the "traveling toothpaste salesman," because previously he worked as international marketing director for Blendex, a German toothpaste manufacturer, in Bangkok. He met Chaleo Yoovidhya, who sold a local tonic syrup called *Kratingdaeng*. Mateschitz tried it and was totally "hooked." Later he discovered that Taisho Pharmaceuticals, producer of the Livita tonic drink, was Japan's biggest corporate taxpayer and this triggered him to introduce the Thai "tonic drink" into Europe.

Today, Mateschitz is a billionaire (the only one in Austria, apparently). His office is in the quaint lakeside village of Fuschl, near Salzburg, where he houses his collection of 16 airplanes in a steel and glass hangar that also serves as an aviation museum and the home of the Flying Bulls at Salzburg Airport. Mateschitz not only generates brilliant sales and marketing ideas; he is equally talented in the execution of the biggest and boldest business ideas. His latest project involves a US$1 billion motor sport and aviation theme park in Styria, Austria.

Mateschitz is an avid extreme sports lover, who evidently drinks ten cans of Red Bull a day. Well, that's "living the Red Bull brand" alright!

SETTING THE PACE AGAINST THE COMPETITION

The success of Red Bull finally led to its appearance on the beverage big player radar screen. In the United States alone, there are more than 30 brands in the market, and energy drinks dominate the beverage industry with a double-digit growth rate. The energy drink category created by Red Bull has become a new battleground for the big beverage players.

According to Mintel International Group, Red Bull's market share has declined slightly over recent years as the big players such as

Coca-Cola's KMX, PepsiCo Mountain Dew's Amp, SoBe's Adrenalin Rush, and Hansen's Monster and Lost managed to gain ground in this lucrative category. However, Red Bull is still quite dominant in the United States, and sales there increased by 10% in 2003, with a forecasted 33% sales growth in 2004. Figures for 2004 revealed that sales actually grew by 40%, and that Red Bull had a 47% share of the US market in this year.

Although Asia and America have a combined share of 80% in the sports and energy drinks category, the European market is still growing at 15–25% annually. This will give an extra boost for Red Bull to hold its grip of around 70% of global market share, thanks to its strong brand and hard-core cult following.

BRAND ATTRIBUTES, POSITIONING, VALUES, AND COMMUNICATIONS

It is interesting to note that the Red Bull brand, which failed in taste testing (as Coke did and still does), practically invented a new major category, and grew from nothing to a major player in the beverage industry in a short period of time. This growth is due to the skill of the brand builder. Dietrich Mateschitz says, "If we don't create the market, it doesn't exist." In order to make this statement come to life, he has built the brand with carefully constructed elements and messaging. First, Red Bull stresses functional attributes.

Functional Attributes

Red Bull builds on its functional product dimensions and their benefits such as improved metabolism, performance, concentration, reaction speed, and vigilance, while at the same time riding on an integrated marketing platform based around extreme sports to convey the brand's emotional dimensions, as described below. This gives Red Bull a sound bi-cameral brand communications strategy, addressing both sides of the brain.

Brand Positioning

The universal positioning of "Red Bull stimulates body and mind" is translated into the more memorable and inspiring line used in the

United States, Canada, the UK, and Australia: "Red Bull gives you wings!" This relates to the energy lift claimed by the product and promised to the consumer. However, there are some inconsistencies with the application of the slogan—for example, in Malaysia it doesn't appear at all.

Nevertheless, the attributes and positioning are communicated by Red Bull to consumers consistently via the brand values, which take the form of a distinctive personality.

Brand Values (Personality)

Each piece of the Red Bull communication strategy denotes the brand values (or personality). These distinctive traits, which determine how the Red Bull brand communicates with its audience across all media, are:

- individuality;
- humor;
- innovation; and
- non-conformism.

Consistently across the globe in all communications, these values are projected as the heart and soul of the brand, which consumers can relate to and build a relationship with.

Integrated Brand Communications

Red Bull made the wise decision to articulate the brand values and find a suitable and sustainable integrated communications platform to ride on. For instance, the affinity sports event sponsorship, with high-octane media coverage, actually herds the consumer closer to the brand. Red Bull consistently uses affinity sports sponsorships, targeted activities mainly related to sport and relevant to its customer base, to increase the number of its followers.

So, we find that Red Bull is continuing to build its brand through extreme sports sponsorships, and supports close to 500 world-class extreme sports athletes who compete in spectacular and often record-breaking events across the globe. In addition, Red Bull is aggressively sponsoring various extreme and endurance-driven sporting events such as the X-Games and motor sports. These disciplines fit nicely with Red Bull's individualistic brand values. Red Bull has also established its very own Flying Bulls Aerobatics Team, which is recognized as one of the world's top stunt-flying crews. And anyone who has ever seen them in action knows why. Going to the extreme once more, Red Bull took an expensive and somewhat risky opportunity to get a stake in one of the sports with the highest media viewing figures in the world—Formula One.

When Red Bull entered Formula One, it invested £60 million to purchase the Jaguar Formula One racing team, owned by Ford Motor Co. The Red Bull logo and "Red Bull gives you wings" slogan replaced the Jaguar logo on the wings of the silver Formula One cars. Since the demise of Jaguar in Formula One, Red Bull has formed its own racing team and has a partnership agreement in place with Ferrari, whereby Ferrari will supply the team with engines for years 2006 to 2007. If this is successful, and so far in 2005 races it seems to be, then Red Bull will achieve its ambition of propelling the brand image even higher and stronger.

In all the above brand promotional activities, there lingers a sense of fun. This is typified by the co-branding of the Red Bull Formula One team at the Monaco Grand Prix in May 2005 with the launch of the latest in the *Star Wars* film trilogy. Life-size characters from the film (including Darth Vader) were seen supporting the team from the Red Bull pit area, and the Red Bull team cars were painted in *Star Wars* livery.

Away from sports, Red Bull has made sponsorship forays into the "rave" scene—for example, with The Red Bull Music Academy, which is a yearly event that travels the world. Red Bull has decided to support music by "letting you do it your way."

Another Red Bull brand communications image vector is to establish its brand in key nightspots, relying on word-of-mouth to increase awareness. For a personal touch in spreading the word, Red Bull employs consumer "educators" to go to beaches, gyms, airports or "any other places where people may need energy" to promote the product and hand out free samples.

THE FUTURE?

There is no doubt that Red Bull has become a brand phenomenon in the global beverage world, in its specific category. From a dubious-tasting drink it is already a global brand icon, but there are challenges to face, especially from the big brands such as Coca-Cola.

One major challenge for Red Bull is to ensure that the brand rational attributes, especially taste, become more relevant to the consumers. Coca-Cola's KMX has recently got good blind taste results when compared to Red Bull; this will give Red Bull's "cough mixture" taste a hard time. The question is: Will Red Bull change its formula to meet these new tastes, or will it expand its product line? If the changes are unavoidable, the bonus question is: How can Red Bull change and be relevant, but keep the magic alive?

Another challenge is how to grow and set its future after graduating from the novelty-value, trendy new product and maintain power brand status in the market. At the moment, Red Bull sales volume is benefiting from pure product distribution efficiency, with market penetration across the globe. The strength of the brand will be tested when the width of the market is maximized, and the sources of future growth are dependent on building, mining the depths of, and developing the market with brand and/or line extensions. Red Bull has to extend its brand but remain relevant to its basic proposition, as it has basically only one core product brand, whereas its competitors have massive brand portfolios.

Perhaps one part of the answer to the above challenges might be that in June 2005, Red Bull revealed it was re-launching its coffee canned drink. So far, only two brands—Ajinimoto's Birdy and Nestle's Nescafé are regarded as Asia's major players. The re-launch, started in its country-of-origin Thailand. Red Bull sees the canned ready-to-drink coffee category rising at 18% annually compared to the energy drink segment's 2–3% in Thailand. The opportunities globally also look good, given Red Bull's track record.

The legal and health aspects are another challenge that looms over the energy drink category—and over Red Bull, in particular. At present, the Food and Drug Administration (FDA) in the United States has no regulations in place regarding many of the ingredients used in energy drinks. (Red Bull uses taurine, glucuronolactone, caffeine, niacin, vitamins B6 and B12, and pantothenic acid.) Nor are there any regulations regarding the levels of legal use, and what mixtures are safe. This might be of significance, because Red Bull claims, without strong clinical evidence, that the combination of the ingredients can improve metabolism, performance, concentration, reaction speed, and vigilance.

There may come a time when the FDA and other market regulators will impose specific and more restrictive regulations on the ingredients, governing claims such as these made not just by Red Bull but by its competitors also. This may possibly slow down the growth of the market and test the branding and marketing power of Red Bull against its more resilient competitors who have not only deep pockets but also massive political influence and a huge grip on distribution.

However, at present, the "force" is with Red Bull.

Brand strengths

- ◆ Built the category worldwide.
- ◆ Brilliant corporate and brand leader.
- ◆ Brand communications strategy is focused and world-class.

Brand weaknesses

- ◆ Remains in a small part of the energy drinks category.
- ◆ Brand portfolio is limited and needs protection.
- ◆ After being a leader, it is in danger of becoming a follower.

Brand architecture

Product branding.

Sources

- ◆ "The History. The Story," www.redbull.com.
- ◆ "Energy Drinks, 2003," The Beverage Network.
- ◆ "Energy Drinks Add Pep to European Market," www.FoodAndDrinkEurope.com.
- ◆ Wilfried Eckl-Dorna, "Red Bull Lightens up," *Fortune*, September 6, 2004.
- ◆ "Red Bull GmbH Fact Sheet," *Hoover's Online.*
- ◆ "Coke ups the Ante in Energy Drinks," *New Nutrition Business*, www.new-nutrition.com, February 2003.
- ◆ "How Red Bull Woke up in the Teen Market," *The Observer*, December 5, 2004.
- ◆ "Red Bull's Energy-Drink Claims May Be Hype—But Not Its Sales," *Business Week Online.*
- ◆ Gerhard Gschwandtner, "The Powerful Sales Strategy behind Red Bull," www.SellingPower.com.

CASE STUDY 3—AIRASIA

Now Everyone Can Fly

★ ★ ★ ★ ★

THE BRAND PHILOSOPHY

With the tagline "Now everyone can fly," AirAsia's philosophy of low fares is aimed at making flying affordable for everyone. AirAsia also aims to make travel easy, convenient, and fun for its guests.

Director and group chief executive officer Tony Fernandes founded Tune Asia Sdn. Bhd. in 2001 in Malaysia, with a vision to make air travel more affordable for Malaysians. With that in mind, Fernandes and his three partners in Tune Air bought AirAsia Berhad and remodeled it into Asia's and Malaysia's first low-fare, no-frills airline. It was also the first to introduce "ticket-less" traveling in Malaysia and Thailand. AirAsia was named "Asia-Pacific Airline of the Year" for 2003—a recognition awarded by the Centre for Asia Pacific Aviation (CAPA).

As chairman Dato' Pahamin A. Rajab says,

> When AirAsia was launched as a low-fare, no-frills carrier in January 2002, we began operations with the mission to make flying affordable so everyone can fly. With four routes and two planes to start with, our low-fares, no-frills concept was introduced to Malaysians. The low fares were certainly good news to many, a majority of whom had never flown before. Good news certainly spread fast and we saw more and more new faces flying with us.

Since beginning its operations, around six million guests have flown on AirAsia, which now operates over 100 domestic and international flights daily from three hubs—two in Malaysia and one in Thailand. Today, it is a profitable, fast-growing international discount carrier, while Fernandes has driven a dramatic change in civil aviation policy in Southeast Asia. With a view to the long term, AirAsia is planning to collaborate with Malaysian Airlines in promoting the domestic air industry, and to discuss sensitive areas such as anti-competitive pricing and sharing of routes.

AirAsia has thrived even under an extremely competitive environment; for example, just on the Singapore to Bangkok route, there are 14 full-fledged carriers and three other low-cost carriers, yet AirAsia still manages to get an 82% load factor. There seems to be widespread optimism that AirAsia will continue to move forward based on the growth achieved in a mere three years. Fernandes has turned an ailing company into a RM49 million net profit company and has sold AirAsia across borders, such as Thailand and Indonesia.

Tony Fernandes graduated from the London School of Economics in 1987 and worked for Richard Branson's Virgin Records from 1987 to 1989. One could conclude that while he worked in Branson's business empire, he was able to learn and observe how to drive a business through developing brand power. Although Fernandes is a different person from Branson, some of his style is very reminiscent of the billionaire brand owner. And, like Branson, Fernandes has said that he would and should focus on one thing, and one thing only—building the brand.

THE NAME, LOGO, COLOR, AND TAGLINE

AirAsia is a great name. It shows the scope of the business, implies who its customers are, and it gives ownership of the region and its connection to air travel. As the first mover in the regional budget airline business, it gains the company a position in consumer minds that is hard to follow.

The logo? Well, there *is* no logo. The AirAsia name doubles up as the logo, and it was designed in a friendly written font to ensure that it could be used for logo purposes as well.

The color—chili red—reminds everyone of Asian culture; it is an auspicious color in Asia and is associated with good luck and prosperity, and the chili vegetable is a part of most Asian diets. The staff wears red outfits, and the planes have the same red color on their livery. Each plane tends to have different paintwork, however, and some even have advertisements on the fuselage.

The tagline "Now everyone can fly" sums up the brand's value proposition to consumers. It offers the prospect of flying to many people who previously couldn't afford regular airline flights. It has an endearing emotional touch to it, typical of great brands.

AirAsia's Recipe for Success

Targeting Asia

Since the terrible events of September 11, 2001, fears of terrorism have prevailed and impacted on the aviation industry globally. Many leisure and business travelers started to focus on closer destinations in Asia instead of making long-haul trips to North America or Europe. Geographically, in Asia most countries are reasonably close but are separated by sea. So, all in all, targeting Asia makes good sense for a low-cost carrier.

To add to the logic, Asians are now enjoying rising incomes and good economic growth rates, which are empowering more of them to fly, especially in parts of Asia that have a poor rail and road infrastructure. There is a huge, dense population base, and a growing number of people who are upwardly mobile, along with widespread availability of Internet usage (which aids in booking seats via the Internet site). But primarily, AirAsia is targeting a different market segment—those people who have hungered for travel but couldn't afford it. AirAsia targets the masses, who are empowered to travel by low fares.

First Mover Advantage

AirAsia's success can be attributed to one very obvious factor—its first mover advantage in Asia. At the time AirAsia started to operate, only 6% of Malaysians flew (which is 1.5 million people out of the total population in Malaysia). Now, the market has grown to 12–13 million passengers annually, and AirAsia has secured around 30% of the domestic market share.

AirAsia was the first company to introduce the budget airlines concept to the masses in Asia. Where, in the past, people used to take road, rail, or other transportation, they are now flying to save time at virtually the same rates, and businessmen who are traveling can now take their families with them very cheaply. Families can now afford to fly together, and flying is now affordable for students studying away from home, and for backpackers and others. Indeed, the hotel industry is reaping the benefits from people traveling more often through AirAsia.

Customers are very empathetic to AirAsia because the airline has taken on the big players and has done so successfully without massive resources. Fernandes leads by example. He walks the talk. For example, he often moonlights as a crew member in order to meet guests and get their feedback. He is very hands-on, and in his free time is often seen helping to carry luggage and interacting as much as possible with everyone in his company.

When Fernandes makes his occasional appearances at the boarding gates, passengers often congratulate him on the carrier's success and thank him for bringing down fares and enabling them to fly. He is always an obliging and popular figure. He also receives letters of thanks from customers saying that they never thought they would be able to afford to fly; others that now they can take their families for a proper holiday.

There is no doubt that Tony Fernandes is the key person who has influenced and shaped government attitudes and airline industry thinking in Southeast Asia and beyond. For example, in around mid-2003, he engaged the support of the former prime minister of Malaysia, Tun Dr. Mahathir, to network with neighboring countries' leaders toward the development of an open-skies agreement. Now, nations such as Thailand and Indonesia are providing landing rights to AirAsia and other discount carriers.

HOW DOES AIRASIA CONTINUE TO MAINTAIN ITS SUCCESS?

The Essentials

AirAsia's operations are based on the following key strategies:

- *Low fare, no frills:* AirAsia's fares are significantly lower than those of other operators. This service targets the guests, who will do without the frills of meals, frequent flyer miles, or airport lounges in exchange for fares up to 80% lower than those currently offered with equivalent convenience.

  No complimentary drinks or meals are offered. Instead, guests now have the choice of purchasing food and drinks on board. "Snack Attack" is a range of delicious snacks and drinks available at very affordable prices and prepared exclusively for AirAsia's guests.
- *Frequent flights:* AirAsia's high-frequency service ensures that guest convenience is met. The airline practices a quick turn-around of 25 minutes, which is the fastest in the region, resulting in high aircraft utilization, lower costs, and greater airline and staff productivity.

◆ *Guest convenience:* AirAsia believes in providing convenient service to make traveling easier and more affordable for its guests. Guests can make bookings through a combination of the following:

  ◆ *Nationwide call center:* Launched in April 2002, AirAsia's nationwide call center in Kelana Square, in Selangor, just outside Kuala Lumpur (KL), is now fully equipped with 180 telephone lines providing a convenient telephone booking service for guests. The call center now takes an average of 6,000 calls daily.

  ◆ *Ticket-less service:* Launched on April 18, 2002, this concept complements AirAsia's Internet booking and call center service by providing a low-cost alternative to issuing printed tickets. Guests no longer need to go through the hassle of collecting tickets!

  ◆ *Easy payment channels:* In line with its "Easy to book, easy to pay, and easy to fly" approach, on March 1, 2002 AirAsia became Malaysia's first airline to enable its guests to pay for their telephone bookings by credit card or by cash at any Alliance Bank branch.

  ◆ *Internet booking:* As Asia's first online airline, AirAsia offers a new convenience in buying seats by logging on to its website (www.airasia.com). No more phone calls, no more queuing. Since the online sales facility was launched on May 10, 2002, the airline has recorded over RM223 million in sales through the Internet alone.

  ◆ *Reservations and sales offices:* These are available at airports and town centers for the convenience of walk-in customers.

  ◆ *Authorized travel agents:* AirAsia also introduced a direct business-to-business (B2B) engine to its agents. The Internet-based real-time inventory booking engine is the first in Asia. The agents make immediate payment via a virtual AirAsia credit card, developed through one of its strategic partners, Alliance Bank.

  ◆ *Improving customer service:* AirAsia is constantly looking for ways to improve its services and increase savings for its guests. AirAsia is the first airline in Asia to have a multi-lingual website with six languages available—English, Bahasa Malaysia, Mandarin, Tamil, Thai, and Indonesian.

- *Cost control:* AirAsia believes that cost, not competition, is its greatest enemy. It makes money by keeping costs low with mainly short-haul flights, a high rate of aircraft utilization, sales of drinks and snacks on board, marketing tie-ups with other companies, landing at secondary airports wherever possible, using crew to clean the aircraft, and quick turnaround times at airports.
- *Cabin crew multi-tasking:* The cabin attendants have additional roles (such as cleaning the aircraft) compared to cabin attendants working for other airlines, but they can earn a commission on sales of refreshments during flights. Even the pilots sometimes help to clean the planes! Tony Fernandes leads by example, helping occasionally to serve customers' drinks and check-in passengers. The culture is different at AirAsia, and it is this "can-do" attitude that is a critical success factor.
- *Addressing customer concerns about safety:* Low-cost operations can make customers concerned about safety, but AirAsia is very conscious of these worries and manages the perceptions of its existing and potential customers.

AirAsia's cost optimization philosophy is in no way at the expense of the airline's safety. The airline's fleet of 24 Boeing 737-300s complies fully with the conditions of the International Aviation Safety and is regulated by the internationally reputed Malaysian Department of Civil Aviation. In July 2002, AirAsia signed a US$20 million agreement with GE Engineering Services for engine maintenance and, later in the month, a US$3 million aircraft engine and aircraft frame parts leasing agreement with VolvoAero. AirAsia also recently signed a US$7 million agreement with ST Aero, covering the airline's engineering components support for seven years.

THE BRAND CULTURE

Fernandes's whole style of management is based on building a strong brand culture, which he is doing in his own inimitable way. He stresses the importance of departments having close relationships with one another and not becoming compartmentalized. He has commented that in the airline business, "the pilots think they are demigods, the engineers think they are really something, and there are lots of prima donnas around—it is a massive ego business." He proudly proclaims that AirAsia doesn't have that. One way that he keeps the "egos" at bay is by making the pilots cook breakfast for the engineers each quarter to thank them for looking after their aircraft.

There is only one large office, so baggage handlers, cabin crew, engineers, pilots, management, and everyone else, have to communicate with one another. This has led to some interesting romances, but also to some good ideas. For instance, the engineers had an idea that would save fuel costs but were unsure about approaching the pilots with it, as it would mean telling the pilots to fly their planes differently on take-off. Fernandes insisted that the engineers talk to the pilots, who welcomed the idea. AirAsia cut its fuel costs by 20% as a result!

No-frills, But Plenty-of-thrills Cabin Crew

The AirAsia philosophy is that not only should flights be affordable, but also fun and an enjoyable experience. This is why the cabin crews on board AirAsia's planes try to live the friendly and humorous brand character. Fernandes says they are not only attractive and well-groomed, but thinkers, too. "How else can one conduct games and activities, then joke and laugh about it, and serve with a smile throughout, all on board a soaring plane?" Fernandes tries to create an environment that is seriously fun, where every person is valued in the AirAsia business. If the brand can be seen as a fun brand that delivers consistently good value and service, then it is likely to be unbeatable.

Fernandes also provides opportunities for almost everyone to move within the company. At the time I met him in late 2004, former check-in assistants and a former accountant were undergoing pilot training. This refreshing management style has definitely motivated the company employees and helped AirAsia to build care, fun, and passion into every area of its business—from check-in, to arrival at destination points.

THE HEART OF AIRASIA: BRAND VALUES

The company describes its culture and brand values as follows:

> [T]he heart of AirAsia thrives on . . .
>
> *Safety:* We commit to "Safety First," comply with all regulatory agencies, set and maintain consistently high standards; ensure the security of staff and guests. Never compromise safety.

Caring: Maintain respectful relationships with fellow staff and guests. Treat people in the same manner we would like to be treated. Strive to be a role model at work and in the community. Take responsibility for personal and company growth. Be an appreciative person to guests and fellow staff.

Fun: Display a sense of humour and the ability to laugh at ourself. Add personality (be ourself) to the guest experience. Demonstrate and create enthusiasm for the job. Seek to convert a negative situation into a positive guest experience. Create a friendly environment where taking risks is okay.

Passion: Be passionate about everything we do. Crave and deliver superior performance. Use initiative to solve business and operation issues. Understand that there is no substitute for hard work. Champion Team Spirit. Enjoy overcoming barriers to good service.

Integrity: Demonstrate honesty, trust and mutual respect. Give the values of AirAsia a heartbeat. Possess and demonstrate broad knowledge of AirAsia. Commit to self-improvement.

AirAsia Experience: Our unique and wonderful experience. A service that will make a lasting impression. An experience that encompasses the above. Fun, Honest, Caring, Passionate, Humble, Safe, Respectful and Individual.

Brand Personality Focus

In 2005, Fernandes says the key brand personality characteristics for focus in AirAsia will be:

- friendly;
- fun;
- efficient; and
- innovative.

COMMUNICATIONS STRATEGY

In terms of advertising the brand, AirAsia's communications strategy is very consistent—AirAsia only advertises its low fares; nothing else. Its primary aim all along has been to associate the brand name with low fares, so that when people think AirAsia they relate it to low fares. As such, the advertisements are usually very tactically driven, but are often done creatively.

AirAsia is always visible, though, and is involved in many public relations activities. Fernandes is a key figure, appearing frequently in the media and talking up the brand and its values. He makes sure that people see a human side to the brand. He also has a view that internal communication is more important than external messages, and the brand and its strategy are always sold inside the company to employees first.

Typical of Fernandes's approach to living the AirAsia brand values is the painting of the company's 26th Boeing 737-300 plane made public in February 2005, which shows a large number of his staff covering the fuselage. Fernandes said at the time, "What better way to thank and give recognition to the staff of an airline company, than to have their faces immortalized on an aircraft?" Who wouldn't want to work for a brand-oriented CEO like him?

But it's not all a bed of roses. Hard business issues are constantly challenging Fernandes and AirAsia.

MORE CHALLENGES TO BRAND SUCCESS

I have mentioned above some hurdles in the airline industry that AirAsia has overcome. Another challenge is that, in Asia, the aviation industry is governed by a series of bilateral aviation agreements, unlike, say, Europe, which is one big open market. AirAsia believes that Asia is going through the initial stages of liberalization. The company has so far been given landing rights in Thailand, Indonesia, and the Philippines. However, deregulation is occurring at a very slow pace.

The biggest area of concern for a budget airline is keeping its costs down. With rising fuel oil prices, AirAsia is trying to keep rising costs at bay. Other costs that can influence profitability include landing charges or "gateway airport" charges, and navigation charges. Although secondary airports are used wherever possible, there is a lack of them in key destinations such as Bangkok, Beijing, Hong Kong, Singapore, Seoul, and Shanghai, and this makes it very difficult for budget airlines. In fact, in some other cities, the older airports are only used for domestic travel.

Since one of its core benefits is price, AirAsia really has to find ways to reduce costs without compromising on safety of passengers and the quality of crew members. For 2005, AirAsia will focus on its operations in Malaysia, Thailand, and Indonesia, develop and connect new destinations, and provide added frequencies.

AirAsia Goes Public

Perhaps the most remarkable achievement in the short life of AirAsia to date was its successful entry into the stock market as a listed company on November 22, 2004.

The retail price for the initial public offering (IPO) was at first set at RM1.16, below the indicative price of RM1.40. However, after the IPO on Bursa Malaysia, the counter closed the day with a 21% increase over its retail IPO price to about RM1.40, and RM1.45 at its highest. That price valued AirAsia at around 21 times 2005 earnings, a premium to the Kuala Lumpur market's multiple of about 13 times.

AirAsia's executive director, Kamarudin Meranun, said at the IPO that investors should look at AirAsia as not just a Malaysian company but as a regional growth prospect. Chong Sui San, a manager at Allianz General Insurance Malaysia, said: "Any investor planning to buy Malaysia will probably pick up some AirAsia stock."

Since going public, AirAsia was awarded third place in *Euromoney* magazine's poll for "Best Newly Listed Company." Importantly, the same magazine named AirAsia as the "Best Managed Company in the Airlines and Aviation Sector" in its "Asia's Best Managed Companies" poll. Analysts placed the airline ahead of other notable brands such as Virgin Blue, Singapore Airlines, and Malaysia Airlines.

Euromoney's managing director, Simon Brady, said that in a sector known for challenges, AirAsia has shown that bold, innovative management can deliver excellence to its customers and value to its shareholders. Fernandes commented: "It gives us credibility. We are now up there together with previous winners such as Cathay Pacific and SIA." AirAsia has won many more awards, too numerous to mention here.

THE FUTURE?

While there may be many hurdles yet to overcome, Tony Fernandes is optimistic and aggressive—he wants to fly eight million passengers in 2005, up from five million in 2004, and buy 80 new planes to serve them. On December 16, 2004, AirAsia confirmed its purchase of

40 Airbus A320 aircraft, with options to buy another 40. The order was worth US$2.5 billion, the largest placed to date by an Asian carrier. If all 80 are purchased, the total value will be US$5 billion.

To bridge the gap with its ever-increasing customer base, AirAsia needed 12 aircraft urgently when it placed the order, so it will most likely lease some aircraft until it begins to take delivery of its own, the first of which is due in January 2006, with the other 39 coming over a five-year timeframe. Airbus will supply considerable support, including training for pilots, cabin crew, engineers, and maintenance personnel. Meanwhile, the company will continue to add to its Boeing fleet, which stood at 26 Boeing 737-300 aircraft at the end of 2004, and expects to have 36 aircraft by October 2005.

Looking ahead, AirAsia is optimistic, even with the inbound competition. The company has secured rights to fly to six cities in China. The airline should also be flying to Vietnam, Laos, and Cambodia by 2006, according to Fernandes.

First mover status has been an implicit part of the strategy, allowing AirAsia to take advantage of scale faster than its competitors. Fernandes says that his new fleet will enable the company to increase passenger capacity and lower costs per seat. This means that AirAsia's prices "will go down," giving this lowest-cost airline an even greater competitive advantage.

As of August 2005, there are 27 low-cost no frills and low fare airlines operating in East Asia, South East Asia and South Asia with over ten in Southeast Asia. Some have already started to merge, such as Valuair and Jetstar Asia in an effort to gain market position and efficiencies.

Continued Expansion of Routes

Moving faster than the competition is one of AirAsia's brand strengths, and the 2005 focus is to be on Indonesia (a country with around 230 million people), and possible new routes in Indochina, including Vietnam and Cambodia.

AirAsia has a 49% stake in AWAIR, a privately owned Indonesian airline that has been relaunched as a low-cost, no-frills carrier to serve domestic and international routes from Jakarta. It already flies to Medan and Balikpapan in Indonesia, and is working toward flying between Singapore and Jakarta.

AirAsia's joint venture in Thailand (Thai AirAsia) is operating to Macau from its Bangkok base. In its home country, AirAsia is expecting to start new routes in East Malaysia (Borneo), including Kuching–Miri and Kuching–Kota Kinabalu.

AirAsia is always looking for ways to connect people. Sometimes these are unconventional. For example, the airline was the first to fly from Kuala Lumpur (KL) to Bandung, from KL to Tawau, and from KL to Macau. All three routes have proved to be very popular.

So, the brand is really "flying" at tremendous speed, but it is not going to forget what it needs to rely on to survive and prosper as the competition gets more organized. Fernandes says that AirAsia will concentrate on staff training, with the emphasis on quality service— in other words, giving customers a great brand experience!

The phenomenal growth of AirAsia reflects its vision to become a strong regional brand. As one of the leading low-fare airlines in the region, AirAsia is the epitome of ASEAN with its rich cultures and wealth of resources. The airline further aspires to bring low-fare travel to the people of ASEAN, and to encourage and boost trade and tourism among countries in ASEAN.

Brand strengths

- First mover advantage gave it the leadership position.
- Great brand culture.
- Developed a unique brand identity that will be hard to follow.
- Charismatic leader.

Brand weaknesses

- The target for some subsidiaries of big players (for example, Tiger Airways with shareholder Singapore Airlines) who have deep pockets.
- Reliant on maintaining the cost leadership.

Brand architecture

Corporate branding.

Sources

- AirAsia head office.
- Cris Prystay, "Tune Air Founder Goes against the Odds to Establish a Low-cost Asian Airline," *Wall Street Journal*, December 10, 2001.

- Scott Neuman, "Asia Takes to Cheaper Skies," *Far Eastern Economic Review*, February 26, 2004, p. 38.
- "Budget Travel—No Frills, Smaller Bills: Good News for Cost-saving Travellers," *Far Eastern Economic Review*, July 10, 2003.
- B. K. Sidhu, "Bids Pour in as AirAsia Begins Book Building," *The Star*, October 19, 2004, pp. 1, 3.
- Nicholas Ionides, "Man of the Moment," *Airline Business Magazine* (Kuala Lumpur), April 2004.
- "AirAsia to Focus on Indonesia, Thailand and Indo-China," *The Star*, January 8, 2005.
- "AirAsia Named Best Managed Company in Euromoney Poll," *The Malay Mail*, January 20, 2005.
- "Malaysia Stock Market Welcomes AirAsia IPO," *Financial Times*, November 23, 2004.
- "AirAsia Shares Jump 20% in Trading Debut," *Herald Tribune*, November 23, 2004.

CONCLUSION

First mover advantage can lead to market domination and continued leadership, even though competition arrives. In the next chapter, you will read about how companies have to reinvent themselves in order to get to the top.

CHAPTER 3

BRAND RENEWAL

INTRODUCTION

If a company cannot achieve leadership in its category by creating the category or gaining some kind of first mover advantage, then another way is for it to reinvent or renew its brand to change perceptions and gain a fresh and vital image.

Although the title of this chapter is "Brand Renewal," in branding terms I am really talking about how companies reposition themselves.

Brand positioning is concerned with the management of perceptions across various markets and consumer groups, and it has to take into account the brand images of competitors. Positioning is about competitive image creation, and has as its basis two fundamental questions that companies need to answer, namely:

◆ Why is our brand different?
◆ Why is our brand better?

These questions are always the subject of conscious or subconscious thought by consumers whenever they are approaching a purchase decision, especially if the price isn't very low. Good positioning leads to competitive advantage and a superior brand image, and this allows a company to gain premium prices for its products and services.

Having to reposition a brand can be quite difficult, depending on how much damage has been done to the brand image over time. The need to reposition is often signaled by decreasing market share and profitability, and market research can easily reveal whether or not a brand is losing or gaining image power and why. The cause of a loss in brand image power may be declining product/service quality, lack of relevance and modernity, or inadequate brand investment. Usually, these are the outcomes of weak or ineffective brand management.

Brands are like people—if they are not looked after and given care as they grow older, they just fade away. Nissan is an excellent example of how to revitalize a neglected brand. Nissan still faces some major challenges, but its turnaround has been nothing short of spectacular under the stewardship of Carlos Ghosn.

Having struggled for decades with a lackluster image and a heritage of doubtful product quality, Samsung is now reputed to be the fastest-growing brand in the world. How it has transformed itself from a relatively weak brand to a power brand is the basis of the second case in this chapter.

CASE STUDY 4—THE NISSAN STORY

From Rags to Riches in Five Years

THE PAST

In 1999, the French company Renault shocked the Asian automotive industry by offering US$5.4 billion for a stake in Nissan Motor, an automotive manufacturing company that had US$19 billion of debt. The following year (2000), Nissan posted a US$6.2 billion loss. Observers wondered if this audacious move by Renault would work out. But Renault appointed Carlos Ghosn as president in that year, and in 2001 he was made chief executive officer. Renault's investment has now more than tripled in value, and Ghosn has become an Asian management and brand-building legend.

Renault has a 44% controlling share in the Nissan business, which, in the year to March 2004, announced a net profit of 503.7 billion yen

(US$4.58 billion). Ghosn forecasted for the year ending March 2005 that sales would rise 10.5% to 3.38 million units. In fact, they rose by 10.8% to 3,388,000 vehicles and generated a 4.4% increase in operating profit of 861.2 billion yen, beating the forecasted 846 billion yen. Nissan has overtaken Honda and is second only to Toyota in the Japanese market. So, how has this transformation happened on such a scale and with such rapidity? How has the failing Nissan brand been saved and revitalized?

Top-down Brand Management: From Hate Mail to Hero for Ghosn

Many analysts say that the Nissan brand revival would never have happened without the strategic and hands-on capabilities of Carlos Ghosn, and it is easy to understand why this is a common perception.

When Ghosn first started to shake up the company he was literally hated, receiving threats and hate mail. He closed five plants, and reduced the workforce by 14%, purchasing costs by 20%, and the number of suppliers by 5%. As the person imposed by the French company Renault on the traditional Japanese company he was so active in cost-efficiency he became known by the media and others as "Le Cost Cutter."

The first indication we have of Ghosn's thinking about the brand is in 1999, when he was appointed as chief operating officer to the company and declared: "One of the biggest surprises is that Nissan didn't care about its brand. There is nobody really responsible for the strategy of the brand."

Since then he has systematically worked on the brand strategy, but the media has placed all the credit on his ability to cut costs and remove inefficiencies. It is true that he has achieved massive changes in these areas, but at the back of Ghosn's mind all along has been the development of the Nissan brand. In fact, in his Nissan Revival Plan of 1999, Ghosn went as far as to say that "while cost cutting will be the most dramatic and visible part of the plan, we cannot save our way to success." He went on: "The plan was designed to free resources that we could invest in a product-led and brand-led recovery that would put Nissan back on the track of lasting, profitable growth."

As Ghosn said in October 2002, "I hope people will buy Nissan not just because it is a rational buy of reliable quality and low price, but because of other more emotional aspects like design and status."

THE HARD WORK: REBUILDING THE BUSINESS AND REPOSITIONING THE BRAND

There are many aspects to which Nissan has applied itself in turning around the company and the brand, but of note are the following.

Brand Vision

Ghosn began his Revival Plan with a simple strategy for the future that "clearly stated our destination." This was the Nissan brand vision "to enrich people's lives." Product design will play an important role here. As Ghosn puts it:

> Design is key to the revival of the Nissan brand. Not only does it define the first and lasting impression our customers have about our products, but design also plays an important role in expressing the identity of our brands. They realize that a car is much more than metal, rubber, and fabric. It's more than transportation. A car represents freedom, self-expression, even desire.

Product Design

Product design is a key pillar of expansion for the Nissan brand. The aim is to create design that reverberates in the heart, appeals to the mind's eye, and delivers concept and message. Nissan's design will be a creative force that stirs creativity, nurtures innovation, and challenges the conventional to create attractive, distinctive products.

As design appears to be so critical to the consumer purchase decision, Nissan is revamping its whole product range and employing many young, creative designers. As a result, we are seeing some cosmetic eye-catching departures from the normal Nissan line-up, such as orange leather seats in one of the Quest vehicles, and sculptured exterior changes to the SUV Morano.

But despite the importance of design to the future of the brand, Ghosn is very much hands-off in his management of this area of the business, giving designers a lot of freedom as long as the models are not boring and achieve their profit targets.

Product Expansion

In conjunction with the attention to cosmetic design changes, Nissan has to win new customers through its new products. New products are to be launched to help build Nissan sales globally, to achieve the Nissan 180's goal to sell an additional one million new vehicles annually in September 2005. (This requires a sales figure for the year to September 30, 2005 of 3.6 million vehicles.) Nissan intends to roll out 28 new models by 2008.

The ongoing release of attractive new products will not only attract new customers to Nissan, but will also ensure that their next purchase is a Nissan product. The company is still not in all the segments it wants to serve, however; one example is the sub-US$15,000 compact vehicle, a segment that evidently has a growing market and which rival Toyota has filled with its Gen Y Scion brand. But Nissan is determined to fill the gaps with a complete range of what Ghosn calls "segment-defining" models.

The Brand Experience

Sales and service tie the customer more closely to the Nissan brand. Helping to enhance the positive response and service is the Nissan Sales and Service Way (NSSW), a global initiative to firmly establish the unique Nissan method of customer care and relations as one superior to other automakers.

It means knowing intimately the varying lifestyles involving automobiles and needs that the customer may not even have noticed, and then providing personalized care and service that matches the individual customer—and doing so in a swift and responsive way. Another development is the renovation of 10,000 Nissan dealerships worldwide to achieve a common Nissan visual identity.

Product launches are also the subject of change, and the brand experience here is being boosted by more glitz and glamor, including catwalk models and all the marketing skills of showbiz.

New Management Practices

Ghosn established the Nissan Management Way, which is a program designed to increase management quality and increase the speed of decision-making, and therefore to speed response to customers.

The individuals and the organization are more tightly joined, and competencies are enhanced by enforcing two-way communication between employees and management to increase transparency, build trust, and share the best practices. Delegation of authority is practiced to expedite response time to customers.

Ghosn says:

> We have used cross-cultural management, cross-functional teams, and cross-company teams as tools in our search for commonality, for synergy, and for better performance. We have achieved that combination of synergy and better performance in a variety of important areas, from engineering to purchasing, from information systems to manufacturing.

BRAND EVOLUTION: THINK GLOBAL, ACT LOCAL

An interesting and fundamental decision by Nissan was to embark on the "Think global, act local" brand management initiative. Western quality and production platforms were introduced, but the concept of "Japanese-ness" was something of value to retain.

Japanese DNA

The Nissan name is abbreviated from "Nihon Sangyo," literally translating as "Japanese industry," and throughout the rebuilding of the brand, Ghosn has stayed true to his promise of keeping to, and capitalizing on, what Nissan called its "Japanese DNA." The 70th anniversary of Nissan in 2004 was celebrated by a new brand identity according to this Japanese DNA. The Jikoo concept car was the front for this, a symbol that focused on the revival of native craftsmanship.

The interior and exterior design finishes were created by Japanese craftsmen whose skills descend from the Edo period (1603–1867). From lacquer and *karakami* door trims, deerskin stenciled seats from Inden, to parquet flooring, Tokugawa Shogun wheel trims hammered from pure silver with a thickness of only one millimeter, and countless other Japanese parts, Nissan made a statement—its continuing search for its own identity in a global and increasingly commoditized market. The task was to leverage the 2,000 years of heritage and tradition and match this with global consumer contemporary desire. Simply put— treading the tightrope walk of matching tradition with modernity.

The Brand Tagline: "Shift_the Future"

"SHIFT_the future" is the tagline for the repositioned Nissan brand, but as a consumer-oriented company Nissan has taken the time to explain what this means. The way in which this is done skillfully connects the brand to Nissan's product strategy, and relevant attributes and features.

In marketing collaterals, the tagline is well explained multilingually where appropriate. For example, in brochures for the new Cefiro model, a dictionary definition of the word "shift" is given, along with six examples of what this means for the consumer, as follows:

> **SHIFT** *v.* 1. to change. 2. to move to a position that's right for you. 3. to leave the status quo far, far behind.
>
> One of the world's largest automakers, with operations encompassing over 6,000 dealers in 180-plus countries, Nissan is shifting the future of the automobile.
>
> *SHIFT the way you imagine cars to look*
>
> From the overall silhouette to the smallest interior detail, Nissan's innovative designs are creating cars that stand out, cars that show personality, cars that make you smile.
>
> *SHIFT the way you feel about driving*
>
> Driving pleasure is at the heart of Nissan. This passion is apparent everywhere, from the way the car looks to the way it responds to the driver's every command.
>
> *SHIFT the way you think about the environment*
>
> Protecting and sustaining the environment concerns everyone. Nissan approaches this responsibility with the conviction that sound environmental policy is very much at the core of sound business practice.
>
> *SHIFT the way you expect cars to last*
>
> Nissan has always been known for durability and reliability. Now it is raising the bar again, with technological expertise proven in the world's most demanding motorsports events.
>
> *SHIFT the way you stay connected*
>
> IT (Information Technology) is coming to the car, with systems to maintain the flow of information both within the vehicle and with the world around it.

SHIFT the way you consider safety

Under its "Quest for Real World Safety" policy, Nissan aims to provide effective safety technologies based on data from actual traffic accidents.

Sometimes, brands do nothing to explain what their taglines mean and this can result in confusion for everyone who didn't have a part in inventing them. Such appears to be the case with Hitachi's "Inspire the next."

MOVING FORWARD: THE STRATEGIC PLAN

The company now has a forward strategic plan called "Nissan Value Up," which was implemented in April 2005. The plan has three commitments:

- to reach annual global sales of 4.2 million units by the end of fiscal year 2007 (March 2008);
- to maintain the top-level operating profit margin in the automotive industry—this means the achievement of double-digit figures; and
- to maintain a return on invested capital (ROIC) of 20% or higher.

A total of 28 new models will be released during the three years of the plan. Along with renewal of many current models, seven innovative new models will also be released, while other models will expand their geographical reach into new markets.

As part of its future business strategy, Nissan is aiming at non-reliance on the US market, which is showing signs of instability. Being dependent on one main country for international sales is dangerous, and Nissan has announced that it will be adding Russia and Asia, including China, to it sales focus.

ALL VERY NICE, BUT . . . : THE UPHILL ROAD AHEAD

There is no doubt that Nissan is doing well, and if this progress is sustainable it will become a global brand in every sense of the word. However, one threat to the continued rise of Nissan, and one which could indeed destroy it, is the matter of quality. And quality is beginning to haunt Nissan.

Quality

It is a well-known fact that it is impossible to gain power brand status without top-class quality. Quality is a fundamental necessity. In May 2003, Nissan started production with a US$1.4 billion plant in Canton, Missouri and in July 2003 it started a joint venture with Chinese automaker Dongfeng. In April 2004, J. D. Power and Associates Inc. announced that Nissan had dropped from sixth to 11th place in its annual quality survey.

With the bad news circulating the world rapidly, Ghosn conceded that "We've been surprised by the level of deterioration." He said, "We recognize it as a problem, and we will fix it." Most of the reasons for this judgment appear to have their basis in the Canton plant. In dramatic fashion, Ghosn flew in 220 engineers from other plants to do just that.

Critics were quick to blame Ghosn, saying that he has tried to do too much too soon, especially in the United States. In Canton, five new models were launched in less than eight months; a horrific schedule for any company, never mind one that is on the road to recovery. The pressure to get products to market quickly proved detrimental to quality. One executive (who wished to remain anonymous) claimed, "So much effort was spent getting costs down that the quality issue went unnoticed—until it was too late."

The variety of quality problems was indeed a shock to all. But Nissan has not dealt with the issue.

You share the ups and the downs

The quality problem seems instead to have become worse, and it has not been confined to the United States. On December 16, 2004, Japan's Ministry of Land, Infrastructure and Transport announced that Nissan Motor Co. would recall 13,269 cars in Japan to fix faulty welding in the fuel system and defective transmission parts. The recall was to take place the day after the announcement, and affected ten models including the Tiida, Tiida Latio, Cube, and March compact cars built between October 28 and November 29, 2004, according to the ministry. Of these recalls, faulty welding accounted for 13,157 and 112 were subject to transmission defects.

The ministry added that other automakers in Japan had also been required to recall product in 2004. This recall inflation, it said, was partly due to the sharing of components among companies to reduce costs of production. In simple terms, one faulty part from one company spreads quickly to others, and it is more difficult to control quality when parts are arriving from several companies.

Poor quality can destroy brands quickly as consumers lose confidence, especially when ministerial announcements are made. Some may forgive "teething" problems in distant countries with new plants (although they are still inexcusable), but problems in your own country—especially in a market the size of Japan—could be disastrous if they continue. Nissan's share price dropped by around 10% in 2004, and there is no doubt that the company is currently facing a confidence crisis.

No matter where they originate, quality problems have to be dealt with quickly and finally. For instance, Mercedes Benz is currently losing market share and profitability due to this very problem. Daimler Chrysler has also come under constant pressure during the last two years on the very same issue and has failed to deal with it. For example, in November 2004 in Malaysia it was recalling Mercedes cars for braking problems.

With the targets projected and promised by Ghosn, the quality dimension will remain a cause for concern both within and outside the company. And no one knows better than him that poor quality can quickly destroy a brand.

There is a further challenge that threatens to derail the branding effort, and that is the pressure on prices and the need for volume.

The Price–Volume Challenge

Nissan, like any other business, has to constantly move the volume figures up in order to gain economies of scale, cost reductions, and higher profits. But this is a tricky task. In the US market, for example, General Motors and Ford have ruined their profit margins by substantially raising discounts and incentives. In order to compete with downward shifting prices, Nissan is under pressure to do the same. In the United States, Nissan's incentives rose an average of 17% in the six months to September 2004. Figures from NW Market Research indicate that in August 2004, Nissan's incentives were US$1,599 per vehicle and in the following month US$1,853 per vehicle. This helped

US sales figures, but analysts are concerned that if Nissan continues to fight on price in order to achieve its 3.6 million sales targets by September 2005, then the enviable track record of high profit margins that it has built up may be eroded.

Another connected issue is that too much sales discounting tends to dilute brand image. Thus, this balance between volume and price has to be managed delicately. On top of this, there are other considerations in the marketplace that are tending to make life difficult for motor vehicle manufacturers.

Challenging Market Dynamics

More obstacles seem to be looming up for Nissan and other firms, as market conditions change. First, costs of raw materials are being driven up through rising prices of vital commodities such as rubber and steel. Second, higher interest rates and tighter credit in important markets such as the United States and China pose a threat to the demand growth for cars. Japanese manufacturers such as Nissan also have to deal with the weaker US dollar, which makes their products less competitive than those of the indigenous market producers.

Despite all this, Nissan sticks to its promises, and publicly re-emphasizes them. Ghosn says they are "commitments." In fact, he says that if the targets he has set are not delivered, then it would be the end of the road for him and his management team. There is therefore considerable pressure building up in the Nissan camp. The head of global sales, Norio Matsumara, has been quoted as saying, "If I said we aren't feeling any pressure at all—well, that would be a lie," but he also says: "We will definitely make it."

Will Nissan make it or not? Place your bets!

Brand strengths

- Investment in R&D to reach vision. The core concept is that the application of the technology must be real-world, useful, pragmatic, and easy for the customer to use.
- Strong brand image as durable products.
- Improved product design.
- Ability of a charismatic CEO to turn around a loss-making company to profitability in a four-year period.
- Growing presence in the United States, which contributed 28% (highest) to net sales.

Brand weaknesses

- Creeping doubts about product quality.
- As Ghosn assumes total responsibility for Renault as well as Nissan in late 2005, he may find it difficult to run both companies well. The quality of management that will run Nissan under his direction as he is forced to become more "hands-off" with Nissan remains to be tested.
- The pressure for discounting, if not resisted, could dilute the brand image.
- Nissan still does not have the brand preference and loyalty enjoyed by the big brands.

Brand architecture

Corporate shared branding (example: Nissan Cefiro).

CASE STUDY 5—SAMSUNG

Strategy and Speed in the Digital World

In the world of consumer electronics, Samsung Electronics Co. was far behind its rivals for the period spanning the late 1980s and early 1990s, and had been slow to react to market trends—it was without doubt more of a manufacturer than a marketer. As a result of this, and because of its reputation for inadequate quality, its image was poor compared to Sony and other companies that were in the forefront of global growth in the consumer electronics market. But the company has managed in the last few years to predict the future better than its competitors, decrease its reaction time, and become more of a marketer than a manufacturer. Now it has pace and face.

Samsung is reputed to be the fastest-growing brand in the world. And it's not modest about making this claim in some of its television commercials shown in Asia in the last quarter of 2004. It is difficult to argue with the statement. During the last ten years or so, Samsung has become the world's most profitable consumer electronics company. Chief executive Yun Jong Yong says, "We want to be the Mercedes of home electronics." In its home country of South Korea, Samsung accounts for more than 30% of the value of the Seoul stock market and 20% of South Korean exports.

It is number one in the world for color televisions, VCRs, and LCDs, and is rapidly closing on Sony in the production of DVD players. Samsung has moved into mobile phones and is now number two behind the giant Nokia. Its revenues have doubled and profits have increased 20 times since 1999, with a market capitalization of around US$71 billion, ahead of Nokia, HP, Motorola, and other players. Market sources predicted that in 2004 Samsung should reach its targeted operating profit of US$12 billion; it in fact hit US$11.52 billion, which analysts say places it second only to Microsoft on the technology profit ladder.

PRODUCT LINES

Samsung's diversity is shown in its product lines, which include:

◆ *Multimedia and home appliances:*
—multimedia PCs, note PCs, PDAs, DVD players, DVD-ROMs, HDDs, HDTVs, DBSs, DSCs, digital TVs, refrigerators, air-conditioners, microwave ovens, MP3 players, printers, and fax machines.
◆ *Semiconductors:*
—DRAM, SDRAM, Direct Rambus DRAM, DDR DRAM, SRAM, mask ROM, FRAM, flash memory, LCD driver IC, smart card and MCU, media SOC (system on chip), merged memory with logic, Alpha processor, TFT-LCD, MDL.
◆ *Information and telecommunications:*
—HHP, ATM LAN/WAN, key phone, CDMA/PCS cellular, transmission system, WLL/switching systems, optic fibers and components.

THE OPPORTUNITIES

In the huge consumer electronics global market there are some opportunities that can be seized by Samsung as well as other players, including the opportunities arising from the following facts:

♦ In 2003 China had around 270 million subscribers in its mobile phone market, and it is expected that this figure will reach 386 million by the end of 2005, 500 million by 2008, and 580 million by the end of 2010. This creates a huge market for telecommunications services, wireless Internet services, and the equipment that will enable consumers to take advantage of new communications possibilities.

♦ In May 2005, more than 90 out of every 100 Western Europeans owned a mobile phone, according to the British research institute, Analysys. Other research suggests that by 2006, 11.7 million of the 37.5 million white-collar professionals in Western Europe will be using mobile corporate email. 64% of them will use smart phones to check their email on the go. By 2007, Analysys says, there will be more mobile phones than people in Western Europe. This is an opportunity that is aligned with Samsung's strategy to lead the world in digital convergence products. 20% of all cellular handsets sold in 2007 will contain an embedded camera.

As Western Europe embraces "digital freedom," Samsung is poised to lead this consumer movement by providing revolutionary digital convergence products that are ideal for people on the move.

♦ As at April 2005, there were an estimated 135 million DVD players in 73 million US households, and they continue to sell at an average rate of 1.7 million units per month. The digital video recorder (DVR) will be the most successful new TV technology, according to an exclusive *TelevisionWeek* survey of 100 TV executives. Six million video films are rented daily. 99% of households possess at least one television and 66% have three or more sets.

More than 70% of US consumers would like to own a TV screen larger than 40 inches. In American homes, consumers are bringing the world of entertainment into their living rooms and dens by creating home theaters. This is an opportunity, and Samsung is responding with world-leading big-screen TV technology and state-of-the-art home theater systems.

◆ From a geographical perspective, different phases of development in different continents pose many opportunities for those companies that can match these with diverse product portfolios.

As we trace the rise of Samsung and its capability to realize these opportunities, let's look first at the issues surrounding the brand's astonishingly rapid development.

THE QUALITY AND IMAGE ISSUE

In the late 1980s and early 1990s, Samsung had a down-market image, troubled by concerns and doubts about product quality. This was indicated by an unusually high rate of after-sales service repair activity. Chairman Lee Kum Hee, shocked by this state of affairs, initiated a furious drive on quality improvement. Defective products were displayed in public areas of the headquarters, and the head of the mobile phone division had to endure the sight of 15,000 of his products being flattened by a bulldozer and set on fire. Samsung mobile phones are now tested in many dramatic ways, including being run over by vehicles and thrown against walls. These draconian measures have clearly worked.

Samsung had learnt a famous branding lesson—that no company can ever develop a strong brand without top-class quality, as consumer trust disappears as rapidly as quality defects arrive. But during this phase of its life, Samsung also realized that if it wanted to move from being a second-division player to a premier-league brand, there were other key elements it had to put in place.

FAST FORWARD: BRAND POSITIONING

Trailing behind many of its rivals during the last decade, Samsung was seen as a follower and not a leader. Despite huge commitments in R&D, Samsung has caught up to, but not superseded, the others in cutting-edge product development, but it does appear to have predicted the digital future more accurately than its competitors, by recognizing that the convergence of technologies was moving faster than expected.

Indeed, the company's slogan, "SAMSUNG DIGItall—Everyone's invited," expresses this realization and places it as an invitation to the world. The company explains that "SAMSUNG DIGITall" is what happens when information, communication, and entertainment are brought together in revolutionary, simple devices that bring people closer together.

Samsung is leading the digital revolution, not in technology, but in its practical application. It has gained a competitive advantage by reacting faster than its competitors as new technologies come on stream. Indeed, Samsung has used speed as a strategy for brand development. While not inventing the technologies, Samsung has been the quickest to commercialize them.

TWIN STRATEGIES: SPEED AND CHOICE

Speed

The strategy of speed, which Samsung has developed into a fine art, allows the company to take advantage of decreasing product life cycles, which are now reduced in some product categories to a number of weeks. This tremendous life-cycle compression is likely to be a permanent feature of the consumer electronics marketplace, where the sheer ubiquity of mass-customized products paradoxically has led to commoditization. They are now regarded by Samsung (and consumers) as perishable goods.

With this in mind, Samsung has moved away from the lower-volume, higher-priced products to the reverse. Another piece of smart thinking was playing in both the B2B and business-to-customer (B2C) markets, producing not just the end-user products but also the components in them. This has given the company the diversity, massive scale, and cost leadership that generates acceptable margins in commodity markets.

Choice

In commodity markets, Samsung has also realized that more is better. Consumers want choice. They want customized products to reflect their lifestyles and personalities. While some competitors have not got to grips with such market trends, Samsung has used its cost and diversity advantages to produce more products in the categories it operates in. For example, while Nokia launches around 20 new models a year, Samsung produces around 100. This allows its brand to cater for the very fragmented market that now exists in consumer electronics, where individuality is demanded at low prices and where the number of segments is increasing at a rapid rate.

Mass customization is the name of the game and Samsung has been the best at reinventing itself to deal with this through the route of huge design improvements.

A FOCUS ON DESIGN

A large part of Samsung's success as a global brand has been due to its focus on design. According to *Business Week,* since the year 2000 "Samsung has won 100 citations at top design contests in the US, Europe and Asia." It quotes Patrick Whitney, director of the Institute of Design at the Illinois Institute of Technology, as saying: "Samsung is the poster child for using design to increase brand value and market share."

In order to drive innovation throughout the company, many policies have been changed.

- Designers with new product ideas can go direct to top management.
- Young designers can challenge their superiors if they believe that a change is needed. (This goes counter to the national Confucian culture, which stresses order.)
- Engineers have to find ways to accommodate technology into new designs, instead of the reverse.
- Designers are seconded to work at fashion and design houses.
- Consumer insight is the norm, and Samsung studies how consumers actually use products. The idea is to move on from just concentrating on the look and feel of its products to improving usability. In Seoul, Samsung has a "usability laboratory."
- Samsung now has design centers in London, Los Angeles, San Francisco, Shanghai, and Tokyo.

In other words, Samsung has reinvented itself, transforming from a copier to a leader in design, and taking advantage of the other giants such as Sony who appear to have taken their eye off the design ball.

A further catalyst to the achievement of scalability and cost leadership has been the fostering of competition within the company.

INTERNAL COMPETITION

Samsung has four major divisions—telecommunications, semiconductors, digital media, and flat-screen panels. Normally, companies would keep these types of divisions separate in terms of both operations and profitability. In its relentless pursuit of innovation, Samsung has insisted on cross-functional and cross-divisional contests, and that boundaries not be sacrosanct. This can mean that engineers, marketers, designers, and others are engaged in "combat" to prove which products are both the most innovative and the most practical. Samsung has found that this cross-fertilization of ideas leads to common production platforms that generate more economies of scale. In 2001, for example, 18,000 new products were produced with 67,000 parts; whereas in the following year, 30,000 new products were produced with the same number of parts.

THE FUTURE?

One question that has to be asked is, given the downward pressure on prices and margins for digital products, can Samsung continue to succeed? Perhaps it is difficult for any single company to stay with this, and the response from Samsung has been to create strategic alliances and partnerships to share the huge costs of R&D, such as one with Sony on LCD screens, Toshiba on memory devices, and others with the likes of IBM and Microsoft. These initiatives also solve the problem of Samsung not having the first mover advantage, as it is teaming up with the first movers and so will share cutting-edge knowledge.

A second issue is that Samsung has no real "hero brand" to help its corporate branding efforts. Whereas Sony has the Walkman and Playstation, IBM has Thinkpad, and Apple has iPod, Samsung doesn't really have any outstanding product recognition. This is related, to some extent, to the follower brand situation it finds itself in.

There is another, perhaps greater, issue facing the company that outweighs all others. Samsung sounds as though it has everything, but one important ingredient is missing and may hold it back from becoming a truly global brand: a strong emotional connection with consumers. In a bid to gain brand awareness and get on to the consumers' hit list, Samsung is spending US$800 million a year on advertising and promotion, double what it was spending four years ago. It spent around US$10 billion on marketing from 1999 to 2004 inclusive, and around US$15 billion on R&D. Samsung marketing chief Eric Kim says that such spending has met the goal of building awareness for Samsung products. The next step, he says, is to persuade people to seek out Samsung products when they shop for electronic gadgets and appliances.

This level of spending is not likely to be reduced until brand friendship, trust, and loyalty are present. As the head of Samsung North America, Dong Jin Oh, has said: "Our brand doesn't provoke an emotional response. We still have a long way to go to be a tier-one company in the US." He certainly put his finger on the problem—that no company can buy its way into the hearts of consumers—and Samsung has to learn this; hopefully not the hard way, as brands such as Sony are experiencing. As Eric Kim put it, "To be loved, we have to affect our consumers' emotions."

Notwithstanding the challenges ahead, it would seem that Samsung has the guts and determination to become a global brand in every sense of the term. It won't be easy, though, as the 2004 results point out. Net profit for the fourth quarter of 2004 fell by 1.6% from a year earlier, and margins were slipping; but Samsung remains upbeat. It expects its profit margin to grow again in 2005 led by the semiconductor and mobile phone businesses, whereas LCD margins are still likely to remain under pressure. And many analysts are forecasting that Samsung will attain its second-largest annual profit in 2005.

Brand strengths

- Management passion and determination to change the rules and the organizational norms to back up the brand strategy.
- Speed as a strategic competitive advantage.
- At present, competitive design.
- Consistency in brand positioning.

Brand weaknesses

- Still seen as a follower and not a leader.
- Huge, draining annual advertising and promotion expenditure.
- Failure (so far) to reach the hearts of consumers; there is still a lack of trust, loyalty, and emotional associations.
- Country-of-origin; Korea is still not seen as the "king" of consumer electronics, a fact that links to the trust and emotional challenges identified above.

Brand architecture

Corporate, with product descriptors (examples: Samsung Electric Cooker RESF3330DW, Samsung Dishwasher Tall Tub DB5710DT).

Sources

- ◆ Corporate information.
- ◆ *BusinessWeek*, November 29, 2004.
- ◆ *Newsweek*, December 2004—February 2005.

CONCLUSION

Refreshing your brand through a process of rejuvenation is fine if the basic name and identity of the brand is intact. But sometimes a brand needs a name and identity change, and this is the subject of the next chapter.

CHAPTER 4

BRAND NAMING
AND IDENTITY

INTRODUCTION

The rejuvenation process that is successfully being carried out by the brand cases discussed in the previous chapter may sometimes not be enough, and names and identities must be changed for various reasons. Naming and identity changes can help to reduce negative perceptions and might be compulsory for gaining global recognition. This chapter deals with these issues.

Some brand names have become famous and profitable assets, and the brand strategy has been built around them. An exemplary example of this is the Orange mobile telecommunications brand. Orange came late into the mobile telecommunications market in the UK, in 1994, and decided not to compete on price but to build a brand that consumers loved. It based its brand around the concept of optimism with the tagline, "The future's bright. The future's Orange." The name and color were researched and the rest is history. The brand had premium prices and few retail outlets, but was sold to France Telecom in 2001 for £31 billion. Such is the power of branding and naming of brands.

For all the good brand names we see, there are as many poor ones. While the name "Sunday" has done well for the Hong Kong telecommunications company, a near disaster occurred when Pricewaterhouse Coopers Consulting (PwC Consulting) decided to call itself "Monday"; fortunately, the decision was overturned by buyers IBM before it could be launched. Oldsmobile could never revitalize itself, mainly because of name associations with being "past it," reinforced by poor product. Nova, the world car launched by General Motors, never made it in Spain where the name literally means "won't go."

Thus, naming is extremely important and can decide the success or failure of a brand. Good names are short, memorable, meaningful, and above all, relevant.

Unlike the PWCs of this world, who had no real reason to undertake a name change, brand owners sometimes feel the need to inject modernity and relevance into their brands by naming and design changes, and to break away from past images.

In this chapter, I have two interesting examples. LG felt it had to move on from the past and from images that didn't resonate well with the new consumer electronics markets. BenQ is a similar example, but in this case it wasn't so much a poor image that was the root cause, as the need to adopt a different brand name to provide the opportunity to gain global status and to distance a new business from the previous brand owner, Acer.

There is also the issue of whether or not a brand name can travel. Legend found that it couldn't use its name in certain countries where it had already been registered, and so it changed it to Lenovo. (See Chapter 11 for a discussion of this company, which has recently taken over IBM's PC interests.)

While all these examples are of interest, I don't wish to give the impression that great brands are developed from good names and fancy logos. But names and logos do have their place in brand success, as the following cases demonstrate.

CASE STUDY 6—LG ELECTRONICS (LG)

"Life's Good"

LG was founded in 1947 as Korea's first chemical company. It also became the nation's first electronics company when it entered the home electronics market on October 1, 1958 with the name "GoldStar Co.," with radios its first product. The company changed its name to "LG Electronics" in 1995, by which time it was making many products, including refrigerators, batteries, elevators, cosmetics, and plastics in conjunction with the LG Group's chemicals division. But it suffered from image problems; in particular, it was associated with poor quality.

This has happened with other Korean companies that also enjoyed little brand success in the late 1980s and early 1990s but turned themselves around in the late 1990s. Samsung is one example. LG found it necessary to make a name change to escape from the poor image that plagued GoldStar. The change of name and brand identity, described below, has brought the brand back to life.

LG was divided into two holding companies on July 1, 2003—LG Corp. and GS Holdings Corp.—to separate the manufacturing- and technology-related aspects of its business from the service and retail operations. Eight retail firms were merged under GS Holdings, including the retail outlets of the LG Group such as LG Mart, LG Home Shopping, and LG-Caltex Oil. LG Corp. holds the manufacturing companies in LG Group, such as LG Electronics and LG Chemicals.

Although the spin on the split is that efficiencies and added value to shareholders will accrue, it is interesting to note that the Koo family will lead LG Corp. and the Huh family GS Holdings Corp. A lot of Asian companies are "marriages of convenience."

Nevertheless, it is LG Electronics that has spearheaded the LG brand revolution, and this case study is concerned mainly with its activities.

RAPID GROWTH IN SIZE AND PROFITS

LG has a vision to be in the top three global companies in electronics, information, and telecommunications by 2010, a mission to become the digital global leader, and a goal to be a key architect of the digital age. It seems to be on track. LG is now a massive global firm with 75 overseas subsidiaries, 13 R&D centers, and over 64,000 employees. Its corporate strategy is based on two pillars of activity:

- *Fast innovation:*
  —Setting extremely high innovation goals and securing a competitive edge, aiming at 30% more than what their competitors can do.

—30% more sales and improvement in market share.

—30% faster new product development.

—Three years ahead of competitors in technology development and establishment of corporate value.

◆ *Fast growth:* To expand market size and earnings quickly, while improving growth rate in terms of monetary value rather than quantity.

You can see from these company statements that LG is a brand that is very ambitious and in a hurry.

Product Lines

LG's product lines include the following:

◆ *Digital appliances:* Refrigerators, washing machines, vacuum cleaners, air-conditioners, microwave ovens.

◆ *Digital display and media:* TVs, VCRs, CD-ROMs, Audio, PDPs (plasma display panels).

◆ *Telecommunication equipment and handsets:* CDMA handsets, GSM handsets, wireless telephones, WLL handsets, mobile communications, transmitters, switchboards, key phone systems, and PCs.

LG's products are distributed and available worldwide to consumers. LG is also heavily involved in B2B relationships. It has set up a "Global Cyber Service Center" website for B2B strategic partners. LG's joint venture with Philips (LG Philips LCD) is the second-largest manufacturer of liquid crystal displays (LCDs).

Product Development and Business Results

Rapid innovation is a feature of the company, speed to market being critical to success in consumer electronics with the compressed product life cycles that predominate in the industry. Sales-wise it seems to have paid off, with worldwide revenues increasing by 35% in 2003 to US$31 billion, from US$25.7 billion in 2002. The 2004 figures are set to rise another 27%.

LG's appliances business has a profitability of over 8%, which is the highest in the world, due mainly to the brand's image success resulting in its appeal to higher-income groups, especially in Western markets. For example, in the United States LG's refrigerators enjoy premium prices of over US$8,000. Innovations, in the form of Internet displays and quieter compressors, give LG products the edge. As we have seen above and will see later in this case, LG gives innovation a very high priority.

In the mobile phone category it has made enormous strides forward. In 2000 it sold only 6.9 million handsets; in 2004, it sold 44 million units, leapfrogging over Sony Ericsson into fifth place worldwide, behind Nokia, Motorola, Samsung, and Siemens. The mobile phone business provides about 30% of LG's revenues.

Globally, LG has the fastest growth in this segment, and is aiming to be in the top three mobile phone makers, if possible by 2006. LG expects its sales of handsets to grow by 50% in 2005 and to overtake fourth-place Siemens. The aim is for handsets to account for half its sales before the end of the decade. The logic behind the drive to move up in this category is LG's belief that once consumers have bought an LG phone, they are more likely to be brand loyal and to purchase televisions, video recorders, refrigerators, and other LG products. This is an interesting and debatable aspect of consumer behavior that is discussed later in the case.

Its other businesses are also enjoying impressive growth in categories such as air-conditioners, microwave ovens, DVD players, and others. It is the world's leading manufacturer of household air-conditioners, and number three in plasma televisions. Over 80% of sales now come from outside its home country of South Korea, and the brand is available in all six continents.

The only underperforming business is LG Philips, where the company had a 94% drop in fourth-quarter profits for 2004. According to the company, this was due to an oversupply in the industry, which caused LCD prices to fall quickly in mid-2004 and by 20% in the fourth quarter of that year. This is not a brand-related issue, as Samsung and Sony suffered similar fates in this area of their businesses. Although prices are expected to pick up during 2005, LG Philips is increasing capital spending by 20% in 2005, a move that has raised some eyebrows among analysts and investors, who still predict that demand for flat TVs is unlikely to grow quickly in the near future, and don't see the need to throw money in this direction at present.

ESCAPE FROM THE PAST: A NEW IDENTITY

As mentioned above, in an attempt to break away from the past the group chose to change its name officially to "LG" in 1995, and set about establishing a new brand identity that suited its globalization objectives. It is now seen as a major player in the global consumer electronics market, with LG Electronics the star of the new show.

A New Brand Identity

The new brand identity was encapsulated in the words "Delightfully smart," an overarching umbrella for everything the brand LG stands for. LG says it is "dedicated to making life delightfully smart."

Further explanation of the "Delightfully smart" brand identity stems from the spirit that is captured by LG, and described by the company as follows:

> LG is delightful (consumer-oriented) because LG is founded with delight by those who encounter LG products. For people who are inspired by the latest digital technologies, advanced designs and stylings, and innovative yet practical functions, choosing LG is a form of self-expression, and self-satisfaction, an amazing comfort in knowing you made the perfect decision.
>
> LG is smart (product-oriented) because its products are smart and developed fundamentally to provide smart solutions for your everyday problems. "Smart" is the expression of the means and the way that our products are innovated. LG products enhance your life with their intelligent features, intuitive functionality, and exceptional performance.

As well as the change in brand identity and the name change that accompanied it, LG also changed its logo, and underlined all these changes with a new tagline.

A New Name, Logo, and Tagline

Naming

According to Woo Hyun Paik, LG Electronics' president and chief technology officer,

> LG originally stood for Lucky GoldStar. LG Electronics used to be known as GoldStar Electronics in Korea and used to use the GoldStar brand on our products everywhere. Even in Korea. [The electronics company] started 50 years ago with GoldStar tube radios. Seven years ago, we changed the name from GoldStar to LG, because, in part, we felt LG had a more modern feeling.

LG says:

> As LG is not an acronym, there is no full name for LG. On renaming the Group, we considered "LG" to be the most appropriate for a new group name that could integrate different images of two mainstreams of the Group's businesses, the Chemicals led by "Lucky" and the Electronics and Telecommunications led by "Goldstar," while including various brand images of other business fields.

The logo

The company says of the new logo that "L" and "G" represents the world, future, youth, humanity, and technology, while the symbol colored in red represents friendliness and gives a strong impression of LG's commitment to the best.

The tagline and brand promise

A new tagline, "Life's good," was also created to express LG's new brand promise, which is discussed later in this case. The "Life's good" promise is an expression that reflects LG's belief that life is enriched and enhanced by products that are ingeniously designed and expertly built. It expresses LG's will to provide solutions for an enriched, good life by continuously developing innovative and "delightfully smart" products.

Corporate culture

But unlike many companies that change their corporate identity, LG—to its credit—has tried to put substance behind the changes so that consumers didn't just experience cosmetic communications changes.

The revision of the corporate identity was more than a mere name change. It transformed the organizational culture and attitude of its employees, and symbolized the beginning of LG Electronics' journey to becoming a world leader. The corporate culture of LG is described by the company as follows:

- No "no" challenge: We suggest an alternative before saying "no" and aggressively work toward fulfilling our goal.
- "We," not "I": We embrace strong teamwork.
- Fun [place] to work: A workplace where individuals' creativity and freedom are respected and working is made fun.

LG is working hard to get the mindset right, and claims harmonious relationships between management and employees. There is no labor union in LG but, instead, a mantra of "Value creative management and employee relations," where everyone devotes themselves to their duties and places their trust in one another.

This is a good example of where the brand has to be lived internally as well as externally. Life has to be good for employees, or the right messages won't be permeated outside.

ADDING EMOTIONAL APPEAL: BRAND COMMUNICATIONS

The philosophy of the brand's positioning is that it provides people with products that help them to feel that "Life's good." It is clear from the brand communications that LG is trying to establish an emotional connection with consumers, something that has eluded it in the past, but is essential to its future success.

It is always used in communications to highlight the brand's breakthrough technologies and latest products. For example, an advertisement in the January 10, 2005 issue of *Forbes* magazine highlights the LG 3G phone. The copy reads:

> 7 am–10 am: Last minute client meeting in Beijing to discuss major structural change. 11 am–4 pm: Intense meeting with engineers to defy the laws of physics. 7 pm–11 pm: Motivational meeting with contractors to pull off the impossible. (11.10 pm: Angry voice message from fiancée in Los Angeles complaining that you forgot to call.) (11.15 pm: Call to fiancée to show her you never stopped thinking about her for a second.)
>
> The LG 3G Phone enables you to see and talk to someone in real time. When you need to most.

It's just one way LG makes life good. To see more ways, visit www.lge.com.

The brand promise contained in the tagline "Life's good" is always contained in advertisements such as this one, but is physically delivered in real ways, principally through product innovation and user-friendliness.

THINKING GLOBAL, ACTING LOCAL

Market sensitivity is one thing that the brand has not forgotten in its rapid rise to global power and reach. It tailors its products for different markets, and so manages to achieve mass customization, a feat that has defied some other companies.

For example, LG has introduced what is called a "Mecca phone" for the Islamic market, predominantly in the Middle East. Called officially the F7100 Qiblah phone, the product features include a prayer time alarm, a direction indicator, and a built-in compass. Muslims say their prayers five times a day and have to face Mecca to do so, and this will help them wherever they are, in whatever terrain, and across 500 cities as it is a GSM phone. In India, where much of the population eats mostly vegetables and little meat, LG came out with a refrigerator that has a smaller freezer than in the standard model and a larger crisper for storing fresh vegetables. Both of these examples of good consumer insight and consequent product adaptation have been very successful.

LG calls this "customization," and it represents its ability to listen to the needs and wants of various consumer segments, or "field management." The R&D demands are thus very high, and LG spends over 4% of annual sales on this activity, amounting in 2004 to over US$1 billion.

LG isn't thrifty when it comes to marketing spend and is certainly willing to invest in brand building. In the United States, LG has long been regarded as a cheap, follower brand copying products from other companies. In order to portray itself as a premium brand in that country, LG spends more than US$100 million a year. It seems to be working, as its phone sales are rising rapidly despite a price premium of around 15%, with customers such as Sprint and Verizon. It has earmarked US$200 million for mobile phone marketing in

2005. LG has acquired a local US subsidiary, Zenith, to take care of the low end of the market, so that it can keep its own premium brand name and not dilute it, yet still access the high-volume, lower-value mass market.

Product Innovation

The R&D effort backs up this promise to make life good with innovative products. As examples, apart from the "Mecca phone" described above, LG is a pioneer in the introduction of 3G phones. The latest LG mobile phones have MP3 players and high-definition cameras, and LG has brought out the world's first terrestrial DMB-receiving handsets.

On the white goods front, refrigerators include Internet displays that enable users to be on the Net while preparing a meal in the kitchen. The company was the first to bring to market the world's largest 71-inch plasma television, and the world's largest all-in-one 55-inch LCD television that can receive digital signals via a set-top box. LG has also produced a stand-alone digital video recorder with a 160-gigabyte hard drive offering an electronic program guide and connection to television, and a US$180 MP3 player the size of a matchbox. Chief executive Kim Ssang Su wants the innovative part of LG's image to be enhanced. At the huge Consumer Electronics Show held in Las Vegas in January 2005, LG won 16 innovation awards, more than any other company.

There are many other examples of innovative leadership, in which LG has excelled. This isn't ad hoc product enhancement, but an extremely focused part of LG's brand strategy, the aim of which is to capitalize on convergence and let LG brand owners do many things at one time, so that life is good.

Making the Complex Simple and User-friendly through Product Identity

One of the keys to the brand's success in making life good is simplicity. LG focuses on not just the visual identity of its products but the user interface. In building what it calls "product identity," LG always ensures that its products are:

- *User-friendly:* Comfortable fit, intuitive and efficient, safe.
- *Solid:* Accurate with fine details, confident and firm, fine finishing.
- *Expressive:* Advanced, attractive, with originality.
- *Reflecting lifestyles:* Needs, value, with vision.

But technology is nothing without skillful brand marketing. LG has improved in this area, particularly in getting close to the consumer (as mentioned above), but there are many more improvements that need to be made. With this in mind, LG knows it has to gain more global awareness. Importantly, it has to strongly differentiate itself from the competition, which is fierce.

EXPERIENTIAL BRAND MARKETING

As companies such as Sony have found to their cost, it is not enough to have good-quality, innovative products; a brand has to develop friendship with and loyalty to the consumers it wants to become lifetime customers. If this fails to happen, then there is much more likelihood of them switching to competitor brands as new products and technologies appear. I believe that LG understands this and is trying to build up that elusive emotional association with consumers that many companies have; however, it has not quite got there yet.

More efforts are being made to gain "share of voice" and "share of heart" on the way to gaining "share of wallet." While LG does use mass advertising to create brand awareness, it also gets involved in what is sometimes called "experiential marketing," which means using event-based marketing, grassroots campaigns, and cause-related activities to foster customer interaction. Currently it is targeting the youth market, but only time will tell if this will be a "delightfully smart" move.

Targeting Youth via Sport: Closing the Gate, or Opening the Door?

The experiential marketing approach has been most evident in LG's push to get a share of the youth market. Campaigns have taken several forms, but one of the main initiatives has been in the area of sports marketing, where LG has chosen action sports such as skateboarding and BMX bike riding. LG sponsors the LG Action Sports Championships in the United States, having secured sponsorship of this event through to 2008, as a way to aim its brand at technology-savvy young people.

LG says that "action sports have 150 million participants globally, and the category is growing at around 30% per year. 85% of the participants are aged between 12–34 years." Jae Bae, executive vice president for global strategy and business management, says: "Research showed us that 'action sports' are well established in many markets and are either growing or have huge potential in many other markets."

There are two reasons for LG choosing sports that are not "mainline." First, other big firms such as Samsung have tied up main attractions such as the Olympic Games. Second, youth is more susceptible to brand-marketing initiatives as, unlike older segments, they are more open-minded about brands they will try. By targeting the young or "young-at-heart," LG hopes to raise its global brand awareness and tap into a large demographic. The challenge is to tap into the values of youth. If LG can do what MTV has done with a similar age range, they will have made a wise choice. But few firms understand youth like MTV, and this represents a challenge to any company targeting this universal segment.

To date, LG's overall brand communications have not been really in tune with youth, and many believe that sponsorship isn't enough. All disciplines have to be consistent in order to capture that segment.

In areas other than sport, LG is also working hard to get close to the customer. In the Middle East it sponsors a Digital Music Festival, and in Mexico it supports local schools. As with its products, LG knows what each market likes and wants, and aims to be seen as a brand that cares about local people.

In looking at the challenges facing the LG brand, the need to address various markets—and not just youth—is one of them.

CHALLENGES

Life may be good, but it is not without its challenges. LG has at least four main challenges, one of which is its home-grown competitor, Samsung, and the second a much closer relative. But let's deal with the most important one first—how can LG position itself across a broad range of products and emotionally connect with all the segments it is targeting?

Brand Positioning and Segmentation

"Life's good" is a broad enough and interesting value proposition, capable of multi-segment appeal; but the devil is in the detail. A massive brand promise such as this has to be capable of execution in all markets.

One of the questions that LG must be debating now is how to target youth with all its fickleness, understand and appeal to its values, and yet still target other demographic segments with product ranges that don't interest youth. The "Life's good" brand promise is capable of this, but a comprehensive communications strategy is needed to pull everything together. So the question is, how can LG wrap this around every brand conversation it has with every target audience, and make it both meaningful and relevant?

Brand Personality

At present, LG appears to be trying to base its brand-building effort on leadership in product features and benefits, but this can never be sustainable, as other big brands such as Sony have found out. Being state-of-the-art is necessary in technology branding, but what LG seems to be missing at the moment is emotion in its branding. Until now, there has been a lot of concentration on product, perhaps at the expense of brand personality development. A strong corporate brand personality would help to add the much-needed emotional dimension to the "Life's good" proposition and enable LG to be flexible and appealing in addressing all markets. Its home rival has the same challenge of increasing its emotional connection with consumers, but is still ahead on the numbers side.

Outpacing Samsung

Samsung has never been the leader in technology (see the case on pages 42–50), but it has been fast to adopt new technology and get it to market. LG has that same challenge—how can it make new technology applications faster than others, especially Samsung? LG knows that a low-price, high-volume strategy won't give it the brand image it desperately seeks, and so it has to produce sophisticated and stylish products that are more costly.

Quality isn't a problem, but it appears that design is vital for success in defeating its rival. As chief financial officer Kwon Young Soo says, "Our quality is almost the same, but design-wise Samsung is better." LG has now increased its design team to 500 people, and it sees design as a vector of perceived value by consumers.

Moreover, unlike Samsung, it doesn't have a semiconductor division, although it still produces chips, so it cannot manufacture some product parts that are very profitable and could subsidize its higher aims. It therefore finds itself with some limitations behind its unrelated "big brother."

Some analysts wonder if LG has the cash to keep up the investment needed to stay ahead of its rivals and catch the likes of Samsung. This doesn't seem to be worrying LG right now, but with the Chinese fast catching up and the Japanese also looking at the same markets, LG must continue to invest in R&D if it is to keep its lead in 3G technologies. It has said that it will spend US$1.73 billion in R&D in 2005, which will be about 6% of sales. Samsung spends 7.5% of its sales on R&D, and its sales are bigger. Most of LG's R&D spend is likely to go on the next generation of mobile phones, digital televisions, flat panels, and network products.

There is one final irritation for LG that seemingly will just not go away, and that is one of the former LG Group subsidiaries, where there is still some involvement.

The Joker in the Pack

While the pressure has been on to boost LG's image, there is a problem which, as yet, is unresolved: LG Card. At the time of writing, a rescue deal costing US$965 million is being put together to save one of Korea's largest credit card issuers from insolvency.

That issuer is LG Card Co. and LG Group, the former parent, along with its connected companies, has found itself involved in the bailout. LG Electronics has tried to distance itself from the scandal, which has been going on now for around four years, by refusing to put up more money than it has offered previously, as has LG Chem. Nevertheless, in the final declaration, companies in the LG Group and the creditors will each contribute 500 billion won of the debt repayment in the hope that the problem will then be resolved.

In the meantime, the market capitalization of LG Card has been steadily falling and fell again even after the bailout announcement. This whole area of bailouts, corporate governance, and transparency associated with the Korean *chaebols* has been holding back the image development of many Korean companies over the last two decades or more, and investors usually factor in a discount figure for them.

With respect to LG Card, the final outcome may be satisfactory, but the image transference is present with the "LG" naming link. It must be a source of frustration for all the winning LG companies that a sibling has caused so much embarrassment and dogged the overall LG brand image. The protagonists against corporate branding will use this in their arguments against this form of brand architecture—for if one product, sub-brand, or related brand fails, then it rebounds on the corporate brand name.

THE FUTURE?

Looking at progress so far, LG is a brand on the move. In the long term, life certainly seems as though it could be good for LG, and among its well-earned accolades it was voted as number 1 in *BusinessWeek*'s "Information Technology 100" in June 2004. It should overcome the stigma of LG Card and is good at turning consumer insight into product with speed. The new logo and tagline, backed up by delivery on the brand promise they contain, should therefore work if brand management is strong. LG seems destined and determined to be a major global Asian brand.

Brand strengths

- Key strength: digital technology leadership (for example, world-class CDMA).
- Product innovation. (LG was the first company to commercialize a full line of Web-enabled home network appliances, including refrigerators, washing machines, microwave ovens, and air-conditioners.)
- Aggressive investment in R&D to reach the vision of global brand leadership.
- Strong product presence and acceptance in North America and Europe.

- Enterprising marketing strategies.
- Good global–local balance and understanding of multiple markets and segments.

Brand weaknesses

- Brand marketing and management capability. For example, on a macro-scale, the issue of global multi-positioning has yet to be dealt with. On the micro-scale as well, there are still some brand management inconsistencies—for example, in website design.
- Connected with the point above, there is still some way to go in the emotional brand area when compared to competitors such as Nokia. Brand trust has to be developed and nurtured.
- The country-of-origin effect is still a problem, but this is not LG's fault. South Korea still has to convince the world that it is as good as Japan and other high-tech countries, where corporate governance and transparency are rated more highly. This results in downgrading by analysts and investors—sometimes referred to as the "*chaebol* factor." LG could, with Samsung, be a great brand ambassador for its country and change global perceptions.
- Tough competition from various determined players in various categories concerned with the digital revolution, including its home rival, Samsung.
- Current perceptions of LG Card, a failed brand associated by name with the main LG brand. As long as the card company is in troubled waters, there remains the possibility of image problems for LG.

Brand architecture

Corporate, with product descriptors (example: mobile phones—LG C1200). Shared branding with company sub-brands (example: LG Home Shopping).

Sources

- *Asian Wall Street Journal,* January 3, 2005.
- Bloomberg, "Business Asia," *International Herald Tribune,* January 3, 2005.
- *BusinessWeek,* January 24, 2005.
- *Newsweek Special Edition,* December 2004—February 2005.

Case Study 7—BenQ

Who?

★ ★ ★ ★ ★

Writing about the Taiwanese BenQ brand has been a little frustrating at times. I put this down partly to my inability to understand some elements of BenQ's brand strategy, and partly to the way in which it has been publicly explained, mostly by the company and in media interviews that, without doubt, lack something in the translation. BenQ is a relatively young brand that is trying to grow very quickly and is still evolving.

In analyzing BenQ, I can see a myriad of brand-related references, statements, and characteristics, including some on brand mission, corporate mission, brand spirit, brand identity, brand personality, desired brand image, brand core value, corporate culture values, visual identity, and more. It occurs to me that BenQ seems a bit like an awkward teenager, constantly searching for its own "identity" but pulled this way and that by lots of interesting diversions; knowing a little about a lot of things and sometimes wondering which path to walk and anxious to explore.

But this is what makes BenQ interesting—it is an ambitious and talented "youngster" that is quickly making an impact on the world stage. I hope that my interpretation of the brand strategy and its constituent elements is illuminating for the reader. In watching BenQ, we are watching the formative years of what could be a great brand, or what might turn out to be just another consumer electronics company. Here is the history behind the brand.

The Spin-off

Taiwan's ACM (Acer Communications and Multimedia) changed its name to BenQ Corporation on December 5, 2001. Acer retains a stake in BenQ, but the two companies operate completely independently and have separate stock quotations on the Taipei stock market. All previous business groups that now make up BenQ Corp. include:

- AU Optronics Corp.: Has technology to manufacture a complete line-up of TFT-LCD modules. Committed to being the global leader in flat display technologies.
- Darfon Electronics Corp.: Specializes in R&D and manufacturing of professional communications devices and high-precision electronic components.
- Daxon Technology, Inc.: Specializes in development of thin film technology.
- Airoha Technology Corp.: First manufacturer in Taiwan to successfully produce integrated circuits GPRS/GSM tri-band and wireless LAN radio frequency transceiver capabilities.
- Copax Photonics Corp.: Supplier of high-performance optically active components.
- Darly Venture Inc.: Strategic investment center for cultivating new business and technology (IT).

The chronology of this is as follows:

- The company was originally established in 1984 as Continental Systems Inc.
- It changed its name to Acer Continental Inc. in 1989.
- Acer Peripherals Inc. was established in 1993.
- It changed its name to Acer Communications & Multimedia Inc. (ACM) in 2000.
- ACM changed its name to BenQ Corp. in December 2001.

Spinning off BenQ was Acer's final move in the restructuring to lay out its group organization. To keep its focus on PCs, Acer spun off both its consumer electronics division, now known as BenQ, and AU Optronics. Acer will continue to provide the global marketplace with Acer-brand IT products, including desktop PCs, home PCs, mobile PCs, servers, and Internet appliances.

On the other hand, BenQ's core focus will be on digital lifestyle devices, including mobile phones, networking, LCD and CRT monitors, digital projectors, plasma displays, and optical storage and imaging products. Its aim is to focus on more entertainment-oriented consumer electronics. BenQ will still provide after-sales service for previously branded Acer products. There appears to be some overlap, however, as BenQ is now producing laptop PCs that compete with Acer.

THE PRODUCTS

BenQ's consumer targets are those people who seek enjoyment in life with indulgence of digital products. With this in mind, it markets networked digital lifestyle devices. Its business activities include manufacturing, R&D, sales of computer peripheral and communications and consumer electronics products, and consulting and technical services.

The main product lines include:

- *Imaging network:* Scanners, optical drivers, digital cameras, color laser printers.
- *Digital media:* Digital hubs, projectors, LCD TVs, MP3 players/ USB flash drives, plasma displays, multifunctional DVDs.
- *Network display:* LCD monitors, CRT monitors, smart displays.
- *Networking and communications:* GSM/GPRS/CDMA/ CDMA2000 mobile phones, wireless LAN, home networking, SOHO routers, smart phones, wireless PDAs, wireless modules.

THE RATIONALE FOR CHANGE

Acer Peripherals (Acer CM) gave three main reasons for the change of name to BenQ:

- *Superior customer service:* Launching an independent brand allows us to dedicate our resources to strengthen and build relationship with end-users and resellers.
- *Channel support:* We are now aligned to better serve our channel as an independent entity away from other affiliated Acer companies.
- *Brand identity:* With leading technology designed to encompass and support the digital convergence era, it became essential for us to differentiate ourselves from other entities under the Acer umbrella. To do this we are focusing on the seamless integration of technology and quality of life. Why? Because enjoyment matters . . .

According to Wilbur Lin, a marketing and communications specialist for BenQ, "A lot of people asks 'Who is BenQ?' They say, 'Oh, they are a spin-off of Acer.' But the Acer name no longer is associated with us. They have nothing to do with us or our products. Acer is gone and we are now BenQ."

Nevertheless, BenQ says it will still support Acer Peripherals (Acer CM) products, and that they "are still the same core company and will honor all contracts made by Acer Peripherals (Acer CM)."

The real reason behind the name change to BenQ is to build a global brand. Presumably, with Acer remaining in any part of the company name, this was regarded as a limiting factor. As K. Y. Lee, Chairman and Chief Executive of BenQ Corporation says, "You must have a brand in order to wield any influence." He is critical of Taiwan's companies in that they are often content to stay as contract manufacturers. Lee says:

> At present, Taiwan has only large companies, but they have no influence; they are only big businesses, but no movers and shakers. . . . The Taiwan government should also consider how to consolidate and develop brand-name companies. After all, with contract manufacturing what products you make or which markets you pursue is never your own decision.

BenQ's Goal, Mission, and Desired Brand Image

Overall Goal

The overall goal of the company is to make BenQ an international, globally recognized brand. Its original parent, Acer, never made it as a global brand, but BenQ certainly is determined to do so. As Lee says, a brand is a bridge for communication between a company and consumers. When a company's internal essence is made "visible," it can influence the positive feelings that consumers have toward the company, and such feelings will in the end have an effect on their buying behavior.

The BenQ Mission and Tagline

The mission of BenQ is "To promote enjoyment matters." This apparently means "to realize that consumers can look to BenQ in their daily life of work, study, and entertainment, and thereby enjoy the delights that can be given to them by various types of Web-enabled fashion-conscious products," according to Jerry Wang, vice president of sales operation.

The desired brand image is for customers "to trust BenQ to bring enjoyment to work, leisure, learning, and entertainment with the broadest range of top-quality networked digital lifestyle devices."

Lee says that BenQ puts stress on "Enjoyment matters" because

> . . . lifestyles fall into four categories: work, learning, entertainment, and leisure. We put emphasis on giving everyone a better technological tool. Nowadays technology has widely advanced and personal lifestyles have improved, which leads people to spend more on entertainment. It is difficult to distinguish among entertainment and leisure from work, so technology should provide the means to place both together.

This is the spirit of the BenQ brand—a belief that work and play ought to be intertwined, and can be; hence the brand mission. To achieve an easy linkage between people and digital IT products, so as to enable every person to gain entertainment from work, Wang initiated the idea of "Enjoyment network"—an open standard platform for accessing and sharing data among different types of digital devices that can be easily linked together via a simple user interface, allowing users easily to truly enjoy the benefits of digital technology.

This seems to me to be reminiscent of the many high-tech firms who seem to be trying to bridge the gap between technology and humanity. But, of course, while objectives might be similar, it is how you do it that counts.

BenQ's initial growth strategy has been more sales- than brand-driven, as it needed to rapidly gain brand recognition, but that is now changing. It has established its technological capability and a strong overseas operation, two of the three qualifications for building an international brand, according to Wang. The third qualification is brand marketing.

Tagline

The tagline for the brand is "Enjoyment matters," which sums up BenQ's brand mission, described above. As is normal with any brand, it is one thing to generate strategic thoughts, but the impact is felt when the implementation starts and the marketing strategy swings into place.

THE BRAND MARKETING STRATEGY

Pricing

BenQ was faced with a large problem when it formed the new company and launched the new brand name—no one knew what BenQ was. There were two urgent needs arising from this situation. First, BenQ had to generate an enormous amount of brand awareness to get consumers interested; and second, it had to sell a lot of product from a position of little awareness or recognition at the same time to enable it to survive.

It wasn't surprising, therefore, that BenQ's initial business strategy was to buy market share with a low-price policy. BenQ, however, has stressed that this was merely an initial marketing strategy initiative, and that as its intention is to grow a global brand, it is aiming for a premium-price end game. This may seem logical, but time will tell whether BenQ can pull it off.

A look at branding history tells us that once a market is entered with a low-price strategy it is difficult to pursue a premium pricing policy, which is the objective for all great brands. By contrast, it is a little easier to start off with high prices and reduce them, although even this is fraught with difficulty and may dilute a brand's power.

Either way, there are potential damaging effects to the desired brand image, so BenQ, although it had little choice but to move down the path it has, won't find it easy later on as it seeks to raise the brand's image in consumers' minds. Whether it is successful or not will depend on its capability to understand consumers and get really close to them emotionally. Price-driven consumers are a different breed from brand-conscious ones. BenQ does seem to be addressing this issue.

Differentiation

Jerry Wang sees the flaw in the above strategy but feels it was necessary. He says, "Brand marketing is not simply a matter of blurting out the slogans. A brand must take as its starting point the fulfillment of consumer demand through a brand with a distinctive character that differentiates it from other brands and clearly separates the company behind the brand from its competitors." With this in mind, BenQ built a new brand identity, with its constituent elements of the name, a brand personality, and a visual identity. Wang clearly understands the value of a brand when he says that "consumers love you not simply because of the product, but because of their understanding of the brand and the company." This understanding is the responsibility of brand marketing.

Customer Focus

Perhaps a saving grace here is that one of the core competencies of BenQ appears to be its focus on the consumer. Product development is based on what customers want, rather than on what technology is available. As an example of this, BenQ has established the Lifestyle Design Center in Taipei to conduct consumer trend research on a global basis. Knowledge is power, so they say, and BenQ is trying to gain as much insight into consumer thinking and purchasing behavior as it possibly can. It also realizes that branding is very much a mind game and that consumer perceptions can be managed with skillful brand management and communications.

Brand Communications

As well as using all the traditional media for brand communications in fairly large quantities, BenQ uses sports marketing and was the official IT partner of UEFA EURO 2004. It tries hard to live the brand philosophy, with interactive websites and a "BenQ JoyFamily Smart Manager." Initiatives here include "Liveupdate," which automatically checks and compares the software of your BenQ product with the latest version and tells you if you need to perform updates; and "QMessenger, [which] establishes a live connection between you and BenQ customer service or other 'JoyFamily' friends to enable customers to get answers to queries just when they want them."

Distribution and Outlets

BenQ has established operations globally and has offices in more than ten countries to support its channel partners. K. Y. Lee says that this is an ongoing search; capable partners must continually be brought into the BenQ distribution system.

BenQ has sales operations in Taiwan, the United States, Japan, the Netherlands, and China with Global Logistics to serve customers worldwide, and has set up distribution channels in the US, Europe, and Asia. In addition to brand business, BenQ actively acquires orders from global IT companies for original design manufacturing business. Its main sales regions are Europe and Asia.

BenQ isn't going to pursue the route taken by Sony and other large brands and build a chain of specialty stores. Instead, it is building brand image showrooms to give consumers a different feeling about the brand's products and to raise awareness. So far, although they number less than ten, the showrooms have proved to be successful in their objectives.

Brand marketing needs a brand platform to stand on, messages to communicate, and a means of expressing differentiation. This is where the name, personality, and visual identity play their part.

BRAND NAME, PERSONALITY, AND VISUAL IDENTITY

The Name

"BenQ" stands for "Bringing enjoyment 'n' quality to life." When originally coined, the name was pronounced "Ben K," and existing and potential customers were mistaking "BenQ" for "bank." BenQ tested the name in its home country (Taiwan) in a market research survey. Although one-third of respondents associated it with Acer, which wasn't great news, another third evidently thought it was a foreign brand, which gave management the confidence to change.

It is well known that the company's intention is for BenQ to become a "cool" global technology brand, but naming issues can sometimes create problems. Even up to the last hour prior to the announcement of the new company and its name, chairman K. Y. Lee was still deliberating on how to pronounce it. As he told staff just before the launch, it had to be pronounced as two syllables: "Ben-Q." Interestingly, the apparent ambiguity of the name often sparks off discussion and certainly it is memorable.

The Brand Personality

As thought was being given to the new visual identity, work was carried out on the brand personality that would drive it. The four personality traits that were most suited to the BenQ brand aspirations were:

- vivid;
- original;

+ enjoyable; and
+ genuine.

Wang says:

> A brand can be likened to a person. A person has values, a sense of mission. But without style, there is a problem. Style comes from the influence of values on behavior and personality. If a brand is to be humanized so that people can like it, then the personality is very important.

The brand personality reminded BenQ that, like a person, a brand should be organic, and the visual identity was created on the basis of this concept.

The Visual Identity

Building a brand is all about turning the tangible into the intangible—products into feelings, if you like. This is what BenQ wanted to do with its brand, and this heavily influenced the development of its new visual identity. As a starting point, it was decided that the butterfly was most suitable to express BenQ's transformation, organic growth, and personality. Butterflies were seen by BenQ and its designers as approachable and a pure form of enjoyment. Butterflies are normally brilliantly colored and have a distinctive originality. The changeable wing patterns of butterflies were the starting point for the visual identity design.

While Acer was associated with the color green, BenQ decided to move away from this to purple. Purple was chosen as it represented a combination of red and blue, demonstrating the harmony that BenQ wanted to express. Staff uniforms were changed and a purple butterfly became the company's symbol. The transformational aspects of a butterfly represent BenQ's transformation from a manufacturer to a brand vendor.

At first the butterfly was emerging from its cocoon, but this was relaunched with new butterfly wing patterns instead. The individualistic wings were adapted to suit packaging, display boards, carrying cases, paper cups, cartons, and so on, and different image and color combinations used for different markets, such as male and female consumer segments. What BenQ is pursuing with its visual identity is an organic format, a departure from the norm in most industries, including technology, where visual identity is set in stone and precisely policed.

This is not to say that there is no brand management system, but as Wang says, "If consumers see an organic image and know that it stands for BenQ, not only have we reached an objective for the brand, but it means we have succeeded in our entire branding effort." So complex were the debates and rollout of the visual identity (cocoons, brilliant wings, and so on) that it was only in place finally after the brand had been in existence for a year and a half. This is not traditional, ideal brand management practice, but Wang even has an answer for this: "The birth of a brand is like the birth of a child. Likewise, its character is only obvious after it has grown a little. Only after a year and a half of maturing did its character gradually become clear."

Well, this is not the time or place to go into the realms of child psychology, but accepted clinical data suggests that personality is largely formed by the age of seven years, not 18 months. However, we get the gist. And the failure to get everything into a coherent whole for one launch must have cost a lot of time and money.

BenQ isn't fazed by this and maintains that what matters is that consumers see a new visual identity that is linked to BenQ, and which reminds them that BenQ is trying to make their lives simpler.

THE CORPORATE CULTURE

Being a relatively new company, BenQ is trying to create a new corporate culture that will enable it to build its brand. BenQ says that while it has been trying to generate exceptional speed, flexibility, efficiency, quality, and channel connections that are essential for a global technology brand, it has also been building a specific culture to support its goal. The four core values are:

- ◆ *We care*: we want to have lifelong relationships with our customers, we seek to understand and meet their needs, care about our employees, and are concerned about our environment.
- ◆ *We innovate*: we create, build and market innovative solutions; constantly looking for new and innovative ways to work and new ways to spark new innovation.
- ◆ *We uphold*: we produce reliable products, but quality for us also encompasses the quality of the experience of using the product as part of a total solution that delivers lifestyle benefits.

◆ *We celebrate*: we aim to bring enjoyment and pleasure to our customers as we celebrate the beauty we see in life.

THE URGE TO MERGE

In an extraordinary move that surprised the market BenQ took over Siemens mobile-phone unit, and didn't have to pay for it. Admittedly, Siemens mobile was a fading and loss-making brand with first quarter losses in 2005 of 280 Euros; but not only did BenQ get it for nothing, Siemens even agreed to provide BenQ with US$307 million to help fund the business, in exchange for an estimated 2.5% stake in the BenQ company, and deal with losses until the deal was finally concluded. The acquisition will make BenQ the first company from Taiwan with an annual revenue of nearly US$11 billion (2004, US$10.9 billion). (Source: BenQ Siemens and Wall Street Journal, June 7, 2005).

To Siemens, the main advantage appears to be the relief it will gain from the mobile division's losses that adversely have affected total corporate profitability; the company is really a business-to-business technology infrastructure brand and has never really understood retail consumer electronics markets. BenQ complements this with its retail-savvy management, and the partnership will be able to provide end-to-end mobile communications solutions like Nokia. Also, BenQ is strong in Asia where Siemens mobile is weak, whilst Siemens is strong in Europe and Latin America.

However, the deal will give BenQ several other advantages.

Firstly, it gets BenQ into the mobile phone segment with scale immediately. Normally to get the scale needed to appear in the elite section of global producers this would take up to ten years from a start position, and a lot of funding. The acquisition won't give BenQ the muscle to tackle the top two—global leader Nokia and number two Motorola—but it can now start to challenge brands such as Sony Ericsson, Samsung and LG.

Importantly, as the future of communications without question lies in the mobile phone segment, BenQ just cannot afford not to be present.

Secondly, and this impacts on the above point, the BenQ potential brand portfolio can expand more quickly as Siemens already has 3G technologies and nearly 1,000 patents in hand.

Perhaps the biggest advantage of all is the Siemens brand name, which is seriously respected, despite its monetary failure in mobile communications. Siemens has a good reputation for quality and performance, and BenQ is hoping that it can get some image transference here that will enhance the standing of its brand.

What Will Happen to the Siemens Brand?

According to both parties, the Siemens brand will be available to BenQ for a period of five years, but it appears that BenQ will start to phase it out within 18 months of the start of the partnership, then use a joint brand name mechanism. Eventually it is assumed that the Siemens brand name will disappear from the mobile market.

Clemens Joos, the new head of the post-merger division (and the Siemens president of mobile services prior to the takeover) says, "There will be new products that will go on the market after October 1st exclusively under the Siemens brand." He stresses the Siemens brand will not be represented exclusively by the mobile phone products now on the market, and that "After our co-operation has intensified to a point where the products can keep the planned market promise, we will begin launching them under the new joint brand." On balance it seems that this somewhat cautious approach is best as BenQ has not yet developed the trust and respect it needs in the mobile phone market.

BenQ is therefore taking one more step to achieving its global ambitions as a brand, and attempting to leave the O.E.M. battlefield. The downside is that it has lost its biggest contract customer Motorola Inc. In the short term this will hurt, but in the long term—if BenQ can make it in the big brand league—that should pose no problem at all.

THE FUTURE?

There are now a huge number of IT companies moving into the digital world, but in just a couple of years BenQ has managed to create an internationally known and distinctive brand image. But Lee says that brand recognition isn't sufficient. "We are still very weak in many countries," he says, and names Thailand as an example. He is determined that BenQ's early success won't turn into complacency.

There are some other developments that are still going on with this young brand, but it has a talented team. BenQ could well do what its relative Acer could not and become a global brand.

Brand strengths

- Strong channel management for brand products brings the company close to its clients.
- Excellent technology-integrated ability in different products and industries.
- Investment in key component sectors gives BenQ a competitive advantage in terms of economies of scale, quality control, and flexibility.
- Corporate culture is geared to the fast-paced digital lifestyle devices business, rather than to the traditional consumer electronics and home appliances sector.
- Ability to correspond with the market trend where basic elements of the digital lifestyle are working, learning, entertainment, and leisure.
- Its manufacturing plants in China, Taiwan, Malaysia, and Mexico are among the most advanced in the world.
- It has stable, long-term relationships with all its main components suppliers. For each component, the company keeps more than two suppliers to ensure sourcing flexibility and avoid the risks of single supply.
- Sales have increased every year due to the right management strategy and efforts from all divisions.
- Heavy investment in branding for BenQ from management, such as the chairman and president of global brand marketing.
- Led by a chairman who is aggressive and rarely gives up.

Brand weaknesses

- Brand recognition still weak in some countries.
- Stiff competition in the IT and electronics industry.
- "Made in Taiwan" country-of-origin adverse perception.

Brand architecture

Corporate, with product descriptors (example: BenQ Digital Camera DC C50, DC E40, DC C40).

Sources

Various corporate media releases.

CONCLUSION

Relevant brand naming and identity are essential for success, and sometimes have to be changed, but if these turn out to be successful there must not be complacency as competitors will always try to attack your market position. The challenger brands are always there—waiting in the wings? or hovering like vultures?—as the next chapter will show.

CHAPTER 5

CHALLENGER BRANDS

INTRODUCTION

If you have done all the right things and your brand is in a leadership position, don't feel you can now relax. Develop paranoia instead, because for every brand that makes it, there are several challenger brands waiting in the wings; given a chance, they will eat away at your business and margins. Challenger brands watch, wait, learn, and strike, so complacency isn't an option for any top brand. Their rationale is as follows.

Not everyone can be number one, but being number two or three can be pretty good and very profitable.

In the automobile market, Hyundai has come from virtually nowhere to being a successful regional brand in a short timeframe. It is now making inroads into Western markets. With its interesting and attractive product designs, value for money positioning, and reliability, it has transformed itself from a brand with massive perceptions of poor quality and cheapness to an international quality player. For instance, it climbed rapidly to number one in quality ratings in the United States in the first quarter of 2005, whereas the former top-ranking Mercedes E Class slipped to the bottom of the list, causing Daimler-Chrysler a great deal of financial and brand image problems.

Jollibee, from the Philippines, has found it hard to move outside its home market in terms of sustainable profitability, but it understands its home market best and continues to outplay the US giants of fast food.

PETRONAS is a global oil and gas giant revenue-wise; however, in branding terms, outside of Malaysia it is still a challenger brand to the likes of BP, Shell, and Exxon-Mobil. (See the case study on PETRONAS in Chapter 13.)

The future looks good for all, but can they raise their game even more? Being a challenger brand is always difficult, and such brands often have to fight against the giant global brands, and often on their territory if the challengers have ambitions to become global brands.

The two cases in this chapter are typical of this fight, but both are finding ways in which they can grow and gain global market share. Haier is a white-goods manufacturer from China that has successfully ventured into the United States, which is dominated by brands such as Whirlpool, by doing the opposite of what it does in China. In its home country it operates on a high-volume, low-cost strategy for the mass market. In the US, it uses niche marketing and a more premium strategy, aiming at gaps in the market and essentially disguising its country of origin.

Emirates is growing fast and really has a winning position as it challenges the big international airlines, generating great service at low cost. Its growth rate is phenomenal, and it is now penetrating more Western markets.

Both these cases show that sharp thinking pays off, and that brand building is key to gaining and sustaining momentum in the fight against larger brands.

Case Study 8—HAIER

Haier Takes the Fight from East to West

The Fast Track

As a great deal of my time is spent in Asia, and has been for over 18 years, I often advise would-be global brand players from Asia to get the number one position in their home market, then dominate their region, then go global if need be. The rationale behind this is simply that few global brands have ever become global without first being number one in their home market. Second, while researching foreign global markets, the common-sense approach suggests that you then go for number one in your region. This second step is tough enough, as Asia represents around half the world's population, but the task is a little easier for Asian companies than for Western ones, who may have problems understanding Asian cultures. Finally, when you have size, volume, an established name, and experience, go for the global market if you feel you can support it and make it into the top two or three.

China's top white-goods manufacturer, Haier, is taking the fast track in contrast to the above normal progression. CEO Zhang Ruimin took a non-driven state enterprise making poor-quality goods, made quality the imperative, and produced a company that is now number one in the China market, with market share for most home appliances ranging from around 20% to 70%, and US$8.5 billion in sales worldwide in 2002. It is so popular in China that people pay a premium for the Haier brand, according to Carrefour in Qingdao, where Haier is based. In fact, its washing machine costs more than a similar US Whirlpool-branded model.

According to Euromonitor International Inc., Haier was the world's fifth-largest manufacturer of large kitchen appliances in 2002, and in that year alone increased its global market share from 3.2% to 3.8%. Haier has offices in more than 100 countries and generated overseas revenues in excess of US$1 billion in 2004, mostly in niche market areas.

Haier has made it into the top five makers of white goods in the United States by taking on Western companies, such as GE and Whirlpool, but the brand is still not a household name in Asia. The quality dimension has to be addressed, as no brand can survive without first-class quality, an area with which Asian companies traditionally have not been associated. Zhang has always realized this, and such is his passion that as a senior manager in the 1980s he once gathered his staff together and took to a selection of defective refrigerator products with a sledgehammer to get across his point of view on the vital importance of quality.

According to critics, though, there are still doubts about the quality of Haier's products and its long-term future. Moreover, some analysts believe it doesn't have the cost control, production discipline, market dominance, and sales support to enable it to compete with its foreign rivals outside its home country of China.

COUNTRY-OF-ORIGIN ISSUES

Haier may have solid perceptions of its brand in China, but can this brand perception be carried to overseas markets?

One of the most critical problems facing Asian brands in recent years is the perception of "cheap and poor quality." This perception has proved difficult to shift, even after decades. It took 30 years for the Japanese brands to shift such a perception, but Chinese goods are still in the "poor quality" category, which is why Haier has chosen just this issue on which to fight its battles. And the chief executive really has taken the fight to the commercial "enemy"—the United States—where quality begins at home.

HAIER AMERICA'S OPPORTUNISTIC STRATEGY: MADE IN THE USA, FOR THE USA

The strategy for Haier in international markets has not been to build at low cost and export to the United States products that would be seen as "Made in China." The company realized that while the Nikes of this world could—because of the power of their brand names—market products with the "Made in China" label (or other countries in Asia), the Haier brand name would suffer from the home-country labeling.

So, instead, a strategy was used to reverse the conditions of manufacture so that Haier was made in the US. The company bought land enough for several factories in Camden, South Carolina, and spent US$30 million on the first refrigerator plant. This was an important part of "managing perceptions"—what brand management is all about—and establishing a secure base for the future, albeit at an increased cost of production. This location has now been extended to form the 110-acre Haier America Industrial Park, a state-of-the-art refrigerator manufacturing facility. This was a very smart move, allowing Haier to label its products "Made in the USA."

In terms of commitment to the community, Haier America is staffed almost entirely by local people, so bringing jobs to the United States where other Chinese companies are accused of taking them away. Zhang says, "merging itself with the locality" is important to Haier, and the company was awarded a "Community Contribution Prize" in 2001, and has a road named after it (Haier Avenue). Local relationships appear to be very good.

Innovation and Niche Marketing

Haier claims to have helped grow the market in certain categories, citing the 50% growth of the compact refrigerator market within a year after the brand's entry. Compact refrigerators have done well, and are increasingly to be found in college dormitory rooms, capturing the brand-conscious next-generation segment. Haier is also sensitive to the needs of different markets, and is keen on giving consumers aesthetic value. The introduction of the wine cooler in the United States is a good example of this understanding, with its sophisticated smoked glass door, curvaceous lines, soft lighting, and chrome racks. It is very much an up-market product, selling for around US$400, and featured on the cover of the *International Wine Accessories* catalogue. This innovation was also brought to market quickly, with less than a year from product conception and design to retail availability. A more recent innovation is the Brewmaster, a beer dispenser that brings draft beer to homes, doubling up as a refrigerator when not in use as a beer dispenser.

Haier is aware of the price–commodity trap and is trying hard to avoid competing on price and promotions, through a focus on quality, design, innovation, and giving consumers what they really want. Consequently, products for the US market include:

- wine cellars;
- beer dispensers;
- beverage centers;
- cellular telephones;
- water dispensers;
- dishwashers;
- refrigerators and freezers;
- fans; and
- rangehoods.

All have good design and space utilization to create value for the consumer.

Partnerships and Structure

Haier America Trading has been looking for strategic partnerships that will give its brand both recognition and credibility, and has managed to get Wal-Mart, Lowe's, Best Buy, Home Depot, Office Depot, Target, Sam's Club, Fortunoff, Menard, Bed Bath and Beyond, P. C. Richards, BJ's, Fry's, and BrandsMart, among others, to carry some of its product range, mainly small refrigerators and freezers. Haier adds value to its retailers by providing logistical assistance, inventory management, and stress-free customer service.

Speed to market and product innovation are essential items for Zhang, who claims, "In this information age, whoever is the fastest to meet consumer demands wins. I work with whoever can give me the information and technology to meet consumer needs." It is this reason that has driven Haier to team up with renowned brand names such as Ericsson, the intention of which is to use Ericsson's Bluetooth wireless technology in its products.

Such alliances are giving Haier access to a valuable R&D base that it currently doesn't have. As far as innovation goes, Haier has about 400 new products hitting the market each year. The failure/success rate isn't known, and one wonders if the company can keep up with this rate of change. Zhang's response is, "Wherever we go, the strategy is always to break in with one product, then introduce more and more along the way. The strategy has worked in every market." Zhang says Haier is niche marketing and can produce a run of around 30,000 units of one product before moving on to the next. Some of them are clearly *very* niche—for example, a washing machine with a virtual fish tank! Currently, the company is in around 60 categories of products and is practicing mass customization.

Including international and domestic resources, Haier now has access to 12 technological research institutes, 48 development centers, ten advanced laboratories, and six design centers.

Haier has learnt from the mistakes of others in managing its brand. Typically, Japanese companies operating in the US have a wholly owned subsidiary headed by headquarters executives. Zhang has a different philosophy, and is smart enough to recognize that his staff are still many years behind their counterparts in developed countries, and actively encourages the joining together of foreign experts and his managers.

Haier America Trading is a joint venture between Haier, which has the majority shareholding, and a small group of US investors. The Haier parent company only gets involved in corporate and brand strategy with the US stakeholders, who understand the market and run the operations. They are given a great deal of autonomy, and this enables both speed and flexibility in decision-making. According to Michael Jemal, president and chief executive officer of Haier America Trading, it is "the opportunity of a lifetime to launch a brand, to build a brand, to create a market."

BRAND CULTURE

While Lexus, the company and brand created by Toyota to break into the luxury car market in the United States, sent its managers well ahead of start-up time to understand the market and US consumer behavior by staying with American families, and placed top Japanese executives to run its operations, Haier has again taken a different route. The top managers are American, with Michael Jemal putting together a team of experienced professionals from sales to marketing to finance to product development.

The brand culture is important to Haier, and prospective employees must emerge successfully from an initiation program that lasts 40 hours before they are appointed. This program emphasizes teamwork, safety, and the importance of quality. On the factory floor, memorabilia from the Haier heritage are displayed, including a photo of the Zhang–sledgehammer incident. Some of the employees earn a trip to China to help them appreciate the values of the company and to experience Chinese culture, and say that it is a once-in-a-lifetime experience. So, Haier attempts to blend the best of the East and West in its employee relations.

THE FUTURE?

Haier has plants in 13 countries and sells its products in over 160 countries. It currently has 30% of the small-refrigerator market in the United States. The Haier brand is on TV sets, air-conditioners, mobile phones, and PC peripherals, as well as a restaurant chain and

Haier Brothers cartoons. The financial services category is next on the agenda. Sales in the US are expected to make US$1 billion in 2008, up from US$200 million in 2000. The goal is to get 10% of the US market for standard-sized refrigerators by the end of 2005. Zhang aims for Haier to be among the world's 500 largest companies within the next few years. He also admits that the company is learning much from the power brands such as Nike and Dell, and instead of manufacturing most of its output, will seek more outsourcing opportunities.

Haier wants to be a global brand, like the Asian brands of Toyota and Sony. In terms of makers of kitchen appliances it is already number six, behind Whirlpool, Electrolux, GE, Bosch-Siemens Hausgeräte, and Samsung Electronics. This focus will carry Zhang's brand to reach its goal, but the temptation of brand extensions could lead Haier to try and do too much too soon. For example, an excursion into pharmaceuticals has not been successful. There is no doubt, however, that if it can survive in the United States and not dilute its brand equity too much by trying to be all things to all people, then a global brand will emerge. The passion is there. As a further measure of its commitment to the US market, Haier America invested over US$15 million in its US headquarters with the purchase of the landmark Haier Building in New York City.

This is just one Chinese company building a challenger brand. More entrepreneurs with ambition, passion, and flair like Zhang, controlling huge companies like Haier, will emerge from this amazing country. And China's entry as a member of the WTO may mean the end of the domination of global branding by Western companies in some basic goods categories.

Brand strengths

- ◆ Product innovation.
- ◆ Speed to market of new products.
- ◆ Passion of its people.
- ◆ Niche market strategy.
- ◆ Strength in low-end appliances such as refrigerators for college dorm rooms.
- ◆ Decentralized sales and marketing allow flexibility in terms of local market adaptation.
- ◆ Ability to move the manufacturing plants away from China, to avoid the "Made in China" issue.

Brand weaknesses

- Country-of-origin issue. Even though products are manufactured elsewhere and are selling relatively well in the United States, to a certain extent the country-of-origin issue may still affect the public's perception of their products.
- Consistency of product quality across all markets is still a bit suspect.
- To be really successful in the United States and other Western countries, Haier will have to take on the giant brands in mass—as opposed to niche—product categories, and some observers doubt its ability to do this globally.
- Possible loss of focus in the US market as the brand tries to defend its home market position, where the top world brands are now beginning to take away market share.
- Most design work is still done in China.

Brand architecture

Mainly corporate, with some shared branding (example: Haier Brewmaster) and quite a lot via product descriptors (example: air-conditioner HSU-22CD03)

Case Study 9—EMIRATES

Definitely a High-flier

Dubai is a star brand in its own right (see the case in Chapter 12), but this small destination has another claim to fame—a brand that is the fastest growing in the airline industry—Emirates. Supported by the high-tech, visionary, and outstanding destination brand of Dubai, and one of the finest airports in the world (Dubai International), Emirates is without doubt a world-class brand, and the huge global competitors from Europe and the United States are watching its continued success and growth with a great deal of trepidation.

The tiny sultanate of Dubai seems destined for stardom in whatever it does. Driven by the fear of dwindling oil resources, and the visionary, commercially oriented ruling Al-Maktoum family, Dubai is transforming itself at an astonishing rate. Its airline, chaired by one of the family, is determined not to be left behind in the process.

Emirates started in 1985 with a mere US$10 million investment from the ruling family, and it has paid its way ever since. Competitor airlines complain that the airport subsidization helps its price competitiveness, but that charge can also be applied to other countries, according to Emirates, and Emirates is proud of its consistent profitability, which is independent of the airport and audited to the highest international standards.

Whereas other national and commercial airlines have occasionally run into huge debt and required government subsidies, Emirates has proved that profitability in the airline industry can be sustainable, even in times of turbulence and disaster. In November 2004, it announced a 41% rise in half-year profits with a record US$236 million with sales of US$2.2 billion. The airline has an astonishing passenger traffic record, which has increased by an average of 25% over the last 20 years. Since its inception, Emirates has been consistently ranked in the top five airlines in the world and has won more than 200 awards.

CRITICAL SUCCESS FACTORS

There are a few important factors that can account for Emirates' success—namely:

- ◆ courage;
- ◆ location;
- ◆ airport infrastructure;
- ◆ cost structure;
- ◆ network planning; and
- ◆ brand culture and mindset.

Courage

Given its location in the midst of the Middle East problems, it is astonishing that Emirates' sales have continued to rise over the last few years.

This is due largely to the fact that Emirates continued to fly when its competitors chose to give the region a miss; however, it is also because somehow it has managed the perceptions of travelers with respect to safety. It is a trusted brand and has overcome adversity in highly volatile conditions. On determination and courage alone it deserves credit.

Location

Dubai has always been a trading hub between West and East. Emirates has capitalized on this and taken advantage of the fact that long-haul travelers may need to stop over in the region for business or leisure reasons. So, it fits well with Dubai's business strategy—as a hub for business and leisure; a stopping-off point for world travelers that provides everything they could possibly want. In fact, the airline has a symbiotic relationship with the Dubai brand. Its passengers often stop off in Dubai for sun, shopping, and sport, and the Dubai brand-building exercises provide more seats for the airline. So, "Emirates supports Dubai and Dubai supports Emirates," says Mark Turner, a manager in the airline's crew-training division.

Airport Infrastructure

The infrastructure provided by Dubai International Airport is first class; it is considered the Middle East's premier and busiest airport, and is linked closely to Emirates's success. Open 24 hours a day and handling 20 million passengers a year, it is growing quickly. By 2010 it expects this figure to be 60 million passengers—about the same as Heathrow—and Emirates will have its fair share of this market. Emirates' flight schedule is such that most of its busiest flights arrive and leave during the night, when other airports are not operating. This aids operational flying time, and hence revenues per plane. Under consideration is a larger airport to be situated nearby.

Cutting-edge design, functionality, and a wealth of amenities and services ensure a great brand experience for the airline's travelers who visit Dubai. The experience will get even better in the future, as a US$6 billion improvement to the airport and its shopping mall is planned.

Network Planning

The clever part played by the network planners is the airline's hub strategy. Emirates flies people from its destinations to Dubai and then flies them off again to more destinations, a strategy also employed by Changi Airport in Singapore. By doing so, it can make routes profitable that would otherwise be unsustainable, such as Pakistan and Sudan. Pakistan and India have been involved with Emirates from the start, using Dubai for a trading post. But Emirates has reached out and, for example, now flies to five British airports with 77 weekly flights. It has 49 weekly flights to Australia, and goes to Germany and Switzerland. Dubai is a convenient stopover, and Emirates has global reach.

Its latest development is the US route, where it flies 14 non-stop flights to New York. More US destinations are in the pipeline. Goldman Sachs analysts predict that within the next five years Emirates could be matching or exceeding the number of global seats that British Airways currently has. In addition, 19 African countries are being targeted for the future.

Cost Structure

Flying at times when others don't, acting as a nexus for international travelers, global reach, high total volume and occupancy of seats, and targeting of countries such as those in Africa where competition isn't so fierce are all factors that allow Emirates to have a distinct cost advantage.

There is another smart factor involved in contributing to the low cost structure of the airline and that is its human capital policy. Emirates staff are employed from around the world, and incomes are set at the levels in each home country. Many staff come from low-wage-earning countries, and whereas some airlines are weighed down by people costs that can reach as high as 35% of total costs, Emirates boasts of the same costs being below 20%, a significant competitive advantage. This means that Emirates can offer the same luxury travel as other more famous airlines at a much lower cost to the customer, in some cases as much as 40%. This gives Emirates a value-for-money marketing proposition. Dermott Mannion (who runs finance and support services for the airline) says, "It's a significant advantage over the competition."

Indeed, this winning position has led some analysts such as Goldman Sachs to say that the long-haul margins for the big airlines such as Lufthansa are going to be eroded, just as the low-cost, no-frills airlines have eroded margins on short-haul flights.

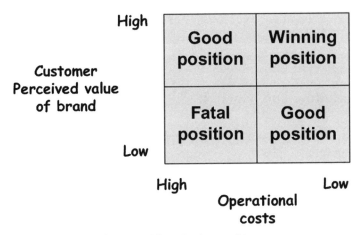

Figure 5.1   Brand power: The winning position

THE WINNING POSITION

In fact, if we look at what makes a winning position for a brand, as shown in Figure 5.1, we can see that Emirates is definitely heading for the top right-hand corner.

To explain, if a brand is in the top left-hand corner it will do well, as consumers perceive the brand to be giving them high value, both tangible and intangible. It will never be a world-beater, though, as it has a very high cost base. By contrast, a brand in the bottom left quadrant will probably go out of business as it has a high operational cost and a low rating in terms of consumer perceived value. A company that finds itself in the bottom right of the diagram could survive, but it and its products/services will be seen very much as commodities, with little differentiation. The only way to make a good living here is to consistently outperform the competition in term of costs. It is a high-volume, low-margin business. In other words, the company must always possess cost leadership, something that is very difficult to get and then to maintain. The winning brands in the world are those that have a combination of low operational costs and high perceived value from consumers, and this is where Emirates is aiming to be. In fact, it is moving into this top right-hand quadrant now.

Emirates has a prestigious brand image, but its price positioning places it between the giant airlines and the low-cost, no-frills airlines—a winning position.

Brand Culture and Mindset

Emirates is sensitive to the needs of both its internal and external customers. It has a distinctive multi-cultural flavor to its service. It has a reputation for being a "great place to work," and employees from multi-national companies have been known to leave and go to Emirates after hearing about its culture. With 5,500 employees from nearly 120 countries, it is a melting pot of people that can enhance the customer experience. By 2012 Emirates intends to have around 15,000 flight crew, and it currently receives around a quarter of a million job applications per year!

From toilet flushing instructions in eight languages, to flight attendants who speak an average of ten languages on each flight, to outstanding in-flight service and amenities, who could ask for more?

LOOKING AHEAD: FLYING HIGHER AND FURTHER

There is no doubt that Emirates is destined to be a major international, and maybe a global, brand. It has used niche marketing to learn about the right business model to use, and is now deploying it across the world. Its combination of a low-cost, high-value brand proposition contains all the elements of a winning brand. As a statement of intent, Emirates has placed the biggest order for the world's biggest plane, the Airbus A380; 45 of the huge double-deck aircraft will be taken into use.

Brand strengths

- ◆ Emirates has a brand name that has global awareness.
- ◆ It is based in Dubai, a strategic location with a massive program of national development that will attract more and more travelers. (See the case on Dubai in chapter 12)
- ◆ Dubai International Airport adds to the brand experience.
- ◆ It has low operational costs and a prestige brand experience.

Brand weaknesses

It is a niche player, and becoming a global brand may be difficult as it will mean going head-to-head with the big players in Europe and the United States. In the meantime, it will have to watch out for the low-cost carrier invasion in the region.

Brand architecture

True corporate branding.

Main source

The Asian Wall Street Journal, January 12, 2005.

CONCLUSION

Challenger brands can only be successful if they position themselves correctly. They have to own a position that the leaders don't possess, and that position has to be relevant and meaningful to consumers. Positioning is explained in greater detail with cases in the next chapter.

CHAPTER 6

BRAND POSITIONING

How Does Positioning Fit into Brand Management?

The importance of positioning your brand well has been referred to in previous chapters and is now explored in more detail. How you position your brand against the competition is crucial as it is concerned with differentiation, an issue that is critical in crowded markets. This chapter looks at the options available, with examples.

Positioning is vital to brand management because it takes the basic tangible aspects of the product and actually builds the intangibles in the form of an image in people's minds. It focuses on the chosen target audience(s) and influences their thoughts about the brand in relation to other brands. Through the strategies described in this chapter, positioning seeks the best way of convincing people that this particular product is both different from and better than any other. This chapter explains how and why brands are built, and the critical role played by the positioning process in helping to make the strategic leap from being perceived as an ordinary brand to being seen as world-class, with all the rewards this brings. Strong—or even world-class— branding is impossible without powerful positioning.

In positioning a brand, the brand's actual performance can be introduced as well as its personality. Here are some of the more common strategies that have proven themselves.

Thirteen Power Positioning Strategies

There are 13 strategies that can be used (some in combination) to establish powerful positions. The fundamentals of these are described below, together with some of their advantages and disadvantages.

1. Features and Attributes

This is probably the most obvious strategy and traditionally the most frequently used in many industries. With this strategy the focus is on those characteristics of the person, company, product, place, or whatever, that can be used to endorse the perception that here is something that is different, or better, or both.

The motor vehicle industry is a typical user of this strategy, and most car manufacturers have used it to stay in the forefront of people's minds. Volvo is one of the best examples, having for many years positioned its vehicles as being the safest on the road. Service companies are also frequently users of the strategy, an example being The Ritz-Carlton hotel group advertising its uncompromisingly high service quality standards. It gets its staff to think in this way by instilling in them the concept that, "We are ladies and gentlemen serving ladies and gentlemen."

Advantages

With this strategy there is the potential to own it for a long time, as with Volvo, or it might last only for a short period of time, as in the case of laser jet printers, or 3M with nasal dilatory strips. In either case, it can result in the creation of a rapid market share, particularly if your product is first into the market with a new and distinctive feature or attribute.

Disadvantages

Features and attributes can be copied sooner or later (with increasing speed as technology advances), and this will erode market-share gains. Competitors may produce enhancements that cause your offer to be obsolete, and repositioning might consequently be difficult. Technological change is militating against this strategy by accelerating the speed with which products can be copied, and thus reducing life cycles.

2. Benefits

This strategy takes features and attributes to the next stage by describing what benefit(s) the customer will receive as a result—for example, a toothpaste containing fluoride (feature) helps to fight decay (benefit), or contains a whitening agent (feature) for sparkling white teeth with no stains (benefit).

The benefits positioning strategy answers the question consumers have in their minds: "What's in it for me?" The safety feature of a car means protection. The introduction of airbags into cars as an additional feature might mean more expense, but in the consumer's mind the benefits of a life-saving attribute outweigh the cost.

Advantages

This strategy helps to give a company and its products more appeal by allowing people to see clearly what the features actually mean. Like features, benefit positioning can establish short-term competitive advantage, and can lead to market leadership and quick gains. It is a reasonably flexible strategy, and can be extended in a clinical, logical way (aimed at the left brain) and in a more emotional way (aimed at the right brain).

Example

Feature	Rational	Emotional
Safety	Protection	For your family

Disadvantages

As with the features strategy it can be somewhat short-lived, and what is a benefit and competitive advantage today is part of tomorrow's basic product. It is based around the concept of a USP (unique selling proposition) that is vulnerable these days to easy replication, further enhancements, and technological innovations. I can buy the latest personal computer with the highest processing speed or hard disk capacity, currently state of the art, only to find four months later that there is a new industry standard for that product category.

3. Problem–Solution

This is another widely used and often highly effective strategy. It is based on the premise that consumers don't necessarily want to buy a product or deal with a company strictly for that purpose. What they really want is a solution to a problem they have that can be provided by the product or company. Here are some examples.

People often regard some banking products as a necessary evil. It is highly unlikely that they will wake up in the morning and shout gleefully, "What a great day for an overdraft!" More likely they will wake up at three or four in the morning worrying about how they are going to solve an immediate financial problem to which an overdraft might be the solution.

Oracle and many other companies also use this strategy. (See the book by myself and K. C. Lee entitled *Hi-Tech Hi-Touch Branding* (Singapore: John Wiley & Sons, 2000) for many more examples of technology companies that are using this positioning strategy.)

Advantages

This strategy is clearly appropriate for certain industries such as financial services, IT, and communications, but it is also widely applicable. Because problems always have an emotional consequence or impact on the consumer, it is a useful strategy because emotion can be built into this positioning, being often accomplished by suggesting an emotional benefit attached to the solution.

Example: Life insurance

Problem: What happens to my family if something happens to me?

Solution: Life insurance

Emotional benefit: Peace of mind if a disaster occurs

Disadvantages

Other competitors can also solve the same problems consumers have, perhaps even improving on the solution. In technology-led industries, this strategy is now becoming so overused other means of differentiation are essential.

The big crunch can come if you claim the solution approach but don't deliver—for example, with warranties that don't perform. Also, to maintain brand credibility with this strategy (particularly in technology-driven industries), new product development is vital because life-cycle compression means the rapidity of new product innovations makes today's problems disappear quickly. The pace of change also brings with it new and different problems. You have to stay on top of the game here.

4. Competition

Every company must always be aware of the competition—what it is doing and what it intends to do. Depending on competitor strategies, it may be necessary to change your position. This would be a reactive strategy. On the other hand, it is possible to be proactive and change your position and so disadvantage the competition. For example, on the Motrin website (www.motrin.com, accessed June 8, 2005), Motrin claims that "Nothing is faster, or stronger on tough muscle pain than Motrin—not Advil, not Aleve," the latter two being competitor brands. You can't get much more direct than that.

Advantages

Competitive strategies tend to be better for positioning companies and more difficult for products. Corporations tend to have more unique characteristics in the form of personality, culture, size, and visual identity that people can more readily associate with, and an image that can help to keep a company one step ahead when managed well.

However, with products there is often less to work with in terms of differentiators, especially in today's increasingly cluttered markets. Notwithstanding this fact, if based on the truth or statistics, it is possible to own a position, as demonstrated, for instance, in the case of taste tests.

Disadvantages

Competitive positioning can invite retaliation, and in some countries it is prohibited. It can lead to a lot of wasteful expenditure and to embarrassing public incidents, as in the case of ambush marketing. The message here is that you had better be sure your product or company has something to offer to your target audience that others cannot match.

5. Corporate Credentials or Identity

Some companies rely on the strength of the corporate name to endorse products, positioning them by the house brand reputation. This can be very powerful, as demonstrated by companies such as Sony, Canon, and Nestlé. The sheer power and ubiquity of the parent can make life very difficult for would-be competitors trying to establish their own position.

Advantages

The power of the corporate name can help to strengthen or make a strong position for even an average product. A well-known name can cross different markets and, in some cases, create global product positions, as in the case of Sony moving into the entertainment industry from consumer electronics.

Disadvantages

If the company has a bad time, so does the product, and the position can lose its credibility. A badly managed corporate image will make life very difficult for products positioned around the strength of the parental name and reputation. It can also work the other way round, as was the famous case with Firestone tires. In January 2000, after a television station in Houston aired a 90-minute story on thread-separation accidents in Texas, many people called the station to relate their stories of Firestone tire failures. A total of 6.5 million tires were recalled. Bridgestone/Firestone officials accepted full responsibility and admitted that the company had made "bad tires." Since the recall, both companies have faced an estimated 300 law suits stemming from deaths and injuries resulting from tire-separation incidents. The first of these, in August 2001, went to trial but was settled out of court for US$7.85 million. Ford, also named in the suit, settled out of court for US$6 million before the trial began. By the time of settlement, federal regulators had recorded more than 203 deaths and 700 injuries in vehicles—primarily Ford Explorers—equipped with Firestone tires. Opinion polls suggested that the public had lost faith in the companies and that consumers were worried about the safety of Ford Explorers (www.e-businessethics.com/firestone.htm, accessed on June 8, 2005).

6. Usage Occasion, Time, and Application

This strategy can be an effective differentiator, but it is more appropriate for products and services than for companies and larger institutions. The strategy gains its value from the fact that people not only use products in different ways, but may do so on different occasions and at different times. For instance, some people will eat a Kit Kat for a between-meals snack (time usage). A nutritious chocolate drink is used by some people before going to sleep (time), and by others as a food supplement at various times of day (application). Champagne is enjoyed usually only at celebrations (occasion usage).

Advantages

Products and services can gain a market position that is more easily defendable, and the strategy is as flexible as the capability of the product's possibilities for different usage situations. One product can attract many different target audiences once relevance has been established. For an example, see the Tiger Balm case on page 115.

Disadvantages

Products with more effective usage may usurp the position, and as consumer behavior changes over time, the time or nature of usage might change.

7. Target User

The target user positioning strategy is a very good example of focus in marketing. Companies who know their target audiences well can be effective in positioning a generic product to many customer groups, as with the case of Nike, who basically has the "trainer" footwear dedicated to each relevant sports group.

Advantages

This strategy is good for getting into and defending niche markets, and for building strong customer relationships. It is clearly a winner for developing a product range where a wide range of customer groups exist for a generic product, but where slightly differing needs or applications allow a wide, low-cost product range.

Disadvantages

The strategy relies on accurate segmentation, and therefore on research. Companies that don't understand the customers' real needs and wants might know the market structure and dynamics but may still become unstuck. It can be limiting, and user profiles will change over time. Nike, for instance, found it relatively easy to go from trainers to sports apparel, but found it less easy to shift to leisure apparel.

8. Aspiration

This is a strategy that is gaining more and more favor as the world, in every sense, becomes more competitive. Aspirational positioning can be applied in many forms, but the two common ones are concerned with:

- status and prestige (related to wealth achievement); and
- self-improvement (related to non-monetary achievement).

In both cases, the strategy relies on self-expression, and as most individuals have a need to express themselves one way or another, associating themselves with companies or brands that facilitate this is helpful.

With respect to status and prestige, Rolex and Mercedes are power brands that people use to make a statement about their financial achievements in life, among other things. On the self-improvement side, Nike's "Just Do It" tagline urges people to get the best out of themselves.

Disadvantages

Not everyone sees himself or herself as a winner, and it can thus be a turn-off for under-achievers. It is essential, therefore, to know your target audience.

9. Cause

This positioning strategy is also linked to emotion, and focuses on people's beliefs hierarchy and their need to belong. Avon, Benetton, and other companies target customer groups whom they believe will subscribe to a certain philosophy or want to relate to a specific group or movement. Avon targets women and support women's causes—for instance, by conducting a survey of 30,000 women in 43 countries to discover what they feel are their greatest challenges, what is needed for personal happiness, and what things are most important in their lives. This strategy is becoming more widely used and important, as it relates to freedom of thought and speech, democracy, the liberation of women, and other social trends.

Advantages

Companies can own a strong position through this strategy. It can be very powerful when linked to other strategies concerning applications, target users, and emotion.

Disadvantages

Causes can go in and out of fashion, and while welcomed by some they might offend others—proper targeting is vital. Additionally, while in vogue, the "bandwagon" effect often occurs, as is the case now with literally hundreds of companies giving us steadfast promises that they will do everything they can to protect the environment. If you embark on this strategy with your brand, you are also committed to the long term and a high marketing budget in order to prove to the cause audience that you really mean what you say.

10. Value

Value is often related to what people pay, but this strategy isn't just to do with price. There are two main elements of value positioning.

- *Price/quality*—that is, value for money, a positioning used by Virgin and Carrefour.
- *Emotional value*—that is, the association people have when they own, for example, a Mini car. BMW is trying to bring back these memories and emotions with its range of Mini and Mini-Cooper cars, fighting on the nostalgia platform with Volkswagen's Beetle.

Advantages

It is a good strategy when it combines the two elements, and can also be used tactically via promotions. The key is to concentrate on "value," not "price."

Disadvantages

It tends to be commodity-oriented when it concentrates on price, and not suitable for those building a power brand looking for high premiums.

11. Emotion

As a positioning strategy this can exist on its own, but it is often used as an overlay position, adding value and strength to other strategies, as previously mentioned. It is highly important because, as research shows time and time again, emotion sells. Haagen-Dazs ice cream is positioned around the concept of sheer luxury and the enjoyment of the moment. Some of the advertisements portray this with romantic and sexual imagery, and fantasy. The success has been phenomenal. The brand broke into a market dominated by giants such as Nestlé, Mars, Unilever, and others, and sold its products at prices up to 40% higher than its competitors. It was all accomplished through the creation of a unique positioning aimed at carefully selected market segments, and supported by consistent, appropriate advertising, promotion, and distribution.

Advantages

Emotional positioning strategies move people to want things. Emotion creates desire, and when coupled with rational-type strategies (see below) it can be very powerful indeed. Positioning without emotion tends to be less persuasive and to lack motivation.

Disadvantages

As a strategy on its own, it might not sway the minds of the "cold fish"—the more calculating, careful-planning, thrifty types of people. For those who are very price-sensitive the cost will be the decisive factor, overpowering the emotional feelings.

12. Personality

As mentioned in the previous chapter, brand building based on personality creation can be extremely effective, being frequently used by companies to build world-class brands. But people won't respond to a personality they see as being either not relevant or not likeable. Brand personality can be used to position the brand via the brand values (for example, caring), or endorsements by real people (for example, Brad Pitt—Tag Heuer) or fictitious personalities (for example, Adam King in the 2004–05 Guinness campaigns).

Advantages

People are very responsive to this strategy, and when combined with others it can produce high market share, loyalty, and profitability. It is the only way really to gain and sustain a strategic competitive advantage.

Disadvantages

It relies on a very clear understanding of the target audience, and a great deal of investment to make sure that the customer experiences a consistent personality on all occasions. Building a corporate personality, for instance, demands that the entire culture of the organization be changed so that all staff live that personality in their everyday work.

13. Claiming Number One

This is an enviable position to have, as it generates perceptions of leadership. In the high-tech field it can work wonders for the brand and provide a perception of difference, even though product service and quality may be similar between major players. This is essentially what has happened to Amazon.com, which remains the brand leader in its field, even though other companies offer similar products and services. Arthur Andersen, the consulting firm, was the first company to position itself as a technology specialist. Now all the other consulting firms are following and, what is important for the Arthur Andersen brand, are *seen* to be following. The firm's change of name to Accenture has, however, eroded this position.

Advantages

Your brand is widely perceived as the market leader, and if you can maintain constant innovation you could own this position.

Disadvantages

The obvious concern here is keeping ahead of the pack when innovation is happening all the time. You will need to invest considerably in R&D.

GAINING POWER FROM COMBINING STRATEGIES

The power positioning strategies discussed above can be combined in various ways as companies and people wish. A well-known example of this is the sports shoe and apparel manufacturer Nike, one of the world's most admired brands. *Features and attributes* are used, along with *benefits* of improved performance, linked to the *aspiration* of becoming a top athlete, aimed at various *target user* groups, together with *emotion* in advertising pictures and athlete endorsements.

CAPTURING HEARTS AND MINDS

Whatever strategies are used, the key to positioning is capturing people's hearts and minds, appealing to the rational and emotional aspects of their psychological make-up. The astute brand managers are those who understand this, and know how they can combine strategies that satisfy the emotional and rational needs of consumers.

SUMMARY: CHOOSING A POSITIONING STRATEGY

Whatever strategy—or combination of strategies—you eventually choose, there are certain points to be remembered.

- The position must be salient or important to the target audience you are trying to reach and influence. It is no good communicating messages that are of no interest to them, as they will either ignore them or forget them quickly.
- The position must be based on real strengths. Making claims that cannot be substantiated can cause enormous loss of credibility.
- The position has to reflect some form of competitive advantage. The whole point of positioning is to inform and persuade people that you are different from and better than the competition, so the point of difference must be clearly expressed.
- Finally, the position must be capable of being communicated simply, so that everyone gets the real message; it must also motivate the audience. The aim of positioning is to provide a call to action to the target audience, and so communications must be carefully created.

In this chapter you will read about two cases that have used positioning to attract different target audiences. They have used combinations of the strategies listed above. (See if you can work them out.)

The first case is Tiger Beer, a brand that has an international presence but positions itself differently in different target audiences. The second case is Tiger Balm, a brand that has used one value proposition to cover multi-market segments.

CASE STUDY 10—TIGER BEER

"Roaring Loud"

★ ★ ★ ★ ★

Take a trip to Sentosa, go shopping on Orchard Road, eat chili crabs, and get refreshed with Tiger Beer. One would assume that anyone who has visited Singapore would have definitely experienced these things. If you are lucky, you might also visit The Tavern located at the impressive premises of Asia Pacific Breweries, the company that brews and markets Tiger Beer. Tiger Beer has become an inevitable part of the Singapore experience. It has matured into one of Singapore's most powerful brands and is now rapidly leaping across other parts of the world.

THE BRAND STORY—"TIGER ON THE PROWL"

In 1931, Heineken and Fraser & Neave established a joint venture company, Malayan Breweries Limited (now Asia Pacific Breweries). In line with the expertise of the Dutch partner, the beer that was brewed was of a superior grade. It was called "Tiger," a name that in the Chinese culture suggests strength. In 1932, the tap was opened for the public and the first cases of Tiger Beer were seen in Singapore's watering holes. The decision was made to promote Tiger as the flagship brand of Asia Pacific Breweries (APB) and get a strong foothold in the large Asia-Pacific market. APB deliberately didn't want Tiger to compete head-on with the already established brands in the United States, Europe, and Japan.

In a media release issued in 2000, Mr. Koh Poh Tiong, chief executive officer of APB, drew a comparison with a boxing match.

> Tiger was an amateur fighter. So we thought, forget about countries like Japan and the USA with their heavyweight brands. Let's forget about Europe, but focus on Asia Pacific, a very large area. Let's grow in our own front yard and backyard. Markets like Vietnam, China and Thailand—those fit in our strategy perfectly.

The company's name change from Malayan Breweries Limited to Asia Pacific Breweries made perfect sense, keeping in mind the business vision of the company. To some extent, the success of the Tiger brand can be attributed to a focused approach and a realistic ambition.

Today, Tiger has become a pan-Asian beer brand eclipsing the Southeast Asian market and being regarded as a premium Asian beer brand in markets outside of Asia. In 2003, overall volume sales for Tiger Beer outside of Singapore grew by 6%, and revenue grew by 11%. More importantly, Tiger Beer grew volume sales and market share in its two biggest markets—Vietnam and Malaysia. The size of export sales has increased substantially, with the UK leading the pack. While the UK has witnessed promising growth of over 20% for the fifth successive year to 2004, the initial sales in New Zealand have also been encouraging. The flow doesn't stop here, as the brand had an exquisite launch in the United States and is also achieving new distribution in Sweden, Finland, and the Middle East.

Two years ago, the home market in Singapore witnessed a slowdown during the SARS menace, but now everything is back to its vibrant self and the Tiger is roaring louder than ever. While international expansion is high on the priority list, Tiger Beer also stays true to its Asian roots. In 2004, APB started brewing Tiger Beer in Thailand. This was an important milestone to further strengthen the brand's grasp on the Thai market, which was already familiar with Tiger through the export route. The effort aims to get healthy expansion and conversion of the domestic market by offering a refreshing experience.

In a press release on Tiger Beer's marketing campaign in Thailand, Mr. Chris Kidd, director, group marketing, APB said: "We believe that Tiger Beer will appeal to young adults who seek adventure, have achieved some level of success and appreciate the better things in life. Tiger Beer seeks to offer the Thai beer drinker a different experience that will set him apart from the rest of the crowd."

THE BRAND PROMISE

Singapore's beer market is nearly at the same level of maturity as the world market, with mainstream brands such as Heineken and Carlsberg, and specialty brews such as Stella Artois and Hoegaarden, competing for market share. Despite intense competition, Tiger has maintained its market leadership position.

The success of the brand can be partly attributed to an award-winning taste and an extremely strong distribution network, but a large part of the success accrues to the brand-building efforts over the years. The brand has undergone a transformation from being a mass brand to a "masstiege" brand (not quite a mass brand nor a prestige brand, but occupying a space between the two), and is now beginning to gain prestige status in a few parts of the world. This is evident when you observe the brand's evolution.

The brand communication reflects the evolution quite well, and the change in the brand tagline from "Time for a Tiger" in the 1940s and 1950s to the "What time is it? It's Tiger time" campaign in the 1990s has added robust dimensions to the brand personality over the years. The image overhaul was further boosted in 1998, when APB embarked on a global program to revamp its product packaging design.

Tiger's new look is dynamic, distinctive, premium, and authentically Far Eastern, with a more contemporary, eye-catching logo and distinctive bottle design and print advertising. In fact, in early 2005, Tiger Beer embarked on an interesting brand path with the unveiling of "Tiger Nation. The State of Fun." campaign. The campaign is discussed further below.

BRAND PERSONALITY

Efforts have been made to develop a brand personality that appears to be:

- dynamic;
- sporty;

- youthful; and
- aspiring.

The brand personality is brought alive through the various brand touch points that Tiger Beer creates through varied activities. It has a long association with football through the Tiger Cup held in Southeast Asia. In line with the strategy to be associated with the most popular sport in the world, Tiger Beer continued its broadcast sponsorship of the English Premier League (EPL) in 2003 for Asia with ESPN Star Sports. EPL is the world's most popular football league, and the broadcast sponsorship introduced the brand to fans across Asia.

Tiger Beer brought world-class golf players to Singapore by sponsoring Tiger Skins, a premier golf event in Asia, for two years running. This high-profile event drew the attention of avid golf fans and other young professionals in Singapore and the region, and was a positive step toward making Tiger an aspirational brand. Tiger Beer also hosts massive entertainment engagements such as the Tiger Beer New Year Countdown every year. All these activities act as a collective force in strengthening the brand's appeal to a younger, upwardly mobile target audience.

MULTI-PRONGED BRAND POSITIONING

Tiger Beer's brand positioning is rather interesting and invites debate to some extent. Intriguingly, Tiger Beer uses different brand positioning strategies in markets outside of Singapore and Asia. In New Zealand, Europe, and the Americas, Tiger Beer is beginning to be associated with fashion, film, and music, thereby reaching out to trend-setting cosmopolitan and sometimes counter-culture consumers.

By contrast, in Singapore until 2004, Tiger Beer was positioned as a premium home-brewed beer with the "spirit of celebration anytime, anywhere" as its essence. In the UK, Tiger Beer is inextricably linked with "Asian Cool" and is established as a leading player in the niche imported beer segment, offering an exotic and fascinating taste of Asia to UK consumers. The brand communication has a different flavor and tone in and outside of Singapore. Even the websites of the different countries reflect the multi-pronged positioning strategy.

One might wonder about the long-term implications of this brand strategy. On the one hand, there could be confusion in the consumer's mind once the brand crosses geographical boundaries to attain a global status. On the other, it could be argued that Tiger has to take a different approach in foreign markets to avoid competing with huge mass brands—that is, it has to take a niche approach. However, looking at the steady success of the brand until now, it looks as though it is working. One wonders if the multi-pronged approach will be blended into a single brand identity in the future.

A New National Brand Communications Campaign

At this point, it would be worthwhile to critique the newly conceptualized advertising campaign that adorns the streets of Singapore. The brand promise of the new campaign is captured in the tagline "Tiger Nation. The State of Fun." It is an extension of the earlier idea of bringing people together at social and fun occasions but has a refreshing twist. The twist is the effective use of wit, humor, and fun. The campaign headlines—such as "Men demand beer, we supply it"—and creative executions under "Dining in Tiger Nation—seafood tastes better in the state of fun" series are definitely eye-catching. One of the creative executions, titled "Grilled stingray," depicts a stingray chained to a chair and being interrogated by a pair of sharks.

The new brand communication is powerful on two counts. First, within Singapore the "Nation" concept is something that Tiger can legitimately own, as Singapore is the spiritual home of Tiger Beer. It can also successfully add the following personality traits to the brand:

- sociability;
- optimism;
- spontaneity; and
- fun.

These are extremely compelling territories that a brand can own. The impact of the current brand communication will reflect on the brand's health in due time, and it may be that owning the "fun" dimension can be a great differentiator.

The bigger challenge might be that of a strategic trade-off. The brand has to shed some of its older traits in order to have a unique and consistent image in the long run. This thought prompts a second count as to why "Tiger Nation. The State of Fun." is a powerful platform. This platform gives Tiger a window to put "fun" at the core of the brand and move away from a multi-pronged strategy if there is a need for the brand to align all its communication and positioning and have a unified brand identity globally.

CONCLUSION

Today, Tiger is continuing on its path to become a leading global brand with accelerated internationalization in non-Asia markets. With its award-winning taste and differentiated imagery, Tiger Beer has the necessary attributes to compete against any other competitor brands in an increasingly cosmopolitan world. Tiger Beer is an inspiring example of a brand that offers a heady cocktail with potent ingredients, such as the mystique of the Orient, a titillating taste, and a cutting-edge awareness of what is coolest around the world. Cheers!

Brand strengths

- World-class taste and quality.
- Heavy investment in image building.
- Strong distribution network.
- Three hundred and sixty-degree brand efforts.

Brand weaknesses

Different positioning strategies could result in a schizophrenic brand image and lead to customer confusion due to exposure to varied communication. Tiger is still struggling to erase the mass appeal image among discerning young customers.

Brand architecture

Product branding, with product descriptor for variants (example: Tiger Beer Classic).

Sources

- Internal sources at Asia Pacific Breweries.
- APB corporate website—www.apb.com.sg.
- APB marketing.

CASE STUDY 11—TIGER BALM

"Works Whenever it Hurts"

★ ★ ★ ★ ★

Tiger Balm is one of the brands in the healthcare division portfolio of Haw Par Corporation Ltd., a company that has been listed on the Singapore Exchange Ltd. since 1969. The group's core business in healthcare and leisure products promotes healthy lifestyles through health products, dietary supplements, pharmaceuticals, and location-based recreational centers such as oceanariums and bowling facilities. Besides healthcare and leisure products, the group has interests in investment properties, and manages its own portfolio of long-term and short-term investments in securities.

The group's primary corporate strategy is to expand its core healthcare and leisure businesses through product extensions under its own established brands, forming strategic alliances with overseas partners in various key markets and venturing into new growth areas. It also aims to manage efficiently its portfolio of investments in properties, as well as long-term and short-term securities, to achieve a reasonable return.

Tiger Balm has a range of products under the brand name "Tiger," such as Tiger Balm joint rub, Tiger Balm muscle spray, and Tiger Balm Soft. These product extensions are used throughout the world to invigorate the body as well as to soothe away aches and pains. (More details are given about the brand extensions later in the case.) Tiger Balm is a heritage brand with a long brand history. It is now sold in more than 100 countries and is used by millions of customers.

THE BRAND STORY

This herbal ointment remedy is truly an Asian brand, since it was passed down through the generations with its origin in the imperial courts of China, whose warlords and emperors needed relief from aches, pains, and a variety of other ailments.

A Hakka herbalist from China named Aw Chu Kin left China and established a medicine shop in Rangoon, Burma in the late 1870s where he developed and sold the balm. As a herbalist he had studied various remedies and knew from history, plus his own experimentation, that mixing ingredients such as camphor, clove oil, and menthol could bring pain relief. Tiger Balm's unique formulation contains these three ingredients plus cajuput oil. In product extensions, other ingredients are added.

Aw had two sons, Aw Boon Haw and Aw Boon Par. It was Aw Boon Haw who lent his name (meaning "tiger") to the remedy, and after the death of the father, Boon Haw marketed the balm under the brand name of "Tiger Balm." Together with his brother, they moved to Singapore in 1926. The tiger animal is also synonymous with strength and vitality in Asia, and this was deemed highly suitable as the product benefits include strength and speed of healing. Indeed, in the early days Boon Haw would travel with a tiger as a symbol of the potency of the balm.

The springing tiger logo, created by Boon Haw, has always been the trademark of the brand, successfully creating a high degree of awareness, recognition, and recall in global markets. The packaging, consisting of an official-looking imitation paper seal as a sign of approval, has made the brand unique and stands out from other competitors. Hexagonal jars and other more modern packaging are in use, but the tiger always takes the spotlight.

Aw Boon Haw was a savvy marketer and an entrepreneur who leveraged the balm business into an empire with interests in pharmaceuticals, banking, insurance, rubber, and newspapers. In the late 1920s, he looked for more extravagant ways of promotion. For example, he built a tiger-shaped car from which he distributed enameled posters of his pharmaceutical products. He would use every philanthropic act as a promotional opportunity for the brand.

Today, Tiger Balm is reaching more than 100 countries across five continents—from Norway in the north to New Zealand in the south, but naturally it is most popular in Asian countries such as Singapore, Malaysia, Hong Kong, Indonesia, and Thailand.

THE BRAND PROPOSITION

Tiger Balm is focused around one fundamental brand proposition, neatly summarized by its tagline: "Works whenever it hurts." It makes "things that hurt" feel better. Lynn Pan, director of the Chinese Heritage

Center in Singapore, suggests that the product has more mythic than medicinal value. "There's nothing much to Tiger Balm, yet Aw conveyed a feel-good factor. He understood the power of branding."

While this is an ambitious promise and in pragmatic terms unrealizable (Tiger Balm cannot stop many internal problems from hurting), the brand is recognized for what it can do and has succeeded in the "battle of the mind." The positive perception that people have about Tiger Balm is that it helps to cure aches, pains, and other ailments, and that the remedy originated in China a long time ago.

USAGE OCCASION AND APPLICATION POSITIONING: GROWTH THROUGH BRAND EXTENSIONS

The Tiger Balm brand has many product extensions, and each new product is launched using the existing established "Tiger Balm" brand name. Introducing new products with an existing brand name attracts new and existing consumers, giving them confidence in their purchase. The strength of the brand name also gives mobility to Tiger Balm, enabling it to move into new markets more easily.

Growth of the brand has come organically and not through acquisitions. Tiger Balm has been cleverly managed to adopt a positioning strategy that approaches different market segments but is always based on the same fundamental brand promise.

In terms of the positioning strategies outlined in the chapter introduction, Tiger Balm is probably the best global example of the "usage occasion and application" strategy.

Positioning

Tiger Balm has grown by adopting a "usage occasion and application" positioning approach via brand extensions. As shown in Figure 6.1, the different extensions are related to different target audiences and express different benefits. This is a clever way to grow a brand, and in Tiger Balm's case it now covers virtually all age groups, giving it a global market.

For example, in Thailand, the brand is being advertised and promoted heavily in 2005 via a campaign that is intended to appeal to all by stating that Tiger Balm delivers "Versatile, effective remedies for the whole family," backed by its tagline of "Works whenever it hurts."

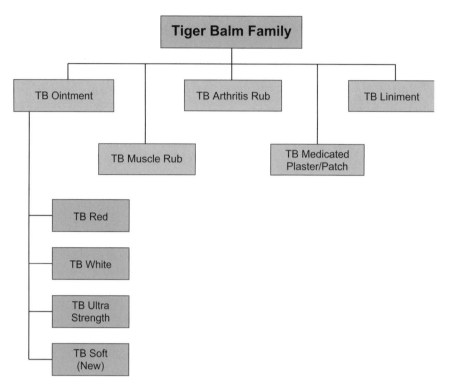

Figure 6.1 Tiger Balm family

In order to fulfill this brand promise, the brand has to prove its worth. The Tiger Balm brand family proposition can be analyzed as shown in Table 6.1.

Consumer Insight Example

Tiger Balm Soft is a very good example of a Tiger Balm line extension that was developed to target today's young consumers, a result of one-and-a-half years of R&D that originated because the original smell was too strong for young adults, who shunned it. This new product not only has a pleasant smell, but also is still effective in soothing headaches, back pain, muscular pain, and nasal and chest congestion.

Table 6.1   Tiger Balm brand—positioned via extensions for different target audiences

TB Arthritis Rub	◆ Alcohol-free cream that provides temporary relief from joint pain associated with arthritis *Target market:* Arthritis sufferers
TB Muscle Rub	◆ An analgesic cream that provides relief for muscle aches and pains due to sprains and strains ◆ A pre-exercise warm-up rub to prepare the exerciser to reduce the chances of spraining or straining the muscles ◆ Easy to apply and non-greasy *Target market:* Sportspersons, athletes
TB Medicated Plaster/Patch	◆ A non-woven material impregnated with Tiger Balm formulation ◆ Effective for the sustained relief of bodily arthritis, muscular aches, and pain sufferers ◆ Special material used allows ventilation and confers greater comfort to the user: being stretchable it can be used over joints such as elbow, knee, and ankle ◆ Two types: cool and warm *Target market:* Arthritis sufferers, especially the elderly
TB Liniment	◆ An effective topical pain-relieving liquid, it provides relief for aches and pains of muscles and joints associated with simple backaches, arthritis, bruises, and strains ◆ Easy to apply over large body areas and is fast acting ◆ Suitable for massage rub and expelling wind from the stomach *Target market:* The elderly and mothers who will buy to apply on their children

(continued)

Table 6.1 (continued)

TB Ointment	◆ A most versatile pain-relieving ointment
	◆ An external preparation for the relief of bodily aches and pains of muscles and joints due to simple backache, arthritis, strains, and sprains
	◆ Also effective in relieving headaches due to tension, itching due to mosquito bites, and flatulence
	◆ Also can be used to clear sinuses and relieve nasal and chest congestion
	TB Red: ◆ Extra-strength ointment (stains on clothing) ◆ Highly recommended for muscles aches. Relieves muscle stiffness *Target market:* Those who want effective relief
	TB White: ◆ Regular strength, gentle, colorless ointment ◆ Does not stain *Target market:* Females
	TB Ultra-strength: ◆ Ultra-strength ointment contains more pain-relieving menthol than TB Red, for deep penetrating relief *Target market:* Those who want a more powerful means of deeper pain relief
	TB Soft (New): ◆ A topical analgesic ointment with a light herbal fragrance and a soft texture *Target market:* Younger consumers, especially those who are active, socially and physically, who in the past have been "turned off" by the smell of the original product

BRAND COMMUNICATIONS

Tiger Balm has an interesting mix of brand communications, some of which are as follows:

+ Tiger Balm rides on the reputation and popularity of Haw Par Corporation, its parent company. For example, in Singapore's Chinatown, at Haw Par Villa, a park that contains mythological art murals on the walls and around the garden, visitors have the opportunity to buy tins of Tiger Balm from park attendants. The founder, Aw Boon Haw, had sculptures erected in the garden to remind people that honesty and being charitable are virtues to pursue—it was his way of repaying society for the profits he has made from his Tiger Balm business.

+ Tiger Balm has been using sports promotions to target customers in the United States. It seems to have positioned itself as the world's leading topical analgesic, perfect for soothing muscular aches and pains for sports enthusiasts and athletes. The name "Tiger" denotes strength and vitality, which seems to complement the characteristics of persons who are sports enthusiasts. In the mid-1990s this could have narrowed the customer base in this lifestyle category to just gym visitors; however, an advertising campaign that targeted golfers helped to change this perception. The advertising campaign featured successful golfers bending over to retrieve their successful putt and giving a twinge of pain. It is a common problem that golfers face. (Ian Woosnam, for example, has played for many years—and still does—with severe back pain.) Audiences were then greeted with the message: "Back ache? Tiger Balm Red & White."

+ Tiger Balm's website portrays its tagline as "The legend in a bottle," to position it as truly an Eastern heritage, stemming from ancient Chinese sources. Legend has it that the remedy was invented for a lusty Chinese emperor who, as a result of his promiscuity, suffered from persistent back pain. The product was thus created, and the remedy was passed on down through the centuries, until the Aw brothers decided to market the ointment.

+ Because of its leaping tiger icon, it is quite natural for Tiger Balm to sponsor causes such as saving or sponsoring tigers as part of a commitment to worldwide conservation and protection of endangered species. In 2002, Tiger Balm gave readers of the *Birmingham Post* a chance to win a "Behind the scenes: VIP tiger tour" with rangers from the Woburn Safari Park, one of the UK's leading tourist attractions.

Summary

All in all, Tiger Balm has gone a long way in a fairly competitive category with some competitors from huge multinational companies. It has extended well, and has kept the Asian appeal intact over its life to date.

Brand strengths

- ◆ Very focused on the brand promise/value proposition.
- ◆ Use of extensive market research to gain consumer insight.
- ◆ Shrewd brand management in launching and sustaining brand extensions and communications that are relevant.

Brand weaknesses

- ◆ Organic growth could be limited by the number of extensions possible without stepping outside of the brand promise.
- ◆ Communications not really creative and exciting—perhaps more investment needed.

Brand architecture

Product branding with product descriptors. Products are always labeled as pain relievers—for example, Tiger Liniment: provides penetrating pain relief; or Tiger Balm Patch: an external pain relief medicated plaster.

Sources

- ◆ Corporate information.
- ◆ "Tiger Balm," *IBRC Regional News*, Vol. 8, No. 1.
- ◆ "Tiger Balm, the Best Stuff in the World—Testimonials," www.ibiblio.org/kelly/tbalm.
- ◆ "Rise of a Tiger," www.asiaweek.com/asiaweek/96/1011/cs6.html.

◆ Azlan Ramli, "New Scent in Tiger Balm Range," *Malay Mail* (Kuala Lumpur), October 4, 2002, p. 20.
◆ "Tiger Balm Eyes 25pc of Medicated Plaster Market," *Business Times* (Kuala Lumpur), July 2, 1997, p. 7.
◆ "Tiger Balm Putts Back into Soothing Sore Golfers," *Marketing* (London), June 23, 1994, p. 5.
◆ "Salving a Damaged Image/An All-out Assault Produces a New Look/Multitech's PR Coups/A Good Corporate Citizen," *Asian Business* (Hong Kong), September 1987, p. 82.
◆ "Competition: Go and Take a Walk on the Wild Side," *Birmingham Post*, June 3, 2002, p. 14.
◆ Michael Richardson. "East Asian Business Searches for Right Brand-name Mix," *International Herald Tribune* (Paris), February 1, 1994.
◆ Hisham Harun "Soothing Balm Minus Heady Scents," *New Straits Times* (Kuala Lumpur), September 21, 2002, p. 8.
◆ Sarah Murray, "Goulish Counterbalance to a Squeaky Clean State: Garish Grottoes and Disturbing Images at a Weird Theme Park in Singapore Give Sarah Murray More than Pause for Thought," *Financial Times* (London), September 4, 1999, p. 16.
◆ "Win Towel and Sports Bag for Gym Visit," *Coventry Evening Telegraph*, October 18, 2001, p. 16.

CONCLUSION

The cases in this chapter have dealt with positioning issues, and have hinted that it is not just rational brand attributes and features that count; there must be emotional appeal also, and this is the subject of the next chapter.

CHAPTER 7

EMOTIONAL BRANDING

INTRODUCTION

After looking at the range of positioning options in the previous chapter, we now focus on the role of emotion in branding and consider how impactful it can be. If you want your brand to get to the top and stay there, your strategy must include an element of emotion. A brand strategy geared toward brand awareness doesn't need emotion, but brand acquisition and retention depend on it. Emotion sells, big time.

Successful brands usually have an element of emotion in their structure. It might be in their brand vision, personality, positioning, or delivery to the consumer, but emotion is a necessary component of power branding.

Hallmark, for example, has an emotional vision of enriching lives, and lives it to the full. Some brands position themselves emotionally, such as the Body Shop, which dedicates itself to the environment and non-testing of products on animals. Some great service brands, such as Nordstrom, deliver emotionally at the point of contact with the consumer. And nearly all of the cases in this book have some brand personality characteristics that are emotional in nature.

There are other brands that derive their emotional associations with the consumer by appealing to people's senses and beliefs. Harley-Davidson appeals to the sense of freedom, BMW to the sense of controlled power, and Dunhill is now basing its brand campaigns around style and nostalgia. Whatever it is and however it is accomplished, emotion sells.

The two cases I have chosen in this chapter are quite different in the way in which they use emotion in the branding process.

In the first case study, the Banyan Tree is really driven by its emotional brand personality, as you will see. It is a niche brand that appeals very much to the feelings of romance and intimacy, but it achieves its emotional appeal by not just capturing it in brand communications but by bringing the emotional dimension to life via "experiential branding"—that is, delivering a physical, sensual and highly emotional experience to the customer.

The second case is Jim Thompson, the luxury silk brand. Luxury has emotional appeal of its own and so do luxury products, but Jim Thompson has the added ingredients of heritage and mystery, through the disappearance of its founder. The emotion of the brand is in this case delivered by a combination of maintaining the intrigue and mystery of the founder via leveraging on the brand story (emotional heritage), and the sensory experience of the beautiful Thai silk products and retail outlets.

Both cases have the potential for global brand status in their own fields, and if managed well should reach their goals.

CASE STUDY 12—BANYAN TREE GROUP

The Stage is Set for Romance

Ho Kwon Ping started up the Banyan Tree resorts in 1995, when he discovered an abandoned tin mine on the Thai island of Phuket and turned it into a five-star hotel with a difference. It was created—and has been managed—as a niche, hotel-type product, as opposed to a brand to be built and nurtured. Banyan Tree was designed as a range of small and exclusive high-quality villa hotels offering seclusion.

Features, attributes, quality of service, customer benefits, and product delivery were uppermost in the minds of management.

This was not to say that Banyan Tree's development was accidental—far from it. There was a gap in the market that the top-class giant hotel chains such as the Sheraton and Shangri-la groups could not provide for. There was a niche market opportunity to be seized and owned, and one where competition was limited. The idea was that there existed a market segment composed of people who wanted to stay in accommodation that offered privacy, seclusion, and luxury in a very special and intimate way.

The success was so immediate and intense that the company expanded rapidly. It did so both with its own product and, because of its reputation and proven track record, by taking up offers from other property groups which outsourced the management of their businesses in a bid to improve their standards. This meant, on occasion, giving away the Banyan Tree brand name along with management expertise. But these joint ventures failed to reach the standards of the original product. The growth of the company and the extension of its brand in this way could have been disastrous for the Banyan Tree image, but the astute realization that the product had become a brand led to the rapid recovery of brand control.

The first hotel, The Banyan Tree, won an environment award, the first of over 100 awards that the Banyan Tree Group has received since. By the start of 2005 the group operated 15 hotels and has another eight to come. It also has 42 retail galleries and 38 spas around the world. In recent months, Ho has announced expansion plans for properties in Mexico, Dubai, Morocco, and Greece.

It has not been a bed of roses, however. The Asian financial crisis of 1997, the global recession that followed, the SARS epidemic, and regional bombings have given the business a volatile ride, but all along Ho has relied on brand building and management as the key to future success. As he says, "When you are new with only one or two hotels, you have to establish a brand and create a name for yourself and especially, stand out above the rest. The answer is through innovation, brand building, and taking steps that are applicable to any business."

There is a lot of sense in this remark, but in some respects it wasn't too difficult for the Banyan Tree to differentiate itself as a brand because few other players were in the category. However, had a brand not been created, then the Banyan Tree would not have been able to withstand the intense competition that has since arrived, with many hotel chains and other companies joining the fray.

Ho saw what had to be done and got on with it. Instead of taking the short-term view of creating a new product, only to take the money and run (which would have been easy), Ho created and has sustained a brand experience that is more or less unmatchable, to ensure the realization of massive brand asset value.

In order to get to the stage where the highest, most breathtaking service levels can be created and maintained, and thus develop a huge intangible brand asset, there had to be a strongly focused brand strategy. This is what has made the Banyan Tree one of the most admired and envied brands in Asia. The strategy itself isn't complicated, as you will see, but the greatness of the brand comes from the execution and management of the strategy, and the ability of management to make sure it evolves, is innovative, and remains relevant to the needs of customers.

Let's look at the strategy for the brand and then at how it has been managed.

THE HEART OF THE BANYAN TREE BRAND

The Brand "Essence"

At the heart of the Banyan Tree brand is the "romance of travel." As Ho says, "It is not about money and we are not about luxury. Yes, high room rates and all this talk about celebrities staying in our hotels are easily associated with luxury. The challenge for us is to sell the romance of travel." Beautiful settings and locations, opulence, and grandeur are highly prized features, but they only serve as foundations that are the building blocks for the unique atmosphere and experience the customer will feel and never forget.

The nearest comparison I can make is the experience of taking a trip on the Orient Express. There is a mystery there, an intrigue, a uniqueness that, once experienced, can never be forgotten. Of course, the brand emphasis isn't the same, but the Banyan Tree creates excitement and delivers on its values in a similar fashion. Ho goes on to say, "As long as we are focused, believe in the romance of travel, and find that going around to see places in the world is exciting, we can convince our guests. The danger is in getting jaded."

This is always a danger for any brand, and themed innovation consistent with the brand values is the best way of dealing with this problem. The values of the Banyan Tree are powerful when applied well, and while few in number, they do allow for considerable creativity and customer focus.

Brand Values

The two core values of the Banyan Tree brand are essentially "romance" and "intimacy," and everything possible is done to bring these two words to life for the guests who visit. The key thing to note here is that they are emotional, not rational, in nature. Emotions appeal to the heart; rational factors to the head. If you want to build a great brand in the service industry, especially hospitality, then the emotional dimension should dominate the brand. Emotion sells, and emotional branding at the Banyan Tree level is about selling dreams and fantasies. The brand landscapes a stage on which the Banyan Tree people are the cast, who help the customers, or principal actors, to live out their dreams.

Your own theater of dreams—the brand experience

Naturally, there are the five-star trappings that all top-class hotels and resorts have: a greeting so warm it makes you wonder why life can't be like this all the time; total recall of your preferences; first-name greetings, and so on. But what differentiates the Banyan Tree from all other "competitors" is that the brand experience is taken one step further. The experience touches your heart and soul, and allows you to live your dreams.

Imagine this. You are in a most beautiful villa, insulated from the world and prying eyes. Your bedroom is set amidst a lotus pool and enclosed by glass. The bed is on a platform in the middle of the room but can be entirely hidden by electrically operated curtains should you so wish. The bed is like an altar, set upon a platform, which can be transformed in the daytime with different adornments to be an eating place, a reading place, or a place for drinks. But at night it is turned into a very romantic sleeping place overlooking the lotus pond.

Select an "Intimate Moments" package, and your villa will be transformed while you are at dinner. Dozens of candles now bathe the room in a romantic glow, a bottle of wine lies waiting, there are satin sheets on the bed, a hot-water bath is ready, and a variety of aromatic massage oils and incense sticks are provided. The rest is up to you! (Or no rest, if you prefer.)

This is not unusual in the Banyan Tree. What is actually happening is the bringing to life of those two brand values—romance and intimacy—but in typical oriental fashion. The mantra is that "It takes two hands to clap." You have your dream and are the main player(s); the Banyan Tree is the catalyst that helps it to come true— the employees are the supporting cast.

Staff inclusivity

One of the keys to this transformatic door is that each member of staff is taught to believe that they have one fundamental role, which is to help guests generate their own romantic dreams and fantasies. As a part of the training process, each staff member spends a night in one of the villas to gain an understanding of what the concept is all about. In fact, the people who work at the Banyan Tree are very much a part of the process of brand management, in providing superlative service and a most memorable experience.

BRAND MANAGEMENT: THE SIX Ps: PRIDE, PASSION, PRIVACY, PERSONAL ATTENTION, PARTICIPATION, AND PERFORMANCE

As mentioned earlier, a good brand strategy is worthless if it isn't executed and managed well, and brand management is a tough job that requires tough decisions to be made. The Banyan Tree team is meticulous about managing the brand, and this stems very much from Ho's philosophy of never becoming complacent. He often refers to brand management in terms of the following elements:

- *Pride:* Employees are motivated to do things well, take personal responsibility, and have to be team players.
- *Passion:* People chosen by Banyan Tree are disciplined and proficient, especially if they are going to work in planning and management roles. Everyone working for the company must be passionate about their ideas and beliefs.
- *Participation:* This comes from the inclusivity referred to above— having a sense of helping to create the guests' experience— generating drama and excitement, and this extends to brainstorming, creative ideation, design, and so on.
- *Personal attention:* Every guest is different—has different dreams, aspirations, visions of desire, and definitions of romance and intimacy. It is up to the employees to find out what these are and to deliver them, and to get to know each guest intimately without being intrusive.

- *Performance:* The whole experience is based on the performance of the "players" (employees), and they are taught to
  think about the experience they are giving their guests as just
  this—they are a part of a theatrical event.
- *Privacy:* Guests pay for privacy—to get away from the hustle
  and bustle, not to mention stress, of everyday life and to enjoy
  their own space. A wedding ceremony can be conducted in the
  guests' villa. Evening meals can be arranged just for two on a
  sandbank, with a fisherman who catches fish and brings them
  just to the guests, and a waiter who walks through the water
  to the sandbank to pour the couple's champagne.

Banyan Tree is the stuff of legends. Nothing is too much trouble.
Each guest is treated as the most important person in the world. Can
it be done like this all the time?

CONSISTENCY AND BRAND GUARDIANSHIP

No brand is perfect, but great brands strive continually for perfection
and consistency. The protection of the brand is now a top priority for
the company. It has made a definitive decision to forego many other
"contract-manufacturing" opportunities that could have been
extremely lucrative, so that the Banyan Tree brand equity that has
been built up won't be diluted. The temptation to go for short-term
profits and revenue enhancement has been rejected on many occasions in favor of building long-term, somewhat intangible brand
value. The brand is everything—an entity to be nurtured, protected,
and allowed to grow in a controlled and consistent fashion.

Experiential Variations and Improvization

Ho says that standards do vary by resort, and he has now brought in
two types of brand managers—those that are marketing-based and
those that are operations-oriented—to manage the consistency issue.
Paradoxically, Ho says the element of difference must remain between
resorts in terms of their locations and cultures, and must be encouraged.
Absolute cloning brings absolute boredom (my words, not Ho's). Each
resort must have its own way of delighting the guests, but this cannot
step away from the central brand proposition of giving every guest at
every resort an experience that delivers theater, romance, and intimacy.

Even on a micro-scale, deviations from the norm are allowed, unlike at most hotels. For example, it is standard hotel practice to turn down the bed at night for the guests and to leave a small gift, such as a flower, on the bed or nearby. At the Banyan Tree, the room attendant can decide, within reason, what the gift should be. They are given the opportunity to exercise their judgment and are empowered to do what they think is correct for their "own" guests.

HOW ARE WE DOING? AWARDS—TRANSITORY, BUT A SIGN OF CUSTOMER DELIGHT

Ho is concerned about complacency. Even with all the accolades that the Banyan Tree has had bestowed upon it, he still has that great attribute of good brand leaders—paranoia. For example, of the 120 or more awards won in only ten years he says, "We don't ever think we have got it right. . . . To us, winning awards is like a surrogate for customer satisfaction. Sure, you can measure your achievement using room rates and occupancy rates, but winning awards is heartening to me . . . a sign that we are doing something right."

BUSINESS DEVELOPMENT AND AFFILIATE BRANDS

In order to expand the business and go into other areas of hospitality and spa operations and management without diluting the Banyan Tree image, Banyan Trees Holdings has chosen to develop an affiliate brand called Angsana Resorts and Spa. The brand has expanded rapidly and now has several locations in the Asia-Pacific region. It is concerned with relaxation, renewal, and rejuvenation, with a concept slogan: "Sensing the moment." It thus has a connection with the master brand to do with indulgence, luxury, and privacy, but dwells less on the romantic, intimate side.

An extension of the Angsana brand is Colours of Angsana, which targets tourists with a sense of adventure, culture, and heritage. It made its entrance into the market in August 2003 in China. This brand contains a collection of small boutique hotels in exotic locations acquired under management or revenue-sharing arrangements. Ho says, "The acquisition of these new properties is part of a larger strategy to position the group in exotic 'frontier' destinations that may not boast luxury accommodations, but offer unique experiences that appeal to adventurous travelers." He goes on to say that Colours of Angsana presents a canvas for painting exceptional travel experiences, leaving an indelible memory of the sojourn.

Ho is conscious of mixed images, and says: "We are also mindful of over-stretching or diluting the scope of our individual brands; hence the development of a collection under the banner of Angsana Resorts and Spa to allow for diversification and growth within the group's central strategy."

The group also has another affiliate brand, Allamanda Laguna Phuket, which "offers the comfort of home and the fun of a resort—giving you the best of both worlds for that well-deserved getaway or family holiday." This resort consists of suites, as opposed to a fully serviced hotel.

Despite the statement about brand dilution, the brands are still linked together, and the only thing that seems to be constant is travel to exotic locations. With any really successful brand, there is always the temptation to extend the offerings into a variety of products, sub-brands, and linked brands. In this case, the target audiences are mostly different, and time will tell if the Banyan Tree brand will indeed be diluted or not.

Brand strengths

- Niche marketing positioning and differentiation.
- Outstanding product quality.
- Unique brand personality backed by the brand experience.
- Consistent and appropriate brand communications.
- Obsessive brand guardianship.

Brand weaknesses

- Brand extension into smaller hotels and associated brands, in some cases not under the control of the master brand, may over-extend and dilute the master brand if the experience is not up to standard.
- Failure to protect the Banyan Tree name—a prominent Indian communications company has the same name and a similar website address.

Brand architecture

Corporate and sub-branding.

Sources

- ◆ *Le Prestige* (Malaysia), February 2005.
- ◆ *Branding in Asia* (Singapore: John Wiley & Sons (Asia) Pte. Ltd., 2000), Paul Temporal.

CASE STUDY 13—JIM THOMPSON

From Authentic Silk to Fashion Icon?

HISTORY

James W. H. Thompson was a former architect who arrived in Thailand just before World War II. An enthusiastic art collector and aesthete, he decided to make the country his home. He discovered Thailand's dying art of silk weaving and sought to revive it. Although he didn't invent Thai silk, as weaving and production of raw silk was already established—especially in the northeast of Thailand, a region that Thompson loved—he saw the beauty and the value in that business; in other words, he commercialized it. The first step into the commercial world for Jim Thompson came when he flew to New York to see if he could interest any of the "movers and shakers" in the silk cloth made by small family weavers. The editor of *Vogue* magazine, Edna Chase, was taken by the beauty of the cloth and featured in the magazine a silk dress created by the designer Valentina, with credit to Jim Thompson, and the rest is history.

Jim Thompson's Thai silk shot to fame when it was used in the stage show and movie, *The King and I*. In fact, the Thai silk industry benefited as a whole from the exposure.

Thai Silk Co., formed by Thompson and other shareholders, was formally incorporated in late 1948, and it was extremely successful. Jim Thompson was at the height of his wealth and fame when, during Easter in 1967, just two weeks after opening his first store, he went on holiday in the Cameron Highlands, Malaysia. On the Sunday afternoon, Thompson left his holiday companions at their retreat and went for a walk alone in the surrounding jungle. He never returned. The day before, he and his companions had become lost during a walk in the same area. It was Thompson who found the way back. Not so the next day. He was 61 years old.

Thompson's disappearance sparked many rumors, from theories that he was a CIA anti-communist agent whose enemies had drugged and abducted him, that he had committed suicide, that he had collapsed after becoming lost and had then died of a heart attack, that he had been eaten by a tiger, that he had fallen into a tiger pit, been impaled on stakes at the bottom of the pit, and then been buried by those who found him there. However, the truth remains a mystery to this day. There is no evidence of where he went or how he died. There is simply nothing—not one piece of evidence or any clue to say that he actually did die. Jim Thompson just disappeared. Debate about what actually happened to him continues to this day.

This exotic history gave the Thai firm a rosy future. According to William Booth, managing director of the brand owner, Thai Silk Co., "The folklore has been very helpful as a selling tool." Many great brands are made up of myths and stories, and there is definitely an aura of mystery around the persona of Jim Thompson. In Thailand, he is still the subject of discussion and speculation. People who visit Thailand inevitably gain brand awareness and visit the outlets. The original outlet is a key attraction for tourists coming to Thailand, and can receive up to 1,000 visitors a day.

But outside Thailand, the Jim Thompson brand isn't so well known. And therein lies the dilemma: how to leverage a brand with top-quality, desired products and a huge potential, but little global awareness and traditional product usage? Furthermore, can this be done without leaving behind the heritage and mystique of the brand, a past that generates its own differentiation?

JIM THOMPSON'S FUTURE: BRAND EVOLUTION OR REVOLUTION?

To date, the success of the Jim Thompson brand has been a result of a niche brand strategy, reinforcing tradition and heritage, along with quality products. (The company uses the latest production technology, from upstream raw silk production through to finished products, to ensure quality and efficiency.) But as the company grows more ambitious, this strategy will come under pressure.

Niche Brand

More than half a century after it was founded, the company has continued to grow and business is better than ever, but it is the brand that really drives the business. It has always been a niche brand. Jim Thompson products are sold in around 30 countries through overseas offices and agents. In Thailand, there are 30 retail outlets and the products are also available for sale online through the website. Even so, the spread of the brand's distribution covers North America, Latin America, Europe, the Middle East, Africa, and Asia-Pacific.

Thai Silk Co. is famous for the shimmer, texture, and colors of its traditional Thai silk. It is a part of Thai culture, and it is very much associated with Jim Thompson and his mysterious disappearance. These have been powerful drivers of the brand's success to date. The company has showrooms not only in Thailand and Asia, but also in New York, Atlanta, and London. The company's clothing line, mainly casual wear for women, evokes mental images of the East with rich silk, bright colors, mandarin collars, and fitted sheaths. The stores are visited by people who are brands themselves, such as Hillary Clinton, Leonardo DiCaprio, and Madonna.

The obvious route to take in promoting the brand internationally would be to take those brand strengths and leverage them. In other words, remain a niche brand and stick to what you are good at—leverage your strategic competitive advantage. Niche global brands are the only way to gain universal success without competing head-on with the giant brands in a category.

However, the company appears to have decided to change the brand's identity and move it away from the characteristics of "mystique" and "authentic silk" to become a younger, fresher fashion icon.

Growth Strategy

Growth for Jim Thompson is through diversification, and the aim is to increase the company's product range in response to the customers' demand. Thai Silk Co. introduced casual clothing, evening dress, furniture, gift products, and photo frames to attract new markets, especially the domestic market. T-shirts made of leftover silk from clothing and tie products were introduced to attract young tourists.

The company has launched a new range of less expensive products under the brand name "Nagara," created by a local designer to tap a new market. Non-silk products were also introduced to attract a new market. The danger here is a possible dilution of the main brand. The diversification into non-silk and lower-quality products might have a negative impact on the original Jim Thompson brand, which is associated very much with premium, high-quality silk products.

Brand Identity Change: Fashion or Failure?

The end game for the development of Jim Thompson as a brand is apparently to create a strategy that results in a younger, fresher image with the help of Thai designers, and this is in line with the government's aims to promote exports of high-quality merchandise. (One of the Thai government's economic and brand objectives is to create an image for Bangkok as a fashion center over the next 10 years or so.)

Possibly with this in mind, Thai Silk Co. hired a London-based designer to move the Jim Thompson brand away from flower and elephant prints and to emphasize bold colors and ultra-chic design. This has resulted in a totally new look under the banner "Living with Jim Thompson." The company also has entered the home furnishings category, as European and American designers have discovered that Jim Thompson's inventive twists on traditional weaves are just the sort of fabric that hotels and wealthy home-owners want.

Essentially, the company is trying to transform a brand name associated specifically with silk fashion garments and accessories loved by tourists from around the world (especially from Japan, for some reason) into a brand demanded by consumers and interior designers in North America, Europe, and Asia. The central idea is to position Jim Thompson as a fashion leader for women's clothing and home furnishings. The main immediate brand issue here is, will this shift destroy or enhance the brand image? It is a fundamental brand transformation, but if executed correctly it could make Jim Thompson a global brand.

There is little doubt that this decision has been made after studying the transformation of once-staid companies such as Gucci and Burberry into fashion icons. The concept may be fine, but getting to the finish line represents a huge task. Even Burberry, the revolution of the decade to date, now finds itself with some irritating image problems as fringe customer segments take control of the brand's destiny out of its owner's hands. And other "authentic" brands possessing strong images from the past, such as Laura Ashley, have tried, and tried, and tried, and failed; so, it will be no easy journey.

Presumably, the management of Thai Silk Co. has carried out extensive research before making this fundamental decision. This is a critical move for the company, and a powerful brand vision, values, and positioning will be required to make the brand strong enough to withstand formidable competition from big players such as LV, Gucci, Hermes, and others. The creation of a very powerful brand image will be mandatory if the company is to differentiate itself from its competitors.

Importantly, deep pockets will be required. The brand-building investment needed to take on the giants of the luxury fashion industry will be very much more than the company is used to making.

Inevitably, the success of the new brand strategy will depend on one thing. Will consumers give the Jim Thompson brand "permission" to move into other categories, where needs and wants are totally different from the world of mystique, exoticism, emotion, and romance?

Jim Thompson is a lovely brand, admired by all. The Thai Silk Co. knows the way through familiar brandscapes, and the future will be a test of skillful brand management as it manouvers through new territory. It's to be hoped that Jim Thompson won't stroll into the unfamiliar brand jungle and disappear, just as its founder did.

Brand strengths

- ◆ Heritage.
- ◆ Authenticity.
- ◆ Mystique.
- ◆ High-quality products.

Brand weaknesses

- ◆ The brand is liked very much, but it's not top of mind when people are not in Thailand. It lacks true global awareness.
- ◆ Consumers may not give the brand permission to change its identity and essentially move into a wider category filled with luxury goods brands.

- Crossing categories needs consumer insight and understanding, which presently the company might not have in depth.
- Has it got the cash to invest in luxury brand management?

Brand architecture

Corporate branding.

Source

William Warren, *Jim Thompson: The Unsolved Mystery* (Singapore: Archipelago Press, 1998).

CONCLUSION

The message in this chapter is that you have to have a healthy dose of emotion in your brand strategy to attract and retain customers. In the next chapter, we look at what this means for service brands.

CHAPTER **8**

SERVICE BRANDS

INTRODUCTION

In the last chapter we looked at how emotion has a pull effect, drawing in customers with various types of emotional appeal. For service brands this element is brought into focus merely by the close interaction between people representing the brand and the customers they serve. For product brands, emotion is built with advertising, design, packaging, and other elements, but with service brands it is the face-to-face relationship that can make or break brand acquisition and loyalty.

Service branding is probably one of the most difficult areas of branding to get right. It really is about consumer touch points. When a large percentage of your staff actually come face-to-face or interact with customers in any way at all, this creates a huge challenge for developing and maintaining brand image.

As consumers of services ourselves every day, we know how frustrating it can be not to have our expectations met. And this is the heart of the issue—the gap between consumer expectations and the ability of brands to understand and satisfy them. In Asia, it is perhaps an understatement to say that there is a long way to go in terms of achieving world-class quality. My opinion is based on 20 years of experience in Asia, most of that time spent living in the region. Taking a more optimistic view, I can see many companies trying to improve, and there are a great many opportunities to grow brands in the service sector.

There are currently two main influences on service brand image—whether those services are under your direct control, or whether they are outsourced. It is clearly easier to control service quality if employees who interact with customers are working directly for your company. It is much more difficult if service is outsourced in some way, via franchising, licensing, or other activities such as call centers. On the other hand, outsourcing companies can make their own brand names via giving great service to the companies they have as clients.

In this chapter, we will look at brands that are trying via both means. In the first case I illustrate the service quality battle that is taking place in the Asian healthcare (wellness) sector, focusing on competition between providers from the leading brands in Singapore and Thailand. The service quality imperative has led to one hospital in Singapore declaring it wants to be the Ritz-Carlton of Asian healthcare. At present, however, regarding the consumer brand experience, Bumrungrad "Hospitel" is inching ahead. The very word "hospitel" demonstrates the trend that is happening in the healthcare sector—a combination of a hospital's rational and technical appeal with a hotel's emotional appeal.

But the key to any powerful brand, especially in the service sector, is the ability to establish emotional connections with customers that will attract them, retain them, and encourage them to be your brand advocates.

THE EMOTIONAL BRAND RELATIONSHIP PROCESS

In order to build an emotional brand strategy there are certain steps brand managers have to take, like the steps of a ladder, as shown in Figure 8.1. Let's think of it as two people, as opposed to a brand and consumers. One person sees another across a room at a particular function, and wants to meet them. Following this awareness, an opportunity to meet may arise, and although the conversation is short, it leads to a decision on whether or not the interest is sufficient to carry the relationship further. Further meetings reinforce this mutual respect, and the two people become friends. If the friendship blossoms, it generates mutual trust and loyalty, and it is highly likely that these two people will become friends for life, or have a lasting relationship.

The brand–consumer relationship grows in a very similar way. Awareness comes first, followed by involvement and purchase—a few meetings—which can lead on to the friendship and trust levels, which in turn lead to brand loyalty and lifetime customer relationships. The

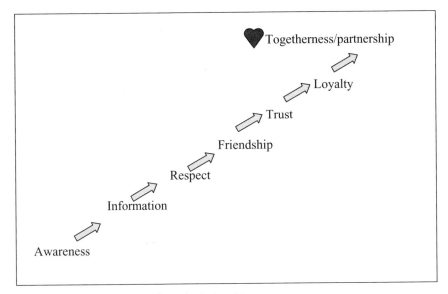

Figure 8.1   The emotional brand relationship process

power brands get to—and move past—the friendship and trust levels; others may get stuck at the first stage. In fact, big spending on awareness follows many brand launches, but the subsequent management of the brand may not take it up the ladder. For example, Lastminute.com (an e-commerce company selling holiday flights and entertainment, etc at the last minute) at one time received 84% brand awareness ratings but only a 17% trust rating. Some brand managers spend millions on awareness—which is an essential step to achieve—but then neglect the emotional side of the brand–consumer relationship, which is necessary for real long-term success.

The pinnacle of service based on establishing emotional connections, as described above, in the hospitality area seems to be the Ritz-Carlton hotel chain. Non-outsourced service brands seem preoccupied with trying to emulate the Ritz-Carlton, and it's not surprising as the company sees very clearly what makes a good service brand—people! Here is an example of what happens on the side of the brand the customer doesn't see—teaching employees to live the brand values.

The Ritz-Carlton stresses its philosophy of explaining to its employees that "You are ladies and gentlemen serving ladies and gentlemen":

◆ Strategy: Employee satisfaction = Customer satisfaction = Profit.

- Twenty-two thousand employees, every one of whom is briefed every day.
- Each day, the briefings focus on one of 20 service principles.

For example:

- *Principle no. 10:* Each employee is empowered. When a guest has a problem or needs something special, you should break away from your regular duties to address and resolve the issue.
- *Principle no. 12:* To provide the finest personal service for our guests, each employee is responsible for identifying and recording individual guest preferences.

It is difficult to fault this strategy, and anyone who has stayed in a Ritz-Carlton hotel will probably say they have had a great experience. If you have stayed at one on more than one occasion, you will know that they know you and your preferences.

Finally, outsourcing is becoming the norm for many businesses that want to grow without adding to their fixed costs. For those companies adept at providing good service, global brand status awaits, especially in the technology sector. India seems to be spawning a lot of good brands here, such as our second case example in this chapter, Infosys.

Case Study 14—BUMRUNGRAD HOSPITAL

The Branded "Hospitel"

Healthcare in Asia

Asia's population will shoot up from 3.2 billion in 2002 to 5.6 billion in 2050, and consumer spending on healthcare products and services will double from US$90 billion in 1999 to US$188 billion in 2013.

Healthcare is an interesting and fast-developing brand arena. As the population and disposable income increases, patients look for better solutions; as they are already conditioned by branded goods, they are looking for branded solutions.

From a Healthcare to a Wellness Perspective

In conjunction with this, marketers have changed consumer views so that they now look upon health from a "wellness" perspective—not just thinking about health when they get sick, but about prevention as well, in all its many forms. Healthcare providers have responded in the public and private sectors by making major shifts in the way they brand and promote themselves. They now offer more subjective, quality-of-life benefits, as opposed to just clinical benefits. They are less focused on technology (except as an enabler), and are more consumer-focused—looking at needs states. For example, in hospital environments now there is a heavy emphasis on design and environmental layout, eliminating barriers such as reception desks, and stimulating easier process flows and greater patient interaction with all levels of staff. Innovations in design enhance positive moods—for example, the ceilings of children's wards are decorated with twinkling stars.

Medical Malls versus Specialist Boutiques

The continuum of wellness provision ranges from the big medical malls that offer every possible service under one roof, to specialist boutique providers, such as spas, skin clinics, laser eye clinics, and other specific areas of wellness. A person can choose, much like choosing a car, whether to have a luxury model or to go for value for money. The range is enormous. But whatever service the provider decides to offer and to what level, there is a distinct trend to focus on innovation, new techniques, facilities, and service. While the first three of these are more easily replicable, it is the service dimension that is the battleground in Asia.

The key differentiator is how well the company understands the customer and gives him or her the best possible brand experience. In this way, wellness providers have learnt many lessons from the modern retail brand leaders.

Competition: Singapore versus Thailand

Singapore and Thailand are two countries that have seen a massive opportunity in the wellness market. Both countries appear to be positioning themselves as the hub for wellness in Asia, but in slightly different ways.

Singapore

Singapore's wellness industry is more strongly connected to government than that of Thailand, and the Ministry of Trade and Industry has stated that it aims to position Singapore as the "Healthcare Hub of Asia" based on two strategic thrusts, which are to:

◆ build an enduring brand name based on clinical excellence; and
◆ attract foreign patients.

As a result, there is a strong focus on expertise, new/first techniques, and specialized research. Staff development is a priority, and there is an increased focus on service. The underlying theme for Singapore is *quality*.

As examples, Singapore's Parkway Group Healthcare—the largest healthcare group in Asia—owns three private hospitals in Singapore: East Shore, Gleneagles, and Mount Elizabeth. Raffles Hospital and Clinics has over 40 clinics and offers convenience. Both are enhancing their expertise and service.

Gleneagles is a good example, as it aims to be the "Ritz-Carlton" of the medical world in the next three years, offering six-star service. Its focus is "Luxurious service, innovative technology." To this end, it says it was the first hospital in Southeast Asia to perform a live-donor liver transplant (1995). It promises:

◆ wi-fi (wireless fidelity-enabled) hotspots at designated locations in its hospital so that customers can log on to the Internet;
◆ free limousine rides home for discharged maternity patients;
◆ a system for logging personal preferences for repeat patients;
◆ shorter waiting times;
◆ support for new parents—Gleneagles Kiddies Club; and
◆ an overhaul of its IT system (S$5–10 million) by the end of 2006.

Mount Elizabeth Hospital strives to be the premier tertiary healthcare provider of choice in Singapore and the region, with its core values of *excellence, customer focus, empowerment*, and *loyalty*.

Among its achievements are:

- the first 24-hour rehabilitation program in Singapore, introducing the country to intensive physical rehabilitation;
- the first artificial corneal implant in Singapore;
- the first private hospital in Singapore to perform fibroid embolisation; and
- the first working Positron Emission Tomography (PET) scanner in Southeast Asia.

Thailand

Thailand is aiming at wealthy Thais, foreigners, and tourists. Hospitals and clinics are offering "packages" so that customers can enjoy several benefits at the same time. As an example, a person can have a child delivery, cosmetic surgery, or dental services combined with a holiday to recover. Check-ups, on-premise spas, and traditional massage are thrown in as well. Even the government is offering upscale services in its hospitals.

While not known for technical expertise like Singapore, Thai providers overcome potential patient worries about safety with ISO certification and accreditation from overseas institutions. As you will see below in the case example, customer relationship management is much to the fore.

Bumrungrad: The Branded "Hospitel."   Founded in 1980 as a local private hospital, Bumrungrad is now Southeast Asia's largest private hospital. It treats over 850,000 patients per year, of whom 275,000 are from 150 different nations. It was the first hospital in Asia to be certified by the US-based Joint Commission on International Accreditation (JCIA).

Bumrungrad Hospital focuses on expertise, luxury, and service, but the emphasis is most definitely on luxury. Comprehensive web-based information is provided, and it offers competitively priced packages (including holiday tours) in an attempt to propagate "medical tourism."

Its renowned "hospitel" (hospital + hotel) concept has been successful in creating the point of differentiation for the business. With its focus on delivering great healthcare with great service, Bumrungrad Hospital has combined different kinds of businesses in its hospital complex, where patients and visitors can find services they have never expected from a general hospital.

This "hybrid business" of Bumrungrad Hospital is designed to respond to the wide variety of needs from customers. It is obvious that the hospital has planned not only to serve the needs of the patients, but also those of their visitors. This far-sighted business strategy has recognized that visitors to the hospital complex typically outnumber the patients. And what is more, it has realized that both patients and visitors like to have available the same things they have when life is normal. Bumrungrad Hospital has used co-branding with other service brands, so that it can offer multiple services.

An example of their service brand extensions is shown in Figure 8.2. Visitors wishing to stay overnight can be accommodated at B.S. Resident—a five-star hotel located in the complex. These short-stay visitors can enjoy browsing around the complex with its retailer brand names such as Starbucks, McDonald's, Au Bon Pain, 7-Eleven, Family Mart, plus many more retail shops in its plaza zone such as florist shops, a fashion boutique, and so on. To serve some special needs, services such as Mandara Spa and Ayame Indian Restaurant are also available. The hospital also offers additional services, such as valet parking, traditional Thai *tuk tuk* transportation within the hospital complex, as well as a digital newspaper and Cyber Corner.

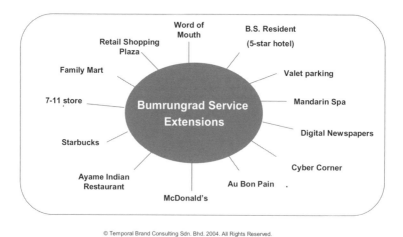

Figure 8.2   Bumrungrad hybrid business model: 'Hospitel'

The branded partner businesses within the complex have been selected with great care. When co-branding is planned, the image of both brands should be compatible to generate an impactful result. Bumrungrad Hospital selected to co-brand with global brands and brands that stand for excellent quality and service standards. With its careful choice of brand partners, Bumrungrad Hospital is able to build and reinforce an image of high-standard wellness services.

Bumrungrad Hospital took off in a regional arena just after the economic turmoil in 1997. With the help of the weak Thai currency, Bumrungrad's quality medical service has become good value for money for regional patients. The disadvantage that Singapore has is its high cost base.

As Thailand has been vigorously promoted as a tourism destination, regional patients well consider this as a bonus to their medical treatment. With that perspective, the road to become a world brand for Bumrungrad Hospital doesn't seem to be far out of reach. But with the same perspective, competition from local hospitals is becoming more intense as opportunities increase.

It requires a different view on branding in order to become a global brand. Although quality is a must and no brands can be powerful without it, quality products and services in modern retailing are no longer a differentiator. They can be replicated, if not improved upon, by the competition. Bumrungrad will have to keep up with the foremost wellness techniques, as well as with great service.

Although Bumrungrad has the edge on service quality at present, further down the road it will need to look for a different route to success if it is to become a world brand. All the powerful brands in the world have a special emotional connection with their customers. It is this emotional connection that makes the difference; it provides the global power brands with brand loyalty and strong viral marketing. It is a big step to become a world brand, but it seems that Bumrungrad is going in the right direction.

Brand strengths

- Good branded business model.
- Clear understanding of customer needs.
- Strong marketing techniques.
- Generating a good customer brand experience.

Brand weaknesses

Concern about how well it can manage the brand going forward under pressure from existing and new competition.

Brand architecture

True corporate branding.

CASE STUDY 15—INFOSYS
TECHNOLOGIES LIMITED

"High on Values, High on Growth"

★ ★ ★ ★ ★

Infosys is ranked 62nd among the "World's Most Respected Companies" in the *Financial Times*–PricewaterhouseCoopers annual 2004 survey and is the only Indian company included in this elite group. More importantly, it is 37th in the list of companies that created the most value for its shareholders. Narayana Murthy, the chairman and chief mentor of Infosys, is among the world's most respected business leaders. These accolades might sound like a routine story for most global companies, but Infosys's story is truly inspiring for all who believe in the power of corporate charisma to achieve market leadership.

THE BRAND STORY: HUMBLE BEGINNINGS AND STILL HUMBLE

Narayana Murthy worked in France as a young man and traveled widely, including to the former Soviet Union. He was greatly influenced by leftist ideologies; however, after visiting countries whose economies enjoyed capitalist success, his belief in communism was shaken. He was determined to create a venture that had a foundation built on the best principles of both capitalism and socialism, with the aim of creating wealth for all its constituents. Murthy still abides religiously by his principles and is credited with establishing a culture at the company that is very distinct. His principles and values have also been well supported by a strong top management that comprises the founder members. The Infosys culture attracts aspiring IT professionals from the premier engineering and management institutes in India, to a company they consider as one of the best places in the world to work.

Infosys Technologies came into being in India in 1981 when seven engineers, working for an Indian re-seller of US-based Data General Machines, were bitten by the entrepreneurial bug under the influence of Narayana Murthy. None of the engineers came from affluent backgrounds, and all had differing skill sets and experience. The binding force was a strong self-belief and a desire to scale new heights in what they did. Relentless hard work and visionary leadership have today resulted in one of the world's largest consulting and IT services providers. Infosys has a presence in 17 countries, 434 active clients, approximately 33,000 employees, and revenue exceeding US$1 billion in 2004.

The Infosys business can be very broadly split into IT services, consulting, and business process outsourcing (BPO). IT services include software development, software maintenance, and re-engineering. The consulting division focuses on two areas—strategic and competitive analysis, and complex operational changes—in order to create a long-term competitive advantage for its clients. India is currently championing the BPO industry, and Infosys is among its major players. Although Infosys offers a wide array of IT-related services, the recent focus is on the Global Delivery Model. This model combines the intellectual capabilities from the various divisions to offer clients an "intelligent work breakdown." Infosys is futuristic and hopes to make a visible difference that can be measured both quantitatively and qualitatively by using the model.

In terms of industries, Infosys has a strong presence in varied industries, including banking and capital markets, automotive and aerospace sectors, health and insurance, among many others. It boasts of long-lasting relationships with global companies such as Bank of America, Goldman Sachs, ConAgra Inc., Levi Strauss & Co., Reebok International Ltd., Apple Computer, JC Penney Company, and The Gap, Inc. Infosys added 38 new clients in the last quarter of 2004, a year that saw a 51% jump in net revenue. The trickle has rapidly turned into a flood.

THE BRAND PROMISE

The ideology of the leaders at Infosys percolates effectively into the characteristics of its corporate brand. The company is known to treat its stakeholders with respect, to abide by the law, and to follow all the fair practice rules. Even the corporate tagline, "Powered by intellect, driven by values," was conceptualized after due consideration.

The company believes that in order to be successful and respected, it has to look beyond numbers and profitability. Infosys is a brand that proudly claims to have high social consciousness. The conscience symbolizes a company that has value systems and unprejudiced practices, a belief in legal behavior and in honoring its commitments to all its stakeholders, and an inbuilt courtesy in its interactions. The value system is a part of every Infosys transaction. The company has experienced situations over the years where it has stuck to its principles and made the right choices irrespective of the monetary implications. For example, in 1995 it disengaged itself from a commercial relationship with General Electric, and talked openly about the change with its customers and the public. In 2001, to the amazement of its investors, Infosys estimated a modest growth of 30%, based on its assessment that the whole IT race was losing pace. There have been many such episodes where Infosys has made choices that reflect its strong value system.

What this means to its customers is that Infosys is a trustworthy brand. If an employee makes a commitment to a client, the company will leave no stone unturned in trying to deliver the solution that is promised. Service delivery is a key factor in the IT business where cost overruns, abuse of timelines, below-expectations end delivery, and cancellation of projects midway after spending millions have become common. In that milieu, if you are a company that is trusted, that honors its commitments, and that delivers on time, then you are building a long-term strategic advantage for the Infosys brand.

BRAND PERSONALITY

The evolved Infosys brand has several brand dimensions. For all aspiring youngsters and IT professionals in India, it is an aspirational brand, one they would like to be a part of. For customers, it is a reliable brand that offers predictable results and, therefore, peace of mind. Similarly, for investors it is a transparent company with high moral standards and no gray areas. Infosys discloses both good and bad news to the market immediately, which is an uncommon practice in today's volatile investment environment.

On the emotional brand relationship ladder described at the start of this chapter, Infosys moved past the awareness, involvement, and respect stages very early in its life. In fact, it thrives on trust and loyalty, which are the highest stages. If we were to sum up the Infosys brand personality, the following characteristics would emerge:

- trustworthy;
- transparent;
- aspirational;
- futuristic; and
- innovative.

THE FUTURE

Infosys has been known as the "company of firsts." It was the first Indian company to list on NASDAQ and to follow the GAAP system of accounting. It was also the first Indian company to place a value on its human resources and to publish its brand valuation with its statement of accounts. The list is long.

Today, Infosys is geared up to become bigger and better. The management is implementing what they call the "Wal-Mart-plus" strategy. Though Wal-Mart and Infosys have little in common, one thing they share is scalability. In the same way that Wal-Mart has scalable engines for retailing, Dell for direct selling, and Louis Vuitton Moet Hennessy for fashion, Infosys believes that it has the scalability for software services. The road to a single-minded pursuit of scale is long and uneven. There is a chance that products or services the company offers may undergo commoditization, which would have a direct impact on profit margins. To stand out in the homogeneous global IT market, Infosys has embarked on a multi-pronged differentiation strategy: applying the global delivery model that works well for it in application development to consulting; and bundling business processes, technology, and transactions into one service that delivers business productivity. Infosys realizes that if it is to achieve continued success in the software business, it will need two key skills: the ability to offer a range of services, and to offer them in increasing volumes; and the ability to take a process, offshore it, and then deliver the desired result to the customer. With a brand that is symbolic of trust, transparency, innovation, a futuristic vision, and aspiration, Infosys could pretty much achieve its goal of being the software Wal-Mart.

Brand strengths

- A charismatic founder.
- A pioneer in processes.
- Delivery champions.
- Futuristic outlook.
- Central focus on human capital.
- High ethical standards.

Brand weaknesses

Founder-dependent.

Brand architecture

Corporate branding for its various business units, including consulting, IT service, BPO, and so on.

Sources

- Corporate website: www.infy.com.
- *Business Today,* August 2004.
- *The Hindu Business Line.*

CONCLUSION

We have looked at emotional aspects of branding and the service dimension, but owners of commodity-based brands find it difficult to apply branding techniques. How can you brand a commodity? The next chapter deals with this issue.

CHAPTER 9

BRANDING
A COMMODITY

INTRODUCTION

Brands come in all shapes and forms. In fact, it is true to say that anything can be branded, as Figure 9.1 demonstrates.

We all know about corporate brands such as Microsoft and Nike, and product brands such as Kit Kat and Pampers. Destinations and

Corporations

Products

Events

Locations

Ingredients

Endorsers

Individuals

Figure 9.1 Brands come in all shapes and sizes

events can also be branded, as is evident with Disneyland and the Olympic Games. There are endorsement brands such as ISO, and branded individuals such as Madonna and Beckham. Even ingredients are branded, such as Lycra and Nutrasweet.

However, the more you get into the area of commoditization, the more difficult it becomes to develop a differentiated brand strategy, as everything is similar. And yet some companies have succeeded. In most cases, if the market has existed for a long time, the only way to develop a brand is to reinvent the category—turn it on its head. To gain the perception of difference in a commodity market therefore needs visionary and creative thinking, together with a good grip on what the consumer really wants.

Strong branding gets companies out of the commodity trap, as illustrated in Figure 9.2.

In this chapter we get a glimpse of how two relatively small companies have done this. BreadTalk has achieved a rapid rise to success by reinventing its category and making clever use of brand management. Size doesn't matter, but brand makes the difference.

We also see how another creative company from Thailand has taken the office and home paper category to new heights. The Advance Agro Public Company Ltd. has created fantastic excitement in what has been traditionally quite a dull category through its Double A brand, principally dealing with writing and copier paper. Both have got out of the commodity trap and are now achieving premium prices, differentiation, profits, and all the other benefits of strong branding.

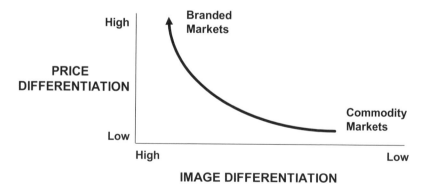

Figure 9.2   Brands versus commodities

Case Study 16—BREADTALK

Branding a Commodity

★ ★ ★ ★ ★

BreadTalk was incorporated in April 2000 and began operations in July of that year with its first outlet at Parco Bugis Junction in Singapore. Since then, it has become an extremely well-known brand in the food and beverage industry in Singapore and subsequently throughout Asia. The reason? It has changed the way people think about and consume a daily staple such as bread. Within only five years, BreadTalk has expanded to 24 outlets in Singapore, with additional outlets in Shanghai, Beijing, and Shenzhen, in China. Through joint ventures and franchising, BreadTalk also has 19 outlets in Malaysia, Indonesia, Taiwan, Kuwait, and the Philippines.

This case study could easily fall under the chapter entitled "First Mover Advantage," as BreadTalk was the first company of its kind to introduce specialty themed breads and buns to the Asian region. Like many great ideas, they appear to be obvious in retrospect. Common sense, if you like; but common sense isn't very common. The idea is quite simple. The French have French bread and eateries such as Delifrance, the Europeans in general have similar bread-based products with local variations, so why can't Asia have its own bread products that are adapted to local tastes?

This touch of clear thinking has revolutionized the whole market for bread products in Asia.

Branding a Commodity by Reinventing the Category

It is true to say that anything can be branded, and essentially BreadTalk has branded a commodity. It has achieved this by totally reinventing the category.

Bread is bread is bread. The bread category has remained much the same for decades with incremental advancements mainly via ingredients. Everywhere there's bread in one form or another—wholemeal, walnut, multi-grain, malt, onion, pizza, and even plain old white! The category's full, isn't it? What's new about that? BreadTalk, that's what. There are many types of retailers who sell bread in Asia with all these features and more, and they all tend to look the same. BreadTalk changed all that almost overnight.

BreadTalk's success is due to its brand positioning and intention to be different from the competition. First, it has transformed a mundane daily activity of buying and consuming bread into an exciting experience. It has been able to do this by giving customers a total experience. From the moment they set foot in the store, to the selecting of products, and using an "open kitchen" process where customers are invited to view how the products are processed—customers are drawn in to experience BreadTalk with the use of all five senses. This leaves a lasting impression in the minds of customers with regards to their experience at BreadTalk, and provides a talking point with friends.

BRAND VALUES AND PRODUCT INNOVATION

One of BreadTalk's greatest strengths and competitive advantages is that everything it does is highly consistent with its brand values, which are seen as *innovative, vibrant, satisfying*, and *simply delightful*. The key value in the branded business appears to be that of innovation, and this is achieved through the company's international R&D team, headed by its official consultant, Noriyasu Watanabe, who provides creative inputs drawn from his culinary expertise.

To further generate ideas and creativity in terms of how to inject life into its bread items, BreadTalk invites other international chefs to showcase creative ways of crafting bread-related products. Its team of culinary experts consistently develops eight to ten new products every three months, making sure that customers always have something to look forward to. This means that the R&D department introduces new, delicious products and flavors that replace 20% of the current range every three months.

Some observers have referred to the brand as a "boutique bakery" or "designer breads," and these descriptions are not far off the mark, because each product is conceptualized and given its own brand plan with a unique name and a prescribed way in which it is presented.

The creative process is aided by an understanding of social trends and by localizing the brand to fit into different cultures. Therefore,

every BreadTalk item on the shelf is a reflection of the currently popular social and lifestyle trends in various Asian countries. In June
2004, BreadTalk opened its first bread boutique in Manila and has
already adapted itself to the local culture, transforming the commonly eaten bread called *tinapay* into an exciting bread item, giving
Filipinos a whole new sense of what it means to eat *tinapay*.

Another aspect of innovation is brand naming. Every BreadTalk
item is interestingly named, making it a great conversation piece for
customers. Names include "Crouching Tiger, Hidden Bacon," inspired
by the Hollywood blockbuster; "Mount Fuji," "Moshi Mushroom,"
"Traffic Light," and the most popular product, "Flosss." BreadTalk
captures the hearts and minds of its customers by making its products appealing to the eye, and titillating to the mind and the palate,
in the process drawing its customers back for more and creating an
emotional tie between them and BreadTalk. It's all about experiencing the lifestyle and the bread shopping experience that BreadTalk
has created.

THE RETAIL EXPERIENCE

This consumer experience starts with the stores. Apart from obeying
the basic law of retailing ("Location is everything"), every store practices an "open" concept. White, sleek display cases highlight each
product, while also communicating openness, freshness, and honesty
to customers. From ceiling to floor, everything is white; and glass is
ubiquitous to create a consistent ambience. Bakers wearing white
outfits and hats craft the delicious bread and pastry products behind
a glass window. This open window concept exudes a spirit of friendliness. It invites customers to peek in and have a look, catches the eye
of passing shoppers, and demonstrates to customers that every product is freshly baked.

The whole baking process, from the preparation of the dough to
the final topping, is done at every individual retail outlet. Through
BreadTalk's open concept, it has proved to be successful at building
emotional ties with current and potential customers since they are
encouraged to interact with and observe the bakers as they create
and make the breads, cakes, and other products. Since buying bread
can also be done on impulse, BreadTalk seizes every opportunity to
arouse the curiosity of passers-by through this open store concept.

Location

BreadTalk's success is not only through managing every consumer touch point with its brand values, but also through choosing strategic and accessible outlets to attract potential customers in areas of high-density traffic flow. For example, in Singapore, most of the company's stores are located at new public transportation systems such as bus terminals, Mass Rapid Transit stations, and Light Rail Transport stations, as well as in well-known malls and department stores, cinemas, and supermarkets. All these outlets provide great visibility for BreadTalk, and also invite potential customers to walk in and be refreshed and revived after a busy day, or simply to enjoy and be tantalized by the appealing tastes and smells of the products as they walk past a BreadTalk store.

THE FRANCHISE EXPERIENCE

The first franchise for BreadTalk was set up in June 2003 in Indonesia. The WC Group of companies has a franchisee in the Philippines called BreadTalk Philippines Inc. and Middle East franchisees are on the way. Malaysia is a recent one and is typical of how the brand works well.

A Typical Franchise Experience

In Malaysia the franchisee, ML BreadWorks Sdn. Bhd., is a joint venture between the international arm of BreadTalk and the well-known greetings card manufacturer and retailer, Memory Lane. ML BreadWorks has plans for ten BreadTalk outlets before 2007, each of which is expected to generate sales of up to RM500,000 per month. In fact, the first outlet—at Malaysia's Mid Valley Megamall—has already achieved its target of RM300,000 per month after only opening in July 2004, and the second outlet is on track to do the same. According to managing director Jo-Ann C. I. Yeoh, the company is set to reach its first-year target of RM4.5 million in May 2005.

The power of the BreadTalk brand name is evident. There have been many competitors following the same path, and in Malaysia BreadTalk was a late entrant into the market. BreadStory, Bread History, Bread Tart, Bread 2 U, Bread to Brag, and Roti Boy are all in the boutique bread segment. But Yeoh says that the brand name of BreadTalk is synonymous with quality bread, and as a result it is taking market share rapidly from the competition. Wherever BreadTalk opens outlets, they take off rapidly Yeoh says, "We sell between 8,000 and 10,000 pieces of buns, cakes, and pastries every day." The decision to local-ize the brand by making it halal to cater for the Muslim market was also a shrewd move.

THE FUTURE? MORE "DOUGH" FOR BREADTALK!

BreadTalk's revenues speak volumes about the public's acceptance and favorable attitude toward it. In only three years, revenues reached S$40 million. BreadTalk has won several awards, including "Singapore's Most Promising Brand" award in 2002. What has been most surpris-ing is its quick move to listing, becoming a public company within a year of its founding.

BreadTalk continues to grow steadily around Asia, managing rapid growth by franchising and licensing agreements, joint ventures, and other direct investments. And curiously, there is hardly a BreadTalk advertisement to be seen. Some limited PR and below-the-line activi-ties and a lot of word of mouth have been behind the brand's growth. BreadTalk is a prime example of the fact that a brand can be built at very low cost, and this should inspire more entrepreneurs and small businesses to start building a brand as early as possible.

BreadTalk proves that you can become a leader through reinventing a category. In 1981, founder and managing director George Quek was in a dead-end job selling dragon candy; today, he's a category leader.

Brand strengths

- A friendly and memorable name.
- Strong brand positioning.
- Strong brand awareness through visibility.
- Consistency in managing all consumer touch points.

Brand weaknesses

- Close "copies" of the concept by more and more competitors requires more innovation.
- Danger of losing brand consistency via franchising.

Brand architecture

Corporate, product brand names adding personality to the corporate brand.

CASE STUDY 17—ADVANCE AGRO PUBLIC COMPANY LIMITED

The Power of Two: Double A

★ ★ ★ ★ ★

You might not be familiar with the name Advance Agro Public Company Ltd., but it owns quite a famous Asian brand name—Double A—a paper product that is approaching legendary status as a branded commodity.

Some things never change. We have been told since the 1980s that we are heading rapidly toward a paperless business world, but this has never happened. In fact, the volume of paper we have to deal with has probably increased. For example, the market demand for commercial and home usage of A4 paper (the most commonly used size) is rising. The increase in size of the market for office and personal computers seems to be a major factor here, contrary to what one would expect.

Double A is likely to be a well-known brand name to anyone who works in an office, at home, at school, or anywhere that involves writing, drawing, printing, faxing, copying, scanning, or any other paper use.

Just as in the previous case (BreadTalk), where bread is bread is bread, we can similarly say that paper is paper is paper; there is seemingly no difference between a huge number of brands on the market. Gram weight, size, colors—all options are offered by most manufacturers and retailers. But a brand is a brand is a brand!

Advance Agro Public Company Ltd. recognized that the only way out of the commodity trap and the path to greater profits is to create a brand; that is, it is only branding that provides differentiation.

Incorporated on March 9, 1989, this Thai company's main objective was to produce printing and writing paper. It became a public company on February 18, 1994. The company's main products are uncoated and coated paper, but it also owns a power plant that produces electricity.

COMMITMENT TO THE ENVIRONMENT AND SOCIAL RESPONSIBILITY

Advanced Agro has an Environment Conservation Standard, which includes an elementary chlorine-free system and other processes that conserve water and minimize pollution. In fact, no treated water is discharged into public water sources. Its R&D unit not only has the remit to develop new and improved products, but also to ensure that all aspects of technologies, processes, production, and products are environmentally friendly. Advanced Agro says that companies in advancing industries will be measured in the future by their performance in environmental conservation and the intelligent consumption of limited resources.

Advanced Agro has agreements with farmers for planting fast-growing commercial trees, and purchasing logs. Over 10,000 farmers and their families are benefiting from this program.

THE "DOUBLE A" BRAND DEVELOPMENT

Advanced Agro's famous brand is Double A, and the company has cleverly positioned this product range brand as a very high quality, reliable paper produced in what it says is its "Mill of Tomorrow." (You can take a virtual tour of the factory via the website.)

The company has spent years on researching breeding techniques to produce seedlings with uniform characteristics in order to arrive at the best pulpwood. This is primarily from eucalyptus logs, which are recognized globally as the best raw material from which to produce high-quality printing and writing products.

The principal market segment for Double A is office premium paper users, and the most popular product is white 80-gram A4-size paper. The products have been carefully developed based on some interesting consumer insights that were discovered through research.

Consumer Insights Led to Product Development

In a market research program that involved interviews with 20,000 consumers, Advanced Agro found certain concerns about paper products held by purchasers and end-users. The main concern was that paper often gets jammed in copying machines. A second issue was the consumer's desire to be able to get high-quality prints on both sides of the paper. A third key concern was that consumers preferred a whiter color paper, as they believe this generates better images.

As a result, the company's R&D unit produced the 80-gram, A4-size, Double A-branded paper. Unusually, the brand doesn't have other variants in gram weight, although it does come in various colors. The brand is very focused in this category, but it has been extended into related categories such as notebooks (see below).

The Double A brand emphasizes various features, attributes, and benefits in its communications, namely:

- extra whiteness and brightness, which leads to:
- sharpness of image in copied documents;
- high opacity, allowing both sides of the paper to be used without ink or toner seeping on to the opposite side, which leads to:
- higher-quality prints on both sides, full usage of paper, and reduced wastage;
- superior smoothness, which leads to:
- reduced paper jams.

It is this last attribute that has become a driving force for some creative brand image development.

The "No Jam" Brand Promise

One of the main driving forces for the development of the Double A brand promise is the fact that, because of the quality and design features mentioned above, the paper has much less chance of jamming in copying machinery. This key message is constantly reinforced through advertisements and other brand communications initiatives. For example, on the Double A website, the words "NO JAM" are right up front on the home page in capital letters. But quite often, the communications are transmitted in a more creative way.

Communicating the brand promise

Double A brand communications are now becoming quite famous, using creativity and fun in an integrated manner. When your products are basically commodities, you have to be pretty creative in attracting customers, and the Double A brand team has certainly developed a core competency here in conjunction with its agencies. Some notable examples are:

- *No Jam Challenges:* Challenges for students and other target audiences have been created, where participants face a series of challenges such as archery, moving through a maze while wearing a blindfold, and shooting paper planes through hoops. Teams compete and win gifts that include cash, scanners, printers, and so on.
- *Twin Angels:* Twin girls, nicknamed Twin Angels as a twist on the brand name, have been used in promotional activities. If consumers spotted them, they received Double A prizes.
- *Creative placement of advertisements:* Double A has used the roofs of Light Rapid Transit trains (above-ground urban trains) for advertising, so that office workers who gaze out of their windows (oh, yes, you do!) can easily see the brand name.

The above are all examples of relevant good interactive marketing activities. On the Internet, greater interaction is now on offer through the Double A customer relationship management rewards program.

CUSTOMER RELATIONSHIP MANAGEMENT (CRM)

It's hard to imagine a loyalty or CRM program for paper products, but Double A has one. There is a difference between a loyalty points-based system and a true CRM system. Double A has a loyalty program that has the makings of a great CRM program. It is worthwhile outlining the difference between the two types of program.

Loyalty Schemes and CRM Programs

Just about every type of retail outlet in every city in every developed and developing country now has a loyalty program (or points scheme, as it is sometimes known). It's pretty hard nowadays to live life without being part of one. You buy groceries, you earn points; you fill up with petrol, you earn points; you fly, you earn points; and so it goes on—hotel stays, car hire, even surfing the Internet now earns you i-points or mouse miles. If it's not points or miles, it's in the Starbucks or TGI Fridays mould of collect a certain number of stamps and the next coffee or meal is free.

Points programs such as these are designed to keep you coming back for more, and it is true that they might influence brand loyalty to some extent, although the degree of influence is debatable.

Do these programs constitute CRM? My view is that they don't, but they can certainly provide a solid foundation upon which to build a CRM program. Normally, these programs have a mechanism— for example, a brief sign-on questionnaire—to collect a little data about the customer and their purchasing habits, but all too often they fail to take the next step that makes all the difference and turns a loyalty program into a CRM program. That step is achieved by capturing that data, turning it into knowledge, and using this knowledge in some way to tailor the product or service you offer to that customer to make it more relevant, more suited, and more specific to their needs. Without this customization, a loyalty program is just a process of "earning and burning" points, and although consumer habits may be affected momentarily, competitors can merely offer more points with the result that the "loyal" customers you thought you had disappear.

Airlines claim that frequent flyer programs are CRM programs because the more points people earn, the more benefits they get—for instance, use of the express check-in or the executive lounge with its free food and drink, extra baggage allowance, and a good chance of an upgrade (though I have never managed to get one).

Once customers have flown a qualifying mileage, they are invited into the upper tiers of a frequent flyer program. Here they will receive a range of program-specific benefits, designed to make life easier and more comfortable for them. At this level, airline staff are sometimes trained to be able to relate to each customer by their preferred name and to learn to recognize regular travelers by sight. The best programs are multi-tiered, with a so-called Chairman's Club at the very top. Here only the most valuable customers get invitations to exclusive events, have direct lines of communication to the chairman's office, and never have to stand in line for anything. If it worked like this it would be good, but the "earn and burn" mentality (see below) destroys the effect it could have and damages brand image.

The concept of lifetime value

Traditionally, most retail companies have only been interested in transactional data—how many units of product have been sold today. Banks are typical examples. Only now are they realizing that by understanding more about the actual person who is buying the product can they make more profit. By getting closer to customers and offering them more channels by which they can do business, a company can help to manage customers over time. The overall aim is to develop such a strong affinity with customers that they not only recommend you to others, but stay with your brand for life. Lifetime value of customers is a reflection of how often a customer buys from you, how much they spend when they do buy, when they last bought from you, and what they are likely to buy from you during their lifetime.

The Double A Rewards Program

Double A has a points-based scheme that is Internet-accessible, meaning that customers can enroll, check their points status, and redeem their points online. The breath of fresh air for customers is that they don't have their points taken away if they don't redeem them in a certain timeframe, as is the case with airlines.

The airline model seems to me to be grossly unfair. By giving customers points, they belong to the customer. Taking them away because of non-redemption is not, in my opinion, ethically correct. And what is more, from personal experience the restrictions imposed by the airline technologies and the rules imposed by management make it difficult to redeem points within the timeframes required. So, essentially, airline "loyalty" programs are de facto discouraging loyalty, or if you like, they encourage disloyalty.

Double A has free enrollment, the usual passwords and user ID's, plus welcome letters. Faxed delivery orders trigger points additions, and redemption doesn't mean having to purchase more paper! Customers can receive travel, food and beverage, or office and home entertainment products through co-branding relationships with partners such as Philips. As well as individuals, corporate customers were given the opportunity to join their own CRM program from July 1, 2004.

But Double A doesn't forget who lines up a lot of its business for the brand and so has a rewards program for its top dealers. For example, the top ten dealers in foreign countries such as Malaysia can, on achieving high-value status, enjoy holidays and luxury trips to Thailand. Charnvit Jarusombathi, executive vice president of marketing, says: "Double A wants to show our appreciation and support to the trade people. . . .They have supported us by making us the office paper of choice and we would like to thank them for their contribution."

The opportunity now for Double A is to turn its points-based CRM scheme into a more loyalty-based scheme, with customer tiering, and so on. It is beginning to do this by customizing newsletters and sales promotion activities to the needs of individual customers. The whole aim of the program is to "create confidence and a relationship between the company and the customer *in the long term*."

GROWTH AND DISTRIBUTION

In moving to markets beyond Thailand, Double A has appointed a number of master dealers and distributors that sell on to dealers who then sell to retailers. In terms of business, the 80:20 rule seems to apply, where over 80% of the business for Double A is derived from what is called the General Trade (consisting of stationery shops and corporate buyers), and the residual amount from the Modern Trade (super- and hyper-markets, chain stores, and department stores).

An innovative and recent development is the introduction of a network of franchised Double A copy centers. This is a very smart move, as to become an authorized franchised outlet certain conditions have to be met, such as a good strategic location, a minimum number of copiers, and volume targets. Double A has created a win-win situation for Advanced Agro and its authorized franchisees, as in return for the franchisee commitments, the company subsidizes outlet renovation, signage, and interior design. This also serves to maintain Double A's brand integrity and consistency, as the blue-and-white brand properties are carefully and systematically controlled.

The standard products and services promised by all Double A copy centers include the following:

- photocopying in any volume using Double A A4- and A3-size paper;
- walk-in and pre-ordered photocopying services;

◆ copying on to white or colored paper;
◆ binding and collection of documents; and
◆ fast, professional service.

This innovative idea has fast-forwarded business growth. For example, in Malaysia alone there are now more than 300 Double A copy centers. The other main area of growth has come from brand extensions.

BRAND EXTENSIONS

One of the characteristics of good brand management is to extend the brand as far as possible in the category, or into other categories, while remaining true to the brand proposition and maintaining relevance to consumers. Double A seems to be doing this well. Treating the category as not just copying paper but stationery, it has diversified into other product areas such as glued binding notepads, mouse and spiral notepads, staple binding notepads, writing books, box files, planning notes, laser paper, and even envelopes.

The company says it is perking up the stationery scene with "some quirky and creative items such as its unique CD notebook with a plastic cover case that stores a CD together with quality notepaper and mouse notepad, which is a handy 2-in-1 invention. Both items come in a variety of designs and make cute gifts." Double A is extending its brand, via creatively designed and colored products, into the gift category. Not bad for a commodity brand!

Even within the more restrictive category of A4 paper products, Double A has brought in more exciting packaging and paper color features for customers, including cartoon-like designs for younger buyers such as students (the corporate decision-makers of the future), and more formal designs for corporate buyers. The original corporate blue-and-white packaging has enormous recognition now among all segments.

In total, Double A has over 40 products.

SUMMARY

It's not easy to brand commodities, but Double A is certainly making the pace in Asia. It has remembered the fundamentals of branding—quality and differentiation—and has brought those to market in its products and communications in an innovative way.

Brand strengths

- State-of-the-art technology backed by commitment to R&D.
- Social and environmental conscience.
- Creative, fun, and quirky brand personality.
- Low-cost, high-value integrated communications.
- Well thought-through and relevant brand extensions.

Brand weaknesses

- Does the company have the cash to invest in international branding?
- Brand growth is being driven to a large extent via franchising, with copy centers that may not deliver service standards that will make Double A a truly great brand.

Brand architecture

Corporate brand association via lettering (AA); product branding is under Double A, enhanced by descriptors and some product names (example: Double A Laser Print Paper and Color Copier Paper).

Source

Advanced Agro Public Company Ltd.

Conclusion

Companies concerned with manufacturing and marketing commodities have specific branding issues to deal with but can be successful, as we have seen. The next chapter deals with companies who are giants, and looks at how conglomerates can brand themselves.

CHAPTER 10

CARING CONGLOMERATES: GIANT BRANDS WITH KIND HEARTS

INTRODUCTION

Some companies are involved in multiple industries with multiple brands. They are so huge that branding isn't the real focus for them—they feel somewhat invincible. Huge conglomerates don't normally take branding to heart. They rely on sheer size and financial muscle to grow and succeed. Their growth is not so much organic, but more by merger and acquisition (M&A). In some cases this means brand warfare, as companies merge for economic reasons and forget about the consumer. This can lead to heated debate and underperformance, as is the case with HP-Compaq.

With multiple brands, disorganized architecture, and ill-thought-out brand strategies, such moves can lead to disaster. At the very least, conglomerate growth, usually by M&A, leads to an underperformance on the stock market. Conglomerates that cannot demonstrate that they have a clear brand strategy are usually discounted by analysts and investors by up to 10%, even though they might be turning in suitable numbers year-on-year.

The more astute captains of conglomerate industry pay attention to branding for this reason alone. They realize that brand building is still important in building their businesses. In particular, the more astute know that branding brings higher market capitalization and returns to shareholders.

In this chapter, we have two cases of conglomerates that actually map out strategies that are designed to demonstrate a caring attitude to their various target audiences, which isn't easy for huge companies. Success can sometimes lead to complacency and a lack of respect for consumers, but here are two brands that have people at the very heart of their brand.

The first case is Siam Cement and the second is Tata, which are the largest conglomerates in Thailand and India, respectively. These huge corporations have not forgotten their roots and are determined to give back to their countries and customers the generosity that they themselves have received.

Case Study 18—SIAM CEMENT ("JAIDEE")

Branding Conglomerates

★ ★ ★ ★ ★

Background

Siam Cement Public Company Limited was founded under the Royal Decree of His Majesty King Rama VI in Thailand in 1913. King Rama VI created the company to end Thailand's dependence on imported cement. Siam Cement focused on cement and related products for more than 60 years before branching out into pulp and paper in 1976. In the 1980s its reach broadened to include petrochemicals, ceramics, iron and steel, machinery, tires, and car parts. Much of the expansion was joint ventures with many of the world's leading companies, including Dow Chemical, Michelin, Toyota, and Hitachi.

Siam Cement became a public company in 1994 and is listed on the Thailand Stock Exchange. The main competitors for Siam Cement are Halliburton, Italcementi, and Ube. Currently, Siam Cement's market penetration is worldwide—North America, Latin America, Europe, Middle East and Africa, Asia-Pacific, and CIS (Commonwealth of Independent States)—and it dominates the market share in Thailand as the country's largest and most advanced industrial conglomerate company. Siam's target segments are mostly contractors, builders and home-owners, and its business types are both B2B and B2C. However, despite its present success, it has not been an easy ride.

In 1997 the Thai baht collapsed, which brought Thailand's economy to its knees. Major conglomerates suffered great losses and were hugely indebted to foreign and local banks. Siam Cement was no different from the other major conglomerates, losing 52 billion baht in that one year. Buried under US$4.5 billion in foreign debt, the company posted a US$1.3 billion loss for that fiscal year. However, instead of hiding from creditors and blaming foreigners for its woes, Siam Cement met with bankers to reveal the full extent of the company's indebtedness and a decision was made to overhaul the group. This effort paid off, as Siam Cement was the largest company on the Thai bourse in year 2000, earning an after-tax profit of US$960,000 compared with a net loss of US$110 million in 1999. Countries all over Asia were facing an economic crisis and the future was grim for Siam Cement, but the company needed to keep short-term credit lines open and promised banks to repay all interest in a timely manner.

The creditors bought the idea, but Siam Cement still needed a recovery plan. In late 1998, the company enlisted McKinsey and Co., Deutsche Bank (DTBKY), and JP Morgan Chase (JPM) to draw up an ambitious restructuring strategy. The strategy was to streamline Siam Cement's core petrochemical, cement, and pulp and paper operations, minimize debt, and sell its non-core businesses. Siam Cement issued debentures that paid more than the prevailing deposit rate in Thailand, which was a boon to investors but still one percentage lower than what banks were then charging for commercial loans. The bonds were structured so that the group didn't need to pay anything back until they matured seven years later. With this strategy, Siam Cement was able to buy time to sort out the group's finances and it raised more than US$2 billion.

More Focus

At the same time, Siam Cement was selling all its non-core businesses. In just 12 months, it sold a gypsum plant in China to Knauf of Germany, and a 50% share in a glass factory to joint venture partner Guardian Industries Corp. of the United States. It also reduced stakes in more than a dozen joint ventures, including those with Toyota and Mitsubishi, by selling the shares back to its partners.

More than US$1 billion worth of assets were disposed of. Siam Cement also offered voluntary retirement schemes to its employees, thereby slimming the group's payroll from 35,000 to 25,000.

These measures reduced the group's foreign hard-currency debt from US$4.5 billion to zero. Its short-term loans accounted for just 10% of its US$2.2 billion in local obligations. With these efforts, Siam Cement had safely tided itself over the Asian economic crisis and slowly regained financial stability for future growth.

Post-recession

By 2003, Siam Cement had profited hugely from Thailand's new residential property boom and China's growing appetite for raw materials, reporting a 4.9 billion baht (US$123 million) net profit in Q3 representing a 34% increase on 2002 profit levels. By comparison with 1997, when Siam Cement had been heavily indebted to banks, it was now able to repay its debts and was ready to bounce back. The tiger began to awake.

STRUCTURE

Siam Cement Public Company Limited now comprises two divisions: a strategic business unit (cement, building products, distribution, paper and packaging, and petrochemicals) and other businesses (property and holdings). Siam Cement also owns several holding companies in the Philippines, Indonesia, and Vietnam. Throughout the years, the company has invested strategically in Thailand, but in recent years it has expanded to investing in Asia. Pantaranji Company, Thailand's largest e-procurement website, is such an investment. This company was jointly founded by Siam Cement, TelecomAsia, CP Group, Bangkok Bank, Siam Commercial Bank, and UCOM Group. Siam Hitachi Construction is another joint business venture between Siam Cement and Hitachi.

Siam Cement Public Company Limited: President

Chumpol Na Lamlieng was formerly a World Bank loan officer with an MBA from Harvard Business School. He joined Siam Cement in the early 1970s and was named president in 1993. He has grown up with the company and is largely responsible for the attitude and success of the Siam business and brand. Chumpol is also a member of the New Pacific Basin Economic Council, and in 2003 he was voted "Businessman of the Year." He is also the current chairman of Singtel (Singapore Telecommunications), a giant brand in its own right.

SIAM CEMENT MANAGEMENT PHILOSOPHY AND VISION

Siam Cement is determined to become a market leader in the ASEAN region by delivering products and services of the highest quality to customers. Achieving this ambition is tough and begins with groundwork, especially setting out management's philosophy for its employees. Siam Cement has ensured that its essence as an ethical company is brought alive by everyone in Siam Cement. "Adherence to fairness," "Believing in the value of the individual," "Concern for social responsibility," and "Dedication to excellence" are at the core of Siam Cement's management philosophy. These are powerful words, and charged with emotion. The ethics encompassed in these slogans are often lacking in today's societies.

A CONGLOMERATE THAT CARES

Few really huge companies are said to be caring companies, although to enhance their brand image they often try to generate such a perception. But to be a caring company there has to be a demonstration of this in many ways, and a sustained effort. With cause-related branding, a company has to be genuine and commit itself to this for the long term, as is the case, for example, with the Body Shop. Siam Cement generously supports the environment and contributes to society in the education, sports, community, and public welfare sectors. It has also set up the Siam Cement Foundation.

An Environmental Brand

Being environmentally friendly has had a positive impact on the brand, especially at times like these when the issue of global warming has reached crisis point. Providing full support to Thailand's efforts to conserve the environment isn't an easy task, however. Instead of just donating funds to environmental causes such as the Royal Reforestation Project and the Volunteer Wildfire Prevention Program, Siam Cement has taken great steps to ensure the health and safety of its employees, spending over 2 billion baht annually. The company has been awarded numerous environmental awards and titles, including the much coveted environmental accolade ISO 14001 certificate of environment management, the Prime Minister's Award for Environment Management awarded by the Ministry of Industry, and EIA Awards by the Office of Environmental Policy and Planning from the Ministry of Science, Technology and Environment.

Brand depth

Not only is the parent company recognized for its environmental efforts, but its subsidiaries also follow the guidelines approved for environmental conservation and safety. Siam Cement is the first conglomerate to have its subsidiaries achieve certificates of the TIS 18000 for their dedication to the safety and occupational health of employees and communities. Siam Cement also conducts the Siam Cement Group Conserves Nature camp annually for Thai youth. The company has thus contributed toward the environment beyond the monetary level, and makes sure that the heart and the soul of its daily operations follow the same path.

An Educational Brand

Siam Cement is utilizing human emotions to portray itself as compassionate, patriotic, and charitable by providing scholarships annually to Thai students at the Sirindhorn International Institute of Technology, Thammasat University for the Engineering Faculty. The company donated a substantial amount (US$250,000–US$499,999) to the Paul H. Nitze School of Advanced International Studies (SAIS) in 2004. SAIS is a division of the renowned John Hopkins University in Washington, DC. Siam Cement's president is also a member of the Sasin Advisory Council for the Graduate Institute of Business Administration of Chulalongkorn University.

Siam Cement is actively participating in educational projects in the hope of enhancing Thai people's knowledge and skills. Some of the ongoing projects are SCG's Apprenticeship Program for Talented and Virtuous Students, IT Genius, the Outstanding Science Teachers

Award, the Outstanding Scientist Award, the Next Generation Scientist Award, Siam Cement Young Scientist Club Contest, Siam Cement Young Scientist's Workshop, and scholarships.

A Youth and Sports Brand

Besides playing an important role in environmental causes and educational programs, Siam Cement also encourages participation in sports among Thai young people. Its objective is to steer youths away from drugs and encourage them to spend their leisure time constructively by learning the value of good sportsmanship. Siam Cement helped to prep Thailand's national badminton players by organizing the Siam Cement World Grand Prix Thailand Open Badminton Championship in 2003. Each year, it organizes the Siam Cement Youth Badminton Project and the Siam Cement Youth Volleyball Project, jointly with the Badminton Association of Thailand and the Amateur Volleyball Association of Thailand.

The community in which Thai youths live is a major factor in exposing them to negative influences. Siam Cement has constantly provided support to activities beneficial to the community by contributing to programs for rural development, community farming, community relations, farmer development, agriculture, and the construction of school buildings and mobile medical units with volunteer doctors. Siam Cement also organizes the Siam Cement Group Conserves Thai Project and the Siam Cement Group Conserves Thai Project for Teachers each year. The company encourages its staff to help Thai society by organizing the Siam Cement Volunteer Camp. It promotes the Siam Cement Project to Relieve Water Shortage and the SCG and Channel 7 Philanthropy Program, where it provides financial support to philanthropic persons or organizations, including running disaster relief projects to assist the victims of flooding, storms, and fires.

BRAND IDENTITY, VALUES, AND IMAGE

A brand's identity is what it wants to be seen as, whereas a brand's image is how it is actually perceived by various target audiences. On the rational side of the conglomerate's identity, it would appear to want to be seen as a stable and reliable company—innovative and creative, but professional, and possessing openness and integrity.

On the emotional side, Siam Cement is projecting itself as environmentally friendly, compassionate, and patriotic, with a passion for knowledge and a vision for the future.

As far as image goes, the company appears to have no gaps between how it wants to be seen and how it is seen, as its brand image is reliable, providing products and services of good quality, a well-established company with a strong connection to the community, and a company that actually contributes back to Thailand's society, its people, culture, heritage, and environment.

Siam Cement is a true philanthropist. There really are no limitations when it comes to its social contributions or environmental conservation efforts. With so many contributions to society, it is hard for consumers not to perceive Siam Cement as having many positive brand attributes, such as being:

- reliable;
- charitable;
- compassionate;
- innovative;
- considerate;
- caring; and
- responsible.

Being a brand associated with positive good feelings, Siam Cement has already "cemented" its position as the largest and most advanced industrial conglomerate in Thailand. As consumers easily relate to the brand and see its positive contributions to Thai society, they are not hesitant in buying its products and services, especially as Siam Cement has maintained an affordable positioning in the pricing of its products and services—another sign of its caring disposition.

BRAND COMMUNICATIONS

Siam Cement uses only traditional mediums such as print advertising, TVC, and outdoor advertising in its advertising and has yet to venture beyond that. This is a sensible strategy, as outdoor advertising is more logical for reaching rural areas, whereas TVC and print advertising are more appropriate for cities and urban areas. The self-imposed limitations here could hinder its image as an innovator, even though the parent holding company has a somewhat sophisticated website.

Overall, though, Siam Cement's branding effort has deliberately not focused on large amounts of traditional brand communications; rather, it has got its message across through its deeds, not words.

Conclusion: A Thai Brand for the Thai People

Siam Cement has been successful in positioning itself as a company with a conscience, doing things for the benefit of the country, society, people, culture, heritage, and environment. These activities have strengthened people's beliefs that Siam Cement isn't just a conglomerate, but a conglomerate that cares. Human emotions are a powerful tool, especially in choosing a product for consumption or usage. Siam Cement has used this route to build its brand by giving multiple customer groups a righteous feeling when using its products and services. In Thai, the name Siam Cement is "Jaidee," which means "a kind heart."

Brand strengths

- Sustained commitment to its causes and beliefs.
- A focus on the brand at all levels of the group.
- Less talk (communications) and more action.
- Emotional brand strategy.
- Connections with the Thai Royal family via investment institutions.

Brand weakness

The national, patriotic strategy will not enable Siam Cement to enter international markets easily under its own brand name.

Brand architecture

Corporate, with endorsed branding for products (cement examples: Tiger, Elephant, etc. Product brands with Siam endorsement via logo).

Sources

- Siam Cement Public Company Limited website, www.siamcement.com.
- "Join the Club," *Far Eastern Economic Review,* June 3, 1999.

- "Big is Better and Back in Vogue," *Far Eastern Economic Review,* December 25, 2003 – January 1, 2004.
- "World Business Briefing (Asia: Singapore: Telecom Executive Named)," *The New York Times,* August 7, 2003.
- "The Stars of Asia—Managers," *BusinessWeek Asian Edition,* June 2, 2001.
- Sasin Institute of Business Administration of Chulalongkorn University, www.sasin.edu/about/advisory/.
- Paul H. Nitze School of Advanced International Studies (SAIS) division of Johns Hopkins University, www.socialfunds.com/page.cgi/companies.html.
- Sirindhorn International Institute of Technology, Thammasat University, www.siit.tu.ac.th/news/pdf/v6n3.pdf.

CASE STUDY 19—TATA

"Improving the Quality of Life"

Like the heavyweight corporate companies of the world, India's Tata Group has an incredible success saga that is rooted in the 19th century. By its own account, Tata Group's 91 operating companies, with a revenue of US$14.25 billion, now represent over 2.6% of India's GDP and 5% of the country's exports. Having served India for 126 years, Tata is now at the center-stage of companies moving away from India-centrism and making a global footprint.

People in India would say that Tata has become a part of their lives, as you are bound to experience a Tata product at least once during the day. This isn't surprising when you look at the expanse of the conglomerate in terms of the products and services it offers. To outline the Tata brand's contact points, it touches 500 million consumers through Tata Tea, 400 million through Tata Salt, seven million through Titan watches, six million through its telecom business, one million through vehicles, and 200,000 through Tata Nova—the group's Internet business. The caring aspect of Tata's branding is that it aims to improve the quality of people's lives in India.

The history of the Tata Group is deeply entrenched in the industrial revolution of India. Jamshetji Tata, the founder, was a nationalist who believed that India must produce its own steel, electricity, and technical education system to attain industrialization. In 1912, when the influence of the British Raj was beginning to weaken, India's first steel was made in a town renamed Jamshedpur after the founder. Today, Tata Steel is one of the lowest-cost steel makers in the world. Be it Tata Steel, started by Jamshetji Tata, or Tata Airlines (now known as Air India), initiated and developed by his successor, J. R. D. Tata, the Tata Group has always been a key contributor to the development of the Indian economy. The efforts of the visionary leaders of the Tata family, who believed that the private sector has a responsibility "beyond business," have resulted in the development of a corporate brand that symbolizes assurance, reliability, trust, a sense of nationalism, and value for money.

THE BRAND STORY

In brand territory, it takes clear-sighted vision to reign supreme. The Tata Group has a strong presence in seven business sectors, including engineering, materials, energy, chemicals, consumer products, communications and IT, and services. Through the second half of the 19th century, the conglomerate had been expanding each year and diversifying from commodity products such as steel, cloth, and hydroelectric power to motor vehicles, wristwatches, and retailing. Despite the continuous growth, the Tata Group's achievement on the brand front is by no means the result of a Pavlovian response.

It was only when Ratan Tata took over the reins from J. R. D. Tata as chairman of the Tata Group in the early 1990s that the conglomerate embarked on a brand-building expedition. The goal was to unify a diverse and dispersed enterprise and enable it to hold ground while the post-liberalization tempest altered the face of the Indian economy. The cornerstone of the brand-building journey was the framing of the Brand Equity and Business Promotion (BEBP) agreement in the mid-1990s. The BEBP was a comprehensive contract that defined the conditions a company would have to comply with to be accredited with the Tata name. Companies had the choice of not signing the agreement, but then they would have to refrain from associating with the prestigious Tata seal. The results of the exercise were not visible immediately, but the hazy shadows were getting clearer with bright sunshine at the end of the tunnel.

The BEBP agreement wasn't just a blueprint left to collect dust. In conjunction with the agreement, the Tata Group rejuvenated its corporate identity with a fresh and modern logo, which now adorns every Tata Group company and is widely recognized by most consumers. It has become a robust symbol that, along with media support, helps in expressing the values of the Tata corporate brand. Corporate advertising, public relations, events, and the Internet are other avenues that the group has used to strengthen its brand equity and highlight its consolidation efforts. Speaking to one of India's leading dailies, *The Economic Times,* in an interview, Ratan Tata stressed the importance of constructing a unified Tata brand: "The intention has been to create a single strong entity that will benefit all Tata companies. . . . If you are to fight a Mitsubishi or an X or Y in the free India of tomorrow, you better have one rather than 40 brands. You better have the ability to promote that brand in a meaningful manner." Adopting this ideology, the mid-1990s saw the corporate portfolio changing from a 40–50% commodity orientation to an equal percentage of brand orientation, and the various services and products starting to reap the benefits of the overarching corporate brand.

Today, the Tata Group is riding the global wave and investing heavily in telecom and IT. Automobiles and IT have been identified as the value growth engines, while salt and tea are the volume-driven categories that continuously build a loyal, mass customer base. Tata Salt was the first branded salt in the country and currently commands 37% of the Indian domestic market. Tata Tea bought Britain's Tetley Tea in 2000 and its various brands have a market share of about 18% in India, which includes the big export market. Tata Motors recorded significant increases in sales volumes across all product groups with a healthy 59% market share of the commercial vehicle domestic market in 2004. The relatively new passenger vehicle business has recorded a 28% jump in market share, which stood at 17.5% in 2004.

The retailing company, the Tata Group-owned Trent Ltd., plans to increase investments in lifestyle store Westside by taking the chain to more than 20 stores operational in seven cities.

Tata's presence is not only felt in the Indian sub-continent, but also across the globe. Recently, Tata Steel bought Singapore's Natsteel in order to explore the markets in China, Australia, and Southeast Asia. Tata Motors acquired the South Korean truck maker, Daewoo, to expand its reach in China, Korea, and Thailand. Tata has had joint venture operations with companies such as Daimler-Chrysler, Hitachi, British Petroleum, and American International Group (AIG), to name a few. Tata's motors are also exported to over 70 countries in Europe, Africa, South America, the Middle East, Asia, and Australia. In addition, the company has assembly operations in Malaysia, Bangladesh, Kenya, South Africa, and Egypt. Similarly, the IT services are spanned across Asia and the United States.

THE BRAND PROMISE

Tata's corporate advertising campaigns have always effectively reflected the brand promise captured in its tagline, "Improving the quality of life." The latest advertising campaign highlights the group's commitment to improving the quality of life through technological innovation. Earlier campaigns have focused on Tata's commitment to continuously pursue excellence in providing world-class services and products to its customers and, in turn, ensuring a better life for its employees and the community. Tata has built its brand blocks slowly but steadily by capitalizing on its real strengths.

Trucks, steel, chemicals, cars, tea, salt, watches, mobile services, infotech, and more—it's a complex portfolio by any standards, and it's a constant challenge to maintain the formidable brand equity. Despite the diverse portfolio, almost 90% of the Tata companies and products share the corporate brand name. This fact highlights the value of the corporate brand and the trust that it has built among consumers over the years. Only a few companies, such as the Indian Hotels Company (Taj Group), IDEA—the mobile services company, Trent (Westside)—the retail company, and the watch company, Titan, don't carry the corporate brand name upfront. This may have been a conscious decision made by management to avoid a rub-off of the group's industrial heritage on its consumer products. However, the

Tata Group has ridden the brand unification cart for some time now, and one might soon expect a stronger endorsement of the corporate brand on its consumer products.

For example, Tata Chemicals, the company that markets Tata Salt, has been leveraging the corporate brand with the commodity product. Tata Salt ranks among the top five fast-moving consumer goods (FMCG) brands in most consumer surveys in India, besides, of course, being the market leader among branded salts. Tata Chemicals recently repositioned Tata's salt as "*Desh ka namak*" (Salt of the country). The company sees this as a successful transformation of a rational product category into one that is based on an emotional bond in the mind of the consumer. There is also talk that Tata Salt could go global, beginning with countries where there is a large Indian population. Tata Salt's brand values are synonymous with those of the parent corporate brand, and the brand communication is a good example of killing two birds with one stone.

While its old-world properties of trust and nationalism remain unchanged, the Tata brand has also added new dimensions. Today, it is increasingly being seen as innovative, forward-thinking, well-managed, aggressive, and high-tech. There have been recent efforts to associate with young icons—the only Indian motor sports prodigy, Narain Karthikeyan, is one such example. The ad campaign for Idea, the group's cellular services venture, themed around "liberation through an idea," is fairly contemporary. In the case of packaged tea, Tata Tea has built a long-term association with the arts and cinema.

THE BRAND PERSONALITY

Tata's brand personality has evolved into a robust one over the last century and has seen the addition of certain positive traits. The key personality traits that are clearly reflected today include:

- trustworthy;
- reliable;
- nationalistic;
- innovative;

- respected; and
- responsible.

These are the attributes that the Tata brand is known for, whether it is through a wristwatch, a piece of software, a group of hotels, or a car. The common fabric that holds diverse products together has been woven by Tata management through its efforts to build a unified Tata brand that benefits all Tata companies. In the liberalized Asian markets where almost all big global brands are making ground, Tata has found the perfect recipe to stand strong in the tumultuous brandscape that promises a world of opportunities.

Brand strengths

- Heritage.
- Visionary leadership.
- Brand guardianship.
- High brand investment.
- Regular brand health checks and revitalization.

Brand weaknesses

- A decade back, one might have described Tata as a middle-aged brand with a fuddy-duddy image. However, the group realized the power of a corporate brand and made intelligent investments at the right time. It is difficult these days to detect any weakness in the Tata corporate brand.
- The Tata family has had a history of nominating someone from within the family to be the "captain of the ship." This could be a sticking point, since Ratan Tata (*Forbes* magazine's "Asia's Businessman of the Year" in 2004) is due to retire in 2007–8. However, one can assume that leadership will be taken care of, as Tata top management has continuously produced the best professionals in the industry.

Brand architecture

Corporate branding, with shared sub-branding for most sub-brands. Product branding for hotels, watches, and retail outlets (examples: Shared branding—Tata Tea, Tata Motors; product branding—Titan).

Sources

- ◆ Tata corporate website, www.tata.com.
- ◆ *Forbes,* January 2005.
- ◆ *The Hindu Business Line.*

CONCLUSION

Businesses can grow to become conglomerates organically or by merger and acquisition. The next chapter looks at how branding can still be relevant to the latter type of growth.

CHAPTER 11

STRATEGIC ALLIANCES, PARTNERSHIPS, MERGERS, AND ACQUISITIONS

Organic growth is a tough route to take to achieve regional, international, or global brand status, and many companies have to resort to other methods, such as alliances and acquisitions. Indeed, as any company that has a global brand, such as IBM or Hewlett-Packard (HP), will attest, strategic alliances, partnerships, and other forms of consolidation are a way of life and a lifeline of support in an ever-changing business environment. They provide a fast-track approach to gaining global branded status.

The first case study could easily have been placed in Chapter 4 on naming and identity, but it has become a global player almost overnight with the substantial acquisition of one "division" of a global brand. That company is Lenovo, and the global brand it acquired is a part of IBM.

I had some hesitation in including the second case, because it is not as yet a star brand. However, it has ambitions to become one, and it is another example of how mergers and acquisitions are increasingly being used as a means of gaining the global reach upon which a brand can be built. SAIC (Shanghai Automotive Industry Corporation) is a Chinese company that is building a global presence and a brand name through this route. It certainly is one to watch.

The third company is Huawei Technologies, a business-to-business communications network solutions brand that already has massive global reach and is partnered by some of the best technology brands in the world.

The last case in this chapter is Phatra Securities Public Company Limited from Thailand. Phatra is probably the most respected brand in its category, and had built its reputation together with Merrill Lynch from the United States. From being owned by Merrill Lynch, to managing a buyout and a seamless transition to an alliance partnership, Phatra has proved that a willingness to change, to learn, and to accommodate a different culture can be done successfully with the right attitude.

CASE STUDY 20—LENOVO

Names and Logos are Necessary,
But not Enough

★ ★ ★ ★ ★

The following is an extract from a press release issued by the Legend Group in 2003.

LEGEND ADOPTS NEW LOGO— ***lenovo*联想**

*   *   *

IN LINE WITH ITS DIVERSIFIED BUSINESS AND LAY THE
GROUNDWORK FOR OVERSEAS DEVELOPMENT

(Hong Kong, April 28, 2003) Legend Group Limited ("Legend") (stock code: 992) today announced the change of its logo to ***lenovo*联想** (pronounced as len'nouvou) to cater for the Group's diversified business development and lay the groundwork for its expansion in overseas market.

Despite the change, both the Chinese and English company names of Legend Group Limited remain unchanged. For its business activities in China, Legend will continue to use its Chinese brand name (i.e. 聯想) while the Chinese logo (聯想) will also be used in combination with the new English logo ***lenovo***. For overseas markets, ***lenovo*** will be used alone.

Yang Yuanqing, President & CEO of Legend, said, "Legend's branding is one of our most valuable assets on which our strength lies. In view of our rapid expansion in recent years, we need a logo that fully captures Legend's business diversification and its goal of internationalization. On our way to become internationalized, we need to have an English brand name that can be used unrestrictedly in markets worldwide in the first place. However, the original English brand name, "LEGEND", has already been registered by others in many countries, making it essential to design and register a new English brand name. Although our business focus is still on China, expanding into the international market is an inevitable path with the globalization of IT industry and for Legend's self-development. That is why we must take proactive action in our preparation."

"*Lenovo*" is a new word coined by Legend. The "le" in "*lenovo*" indicates the connection with "LEGEND" while "novo" is derived from Latin, which means "innovation and novelty." The combination of these two into "*lenovo*" represents "an innovative Legend," which embodies four superb attributes, namely "trustworthy," "innovative & energetic," "professional services" and "easy." Adopting the basic tone of blue combined with a modern design with simplicity, "*lenovo*" is a vivid representation of professionalism, technology, profoundness and wisdom.

*lenovo*联想 and *lenovo* have already been registered by Legend worldwide. The adoption of the new logo will be completed in six months to one year's time. The change will first be made in major cities and key retail shops in the PRC, followed by a step-by-step completion in other cities and regions over the country. The new logo will be used on products which are manufactured from April 29 onwards. With the adoption of a single branding structure, Legend's consumer IT business, corporate IT business, IT services business, handheld device business and all Legend's products will apply the new logo while motherboard business will continue to use the "QDI" logo.

Yang Yuanqing said, "Having fully considered the Group's future strategies and recent development and having made reference to the successful experience of well-known international brands, we decided to choose a single branding structure, which will facilitate us to concentrate our resources on the accumulation of our brand value. During the process of changing our logo, we have conducted extensive market research, and the logo and English brand name were then subject to a serious procedure of justification and discussion. Besides, we have also engaged a world-class branding consultancy whose professional advice helped us accumulate valuable experience, establish and perfect many work procedures related to branding. We believe this will greatly enhance the brand image of Legend and pave the way for our brighter future."

Yang Yuanqing continued, "The change of logo will exert long-term and far-reaching impact on the Group's business development, with our positioning becoming clearer, our company converging greater power, our internationalization process materialized further and our vision getting farther. In future, we will continue to show our commitment to our customers, business partners, staff and shareholders, with our management philosophies and core values."

Liu Chuanzhi, Chairman of Legend, commented, "A brand itself is not merely a logo. Its value is built on the recognition of society and people in general. The older generation of Legend's staff not only longed for making our brand name famous in the PRC but also wish to make it an internationally renowned brand, and making Legend an outstanding representative among Chinese enterprises. Through this, the lofty goal of "Technology Rewards the Country" that Legend set when founded will be materialized. Today, we have already made a big stride towards this goal."

Such was the announcement of the name and logo changes made by this ambitious Chinese company, but what the world didn't know was the speed and strategy that would follow behind these cosmetic changes in Lenovo's bid to become a global brand.

BACKGROUND

Founded in 1984, Lenovo was the first company to introduce the home computer in the People's Republic of China. Lenovo Group Ltd. (formerly known as Legend Group Ltd.) is a leading IT enterprise in China, engaged primarily in the manufacturing and sale of desktop computers, notebook computers, mobile phones, servers, and peripherals.

The "Legend" brand of personal computers has been the best-selling brand in China for seven consecutive years. In recent times, its grip on the market has been loosened by competition from international brands, particularly Dell from the United States. Legend Group has long-held ambitions to become a global brand, but found it difficult to move out of China into international markets with consumers doubting its country of origin and a name that could not be registered across the world.

In 2004, Lenovo had revenues of around US$3 billion, of which 98% was from China. With the advent of the WTO and in-bound competition, this had to change.

A Major Acquisition

In a move that took the markets by surprise, Lenovo announced the largest ever overseas acquisition by a technology company from China on December 8, 2004 with an agreement to buy the PC unit of IBM for US$1.75 billion. The deal was structured so that Lenovo has to cough up US$600 million in shares and cash and take on US$500 million of IBM's debt. IBM has been known to want to get out of the PC market for a few years, where it wasn't performing, and to concentrate on its more profitable service solutions business. This deal also indicated that IBM would gain an 18.9% shareholding in Lenovo. In a more recent announcement, the sum agreed appears to be US$1.25 billion.

The IBM deal instantly gives the company a global brand name with global market access. At one stroke, this seemingly safeguards the future attrition of the national customer base by supplementing it with IBM's global customer base. With this move, Lenovo also became the first Chinese company to acquire a famous global brand name.

Gross margins are reputed to be around 20% in the PC market, compared to Lenovo's 15% margins. Analysts viewed the additional 5% as an incentive for Lenovo to buy. However, IBM's PC business has been unprofitable since 2001, a fact that is discussed in more detail later in the case. Let's have a look at what Lenovo has actually bought.

What Assets has Lenovo Acquired?

According to the sources cited at the end of this case study, Lenovo has acquired the following assets:

- IBM's notebook, desktop business, and related operations;
- 10,000 staff in 160 countries;
- IBM's "Think" brand and related patents; and
- IIPC (IBM's joint venture in China) excluding its X-series server production capabilities.

The partnership will also give Lenovo some additional areas of expertise. IBM will provide marketing support through its existing enterprise sales force of 30,000 people and through the IBM.com channel. Lenovo products will also be retailed by IBM PC specialists. IBM Global Financing will provide leasing and financing services, while IBM Global Services will provide warranty and maintenance services.

The acquisition places Lenovo at the number three position in the world behind Dell and HP, but quite a way behind. Global market share figures for the PC market in 2003 placed Dell at number one with 16.7% and HP second with 16.2%. IBM had 5.8%, while Lenovo had only a 2.3% share.

Nevertheless, the president and chairman-designate of Lenovo, Yang Yuanqing, issued his intention to the other two players by saying, "We are not satisfied to be only number three." With this in mind, he also wants to list the company in the United States in the near future to allow Lenovo to establish itself as more of a global brand. Dell supremo Michael Dell responded in a way that suggested he wasn't worried in the slightest by this latest initiative: "When was the last time you saw a successful merger or acquisition in the computer industry?" Lenovo's share price fell on the announcement of the deal.

Meanwhile, Liu Chuanzhi, the current chairman, said:

> As Lenovo's founder, I am excited by this breakthrough in Lenovo's journey towards becoming an international company. Over the past 20 years, I've watched Lenovo develop into the leading IT company both in China and throughout Asia. Since the beginning, however, our unwavering goal has been to create a truly international enterprise. From 2003 when we changed our international brand name to 2004 when we announced our partnership with the International Olympic

Committee, to today's strategic alliance with IBM, I have been delighted to watch Lenovo become a truly world-class company.

IBM's Stephen M. Ward Jr., senior vice president and general manager of the personal systems group, said: "This is a winning transaction for customers of both companies. Our two companies are a perfect fit sharing a cultural commitment to innovation, customer service and shareholder value." IBM chairman and chief executive, Samuel J. Palmisano, said: "In Lenovo, we have a partner with powerful competitive capabilities in China and Asia and in consumer and desktop PCs. We have worked very carefully with Lenovo to put in place all the elements of a strong, enduring global alliance."

Despite these upbeat statements, Lenovo has it all to do—it has to prove it can make the mixed marriage work and succeed in the global marketplace, while at the same time defend its own decreasing share of an increasing national market. Perhaps some of the biggest challenges it faces are in the area of brand management.

BRAND MANAGEMENT CONSIDERATIONS

One of the most interesting debates going on in the minds of analysts, investors, and consumers is what the post-acquisition period will mean for the company's future market prospects. There are several issues to consider from a brand management perspective with respect to this merger of two extremely different companies.

Timing and Loyalty

One of the issues clearly needing to be resolved is what will happen to the IBM PC brand, as it would be extremely disadvantageous to the brand's relationships with loyal customers and other stakeholders, such as employees, if a trusted brand name that they have admired and/or bought were to disappear. This is of particular concern outside China, where the country-of-origin fear factor strikes at the heart of consumer quality perceptions, but it appears that Lenovo is trying to deal with this. (See the "Trademarking, Licensing, and Architecture Issues" section below.)

There are those who will feel betrayed by IBM, who will doubt that Lenovo can match the quality of IBM, and who will switch their loyalties to other brands. Defending the other goal, so to speak, there will be the Lenovo supporters who may be enthused by the fact that they are taking a step up in the international brand arena by buying apparently better-quality products from a global brand.

The future may well rest outside the China market. If the IBM followers remain brand loyal, then Lenovo will win. However, there are some huge corporate accounts that will be wondering whether the new capability will be up to the mark in terms of production, product development, and distribution. HP is already voraciously looking forward to the prospect of a lot of brand switchers and is saying that if existing customers do switch, then HP will be the beneficiary.

One part of the takeover is to have a transition stage whereby IBM works together with Lenovo. This transition stage is expected to last five years. In fact, IBM will remain the "preferred supplier" of after-sales service for PC products outside China, and is willing to ensure there is consistent customer support.

Part of the solution to this issue of concern is the decision to move the company's headquarters to the United States and to use the IBM management team.

Management of the Business and the Brand

The appointment of IBM senior vice president Stephen Ward Jr. (formerly the senior vice president and general manager of IBM's personal systems group) as chief executive, and the transfer of the head office to Armonk, New York, where IBM is based, is aimed at bridging a large gap in global brand and business management. It is largely expected that a group of IBM top executives with Ward will manage the Lenovo company. Founder and chairman Liu Chuanzhi says, "The most valuable asset we have acquired through IBM's PC business is its world-class management team and their extensive international experience." He has now given up his operational role to become chairman.

This is an extraordinary public admission for a Chinese company—that it doesn't have the capability to run a global brand. To some this implies a loss of face, but to others it appears to be a pragmatic move. Lenovo has a knowledge gap that it feels it can close by learning from IBM, which in 2003 controlled revenues of US$9 billion derived from 150 countries.

However, the downside of this could be that the IBM team has not been able to make profits from those revenues in recent years. In fact, losses for the PC division totaled US$965 million for the period from 2001 to June 30, 2004 (US$397 million in 2001 on sales of US$10.1 billion, US$171 million in 2002 on sales of US$9.2 billion, and US$258 million in 2003 on sales of US$9.6 billion). The loss widened in the first half of 2004 in contrast to the same period in 2003, with a figure of US$139 million on sales of US$5.2 billion, compared to a 2003 first-half loss of USS$97 million on sales of US$4.3 billion. There is then the consideration of the brand name and its importance.

Trademarking, Licensing, and Architecture Issues

Lenovo is trying to minimize the risks on other fronts also, particularly in the area of naming and architecture. It appears that Lenovo has the license to use the IBM brand name for products made by the acquired PC division for five years. But Lenovo is already considering the future architecture and how brand names can transfer, without leaving the matter to the last minute.

For example, Yang says that for a period of 18 months after the deal is finalized the use of the IBM brand name will be unchanged. The ownership of the "Think" trademark will also assist and allow for a transition across the brands. After this time, one alternative that Lenovo has in mind is shared co-branding, such as a distinct "Lenovo-IBM" brand name; another is to use the endorsed branding route, such as "IBM, manufactured by Lenovo." According to Yang, no decisions have yet been made, but the architecture issue and the timing and handling of it will be critical to Lenovo's future in the international arena.

Brand Culture Fit

Another interesting issue is that of human capital, and whether or not the two vastly different cultures of IBM and Lenovo can be brought together to produce a single and motivated brand mindset. Knowing both companies, I would say that this might be one of the most imposing challenges that Lenovo has to face. Lenovo will have around 19,000 employees, approximately 10,000 of whom will be from IBM. The company is already putting in programs to help in the transition period.

For example, each day all vice presidents have to learn English for one hour. Recruits are trained in US-style teamwork and business methods. Careers are at risk if expectations aren't met, but many top managers in Lenovo are already very wealthy and may take the stock options and other benefits, rather than learn all over again. The mindset change is already under way, but will these initiatives be enough and can they achieve the culture change in time? Even with a hands-off attitude, the company is still state-owned.

Advisors and Other Strategic Partnerships

As expected, the advisors are also being recruited in true IBM style, and include McKinsey, Ogilvy, Goldman Sachs, and other specialists. In addition, Lenovo is seeking expertise from other sources. Early in 2005, three buyout funds led by Texas Pacific Group spent US$350 million acquiring a 12.4% interest in Lenovo. The others are General Atlantic Partners LLC and Newbridge Capital LLC. All were strongly in favor of the IBM deal and are experts in cost control, finance, and other specialist areas that will add expertise to help Lenovo move forward into international markets and grow faster. The investing group will have seats on the board of directors.

Lenovo is in a hurry to achieve its global ambitions, and appears to be leaving nothing to chance. But again, questions have to be asked as to whether all that is being attempted can be coordinated and absorbed in order to achieve Lenovo's global brand ambitions.

THE FUTURE?

In the end, as always, the success of the whole initiative will lie in the hands of consumers. Lenovo has failed to make the cut on its own— for example, with mobile phones where it failed to make an impact on Motorola and Nokia. Neither has its PC operations fared well against the likes of Dell, but it should solve any quality problems with the IBM team in place.

To a large extent, brand success or failure will depend on Lenovo's brand management capabilities, especially on how it will manage consumer perceptions and expectations. This is no easy task for a brand with a "Made in China" perceived association, but there is no denying Lenovo's determination and visionary abilities. As with most Chinese brands, this is most definitely a case of "let's wait and see."

Brand strengths

- Management's boldness and determination for Lenovo to become a top two global player in the PC market.
- The purchase of one of the world's most enduring and trusted brands.
- Instant global market access.
- The IBM deal gives a window of opportunity to build awareness and trust.
- Strong advisors and partners.

Brand weaknesses

- Renaming, although essential, makes no difference in China where the company has been losing market share to foreign brands.
- Quality issues in the Lenovo customer experience may not help it pick up home sales, and it is less efficient than some of its peers.
- The Lenovo brand name is unknown in the rest of the world, and there will be country-of-origin challenges.
- Reliance on IBM for managing the brand transition—Lenovo has little international brand management experience, but it is placing its trust in an IBM team that has consistently made losses.

Brand architecture

Corporate, with shared product and product range branding via product descriptors (examples: notebook computers—Lenovo Soleil A 500; mobile phones—ET 560).

Sources

- *Financial Times,* December 9, 2004
- Thompson Datastream.
- Lenovo corporate website: www.lenovo.com.
- *The Asian Wall Street Journal,* January 3, 2005, Dow Jones Newswires.

CASE STUDY 21—SHANGHAI AUTOMOTIVE INDUSTRY CORPORATION (SAIC)

Brand Development through Strategic Partnerships and Acquisitions

★ ★ ★ ★ ★

With the 10th Five-year Plan in place, China's automotive industry is set to address the rising needs of the domestic market through opening up to large foreign automotive players and accelerating "self-development." The development of relevant spare parts will be regarded as the basis of growth, and economy cars will be the focus of development. Basically, the large automotive groups will be the backbone driving the growth of the automotive industry and achievement of mass production efficiencies.

More national technical centers will be set up to enhance technique-innovation and production-development abilities. Market surroundings will be improved, and management based on the legal system will be strengthened to promote fair competition. Greater efforts will be made to exploit comparative advantages and to enhance China's overall competitive ability in the world market.

In 2004, 90% of the passenger cars sold in China were under foreign brand names. General Motors (GM) shifted its Asian headquarters to Shanghai from Singapore, and Volkswagen (VW) has its manufacturing center for the region here. The automotive industry employed 12 million people in 2004.

One of the top three automotive groups in China is Shanghai Automotive Industry Corporation (SAIC). Currently, the group has 55 subsidiary companies in which it has direct investments, and around 60,000 employees. The group's fundamental business is the manufacturing, distribution, R&D, trading, and financing of passenger cars, buses, heavy-duty trucks, tractors, motorcycles, and auto components.

BUILDING THE BRAND THROUGH STRATEGIC ALLIANCES, PARTNERSHIPS, AND ACQUISITIONS

The development and growth of SAIC has been tremendous since its joint ventures with GM and VW that started in 2000. SAIC owns half of the operations and shares half of the profits with its strategic alliance partners, and it now claims to be one of the world's top 500 companies. It is the fourth-largest car maker in the world.

With the strategic alliance model, SAIC's sales revenue reached 186.2 billion RMB and its gross product was 157.8 billion RMB in 2003. In addition, the sales volume of total vehicles reached about 800,000 units and the sales volume of passenger cars reached 597,000 units, creating a historic record with an annual growth of 185,000 units. Hence, the key target SAIC set for the 10th Five-year Period was achieved two years in advance.

The Great Opportunity

With China's WTO accession the country's auto industry is exposed to the full force of global competition and increased pressures for consolidation and restructuring. It creates opportunities to learn new technologies and increase exports. On the other hand, foreign automakers will be able to gain more control over their own sales and supply chains. Chinese consumers will benefit from price cuts and a wider choice of new, affordable family cars. For that reason, SAIC will have to monitor closely and take advantage of the industry driving forces if it is to achieve its goal of launching its own branded car range.

Presently, SAIC is adopting a multi-pronged strategy for its expansion through supporting the growth of its joint ventures with GM and VW, both of which have announced plans to more than double their production over the next three years. This is to anticipate the huge demand from the untapped China market.

SAIC is also targeting foreign markets. As explained below, it is taking a 48.9% stake in South Korea's ailing Ssangyong Motor, primarily a maker of sport utility vehicles (SUV). Besides building Ssangyong sales in China, it can use the brand to gain a presence in the Korean market. With these new initiatives, it would help SAIC to see off the challenges from its chief domestic rivals, First Auto Works and Dongfeng Motor.

The abbreviation of the group name—SAIC—also stands for its unique corporate brand values and practices within the business:

◆ Satisfaction from customers;
◆ Advantage through innovation;
◆ Internationalization in operating; and
◆ Concentration on people.

Aligned with the corporate brand values, SAIC has made efforts to carry out projects that focus on customer satisfaction, overall innovation, global operation, and people-oriented management.

Basically, SAIC is actively engaged in cross-regional assets operations and in further efforts to diversify its business to better anticipate the future trends of China's automotive industry and the competition that lies ahead. At the same time, the group is preparing to shape its own R&D capabilities to provide greater flexibility in its product structure and to develop both domestic and international markets. In short, the three strategic goals that SAIC is currently looking at are to achieve an annual output of one million vehicles, to be one of the Fortune global 500 enterprises, and to produce 50,000 vehicles with its self-owned brand by the end of 2007.

STRATEGIC ALLIANCE BRAND-BUILDING CHALLENGES

While VW and GM are increasingly competing against each other in the same marketplace as they expand their product lines, SAIC plans to launch its own branded car in 2007 and will most likely compete in the same marketplace as its strategic alliance partners. It has set a modest initial sales target of 50,000 units a year. By doing so, the group is exposing itself to the risk of hurting the joint venture relationships with its strategic alliance partners. At the same time, VW and GM are facing the consequences of being forced aside as China's domestic auto industry develops. This provides further reason for SAIC's strategic partners to think twice before allowing SAIC to copy their own creations.

The decision as to whether SAIC will develop its own car, or simply brand and market one of its partners' cars, still remains unclear.

At this stage, the group is experiencing the challenge of convincing the strategic alliance partners to allow SAIC to copy whatever products the joint ventures are making and to put its own logo on them. SAIC has approached the Western companies for assistance in the project but has so far been unsuccessful. The road ahead must therefore lie on the acquisition front.

MERGERS AND ACQUISITIONS

SAIC had a backup plan in place to overcome this challenge with a potential £1 billion investment in MG Rover that would have earned it a 70% stake in the last bastion of British car marques. There were questions being asked about why SAIC should bother to acquire a failing brand in the United Kingdom with a cost base that is many times its own in China. (Labor costs in the UK are about 10 times higher than in China.)

The prospect of acquiring modern technology may be one answer, but perhaps the real intent is to give the Chinese company its own brand capability that it has long desired. However, the deal fell through, but there are still some intellectual property (IP) rights of the MG Rover Group that SAIC appears to hold. The new buyer—Nanjing Auto—faces this issue along with other IP rights claimed by Honda. At present, this is under process, but what this negotiation demonstrates is that SAIC now has the confidence to go out into the global marketplace and start acquiring brands in pursuit of its global ambitions.

In another strategic move to propel it on its way to becoming a global automotive parts manufacturer and assembler, SAIC agreed to buy Ssangyong Motor Co. for US$522 million in October 2004. This followed an initiative in July of that year whereby GM was named as the preferred negotiating partner to buy a 48.9% share of Ssangyong—GM being SAIC's main partner in China. Ssangyong builds the Rexton, Korando, and Musso brands, as well as the luxury Chairman saloon, and has the capacity to make 200,000 vehicles a year.

Additionally, Ssangyong is seen by SAIC as strategically desirable for technology, as it uses Mercedes Benz engine technology. Overall, it adds a technological dimension critical to SAIC in its bid to compete in its home market, which is being flooded with foreign cars offered at descending price levels.

THE FUTURE?

SAIC's future depends on its ability to move into international markets. If the Chinese car market continues to slow and margins to contract, it is vulnerable. For example, even though profitability and net income have not reduced, overall sales for 2004 slowed dramatically. Yet it is an aggressive company and has great determination, and although analysts have mixed feelings about SAIC, it hasn't made many mistakes yet.

It will have to move quickly to outmaneuver the domestic competition, namely Chery (which plans to launch its car models in the United States by 2007) and Geely, both of which make their own branded cars in China. To some extent, while the alliances with overseas brands have done well so far, SAIC needs its own product brands if it is to move ahead.

Brand strengths

- Ambition and perseverance.
- Willingness to try new things.
- Size and cost leadership.

Brand weaknesses

- Heavily dependent on the home market at present.
- Lack of understanding of foreign markets.
- Lack of own product brands.

Brand architecture

Corporate branding.

Sources

- Zhang Da Hong, *Fortune*, October 11, 2004.
- *China Daily* website: http://bizchina.chinadaily.com.cn/guide/industry/industry2.htm.

CASE STUDY 22—HUAWEI TECHNOLOGIES

"Partner for a Networked World"

★ ★ ★ ★ ★

I mentioned in the introduction to this book that I believe Chinese brands will proliferate over the next few years and that some of these will dominate their industries. In this chapter you have read about two such brands. It looks as though the next case—Huawei Technologies—will be another one. In fact, it is very close to reaching global status and leadership in some of its business activities. China needs brands that will act as brand ambassadors for the nation; those that can earn respect in the international business community—and the route to achieving this for the companies concerned is to use alliances and partnerships.

However, Chinese companies are not the only ones to take advantage of foreign partnerships, and it appears that in the era of globalization, to become a strong international or global brand, mergers, acquisitions, and partnerships are critical. Phatra Securities from Thailand, for instance, has been partnering with Merrill Lynch for many years to gain global knowledge and brand reputation so that it can serve its clients well.

It is relatively easy for Chinese companies to pick the relationships they want, as many Western brands are keen to do deals that will gain them access to China's huge market. Chinese companies that demonstrate initiative, speed, and commitment can choose partners that will open the door that leads to instant access to global markets. Huawei Technologies is one company that has led the way.

BACKGROUND

Huawei Technologies is a privately owned company, and still relatively young, having been established in 1988. It is a B2B brand that specializes in the R&D, production, and marketing of communications equipment and network solutions, mainly for telecommunications clients. Typical of the new breed of high-tech Chinese companies, it has no baggage in terms of old technology to weigh it down. A couple of decades ago, China had little technology at all, but it now has all the latest technology in use.

Huawei's business activities lie under the heading of communications network solutions, and the products, which are sold in over 90 countries, are very technical, including:

- wireless networks;
- fixed-line networks;
- optical networks;
- datacom networks; and
- value-added services.

Importantly, the products are based on Huawei's independently designed ASIC chips. This design capability is among the most advanced in the world. These ranges contain a variety of products that Huawei customizes for its clients. The client list is indeed impressive and features blue-chip international brands such as SingTel, Hutchison Global Crossing, Telefonica, BT, Etisalat, China Telecom, and many others.

According to research companies, Huawei is number one in digital switches (Dittberner), number two in ADSL broadband, and number three in optical networks (RHK). It is also one of the few companies in the world to provide end-to-end 3G solutions. The company has over 24,000 employees, 48% of whom are working on R&D, and around 3,400 of whom are foreigners.

GLOBAL REACH

Huawei has gained global reach and status by organic growth and by seeking out smart partnerships.

Corporate Presence

On its own, Huawei has 55 branches overseas, eight regional headquarters, several research institutes, and many customer support and training centers in locations such as Dallas, Silicon Valley, Bangalore, Stockholm, and Moscow.

Passionate Partnerships

Huawei has a policy of partnering with leading blue-chip technology companies to ensure it is always at the cutting edge of its industry and to facilitate growth. Some of these include joint labs and partnership agreements with Sun Microsystems, Intel, Motorola, Texas Instruments, Microsoft, Qualcomm, and Infineon, and it has joint ventures with Siemens and 3Com. It makes the most of its powerful partner brand names in its brand communications and this helps to prove the trustworthiness of the Huawei brand, essential when the origin of the brand is China and where many potential buyers are skeptical of Chinese quality.

In developing its own business professionalism, it has used top consultancies such as the Hay Group and Towers Perrin (human resource management), PricewaterhouseCoopers (financial management), IBM (integrated product development and integrated supply chain), and FhG (quality control).

BRAND VISION AND MISSION

While the mission of Huawei is fairly routine for companies in Asia and elsewhere, the vision is more interesting. According to the company, its mission is:

> To focus on our customers' market challenges and needs by providing excellent communications network solutions and services in order to consistently create maximum value for customers.

While appearing mundane, at least this generates the message to all that the company is customer-centric. It focuses entirely on customers and not on other internal stakeholders, as many such statements do.

The vision is more simple, yet more powerful: "To enrich life through communication."

The important thing to note here is that there is no mention of technology. Like other great brands in the world of technology and communications, such as Nokia, there is recognition that on its own, technology is fairly useless, and that it is what people get out of technology from using it in their lives that is the critical factor.

This brand vision also reminds Huawei and all its partners that the success for any brand, whether B2B as with this one, or B2C as with Nokia, lies in its ability to add value and happiness to the end consumer.

BRAND COMMUNICATIONS

The execution of the Huawei brand vision is best seen in its print advertisements. For example, Huawei occupied a full page in the May 9, 2005 edition of *Forbes* magazine, where it speaks to both its B2B partners and end consumers. In a section of the advertisement, it talks about linking with its customers (partners) "to develop high quality technology solutions, delivered swiftly and at low cost to satisfy real consumer needs." A key message is contained in a highlighted red box exclaiming "Partnership and MORE," but the picture upon which it is placed shows two children engaged in a communications game and really enjoying themselves.

The tagline for the company is "Partner for a networked world."

SUMMARY

Huawei Technologies is a company with a great future. It understands what it takes to make a global brand and is pursuing that path with incredible speed. It also realizes that it needs to understand the end consumer if it is to work with its globally branded partners.

Business is booming for Huawei. Its contracted sales in 2004 reached US$5.58 billion, an increase of 45% year-on-year, of which US$2.28 billion came from international sales. With all that the company has put in place, it is hard not to see a global brand emerging in the near future.

Brand strengths

- Focus on R&D.
- Smart partnerships.
- Speed and flexibility.
- Understanding of B2B and B2C brand marketing.

Brand weakness

Possible over-reliance on partners, making it vulnerable if international markets and the technology sector suffer a decline.

Brand architecture

Corporate, with product descriptors (example: UMT S/HS DPA).

CASE STUDY 23—PHATRA SECURITIES

A Winning Alliance with Merrill Lynch

★ ★ ★ ★ ★

BACKGROUND

Phatra Securities Public Company Limited is one of the leading securities companies in Thailand with respect to investment banking business and the provision of brokerage services to institutional customers, having secured an approximately 10% market share of institutional customers. The company provides a broad range of financial services.

Historically, the company was the securities business department of Phatra Thanakit, which became a member of the Stock Exchange of Thailand (SET) as a broker in 1974. In 1997, the Thai government declared a policy of separating finance and securities businesses; as a result, on September 17, 1997, the company was established as a separate entity in the form of a private company to carry on securities business under the name of Phatra Securities Company Limited.

In 1998, Phatra Thanakit Finance Public Company Limited sold 49% of the company's shares to KASIKORNBANK Public Company Limited, which then held the company's shares directly, and the remaining 51% to Merrill Lynch, following which the company was named Merrill Lynch Phatra Securities Company Limited.

In December 2003, KASIKORNBANK Public Company Limited and Merrill Lynch sold their respective shareholdings in the company to a group of management and employees of the company, and the company reverted to its original name of Phatra Securities Company Limited (Phatra). Despite the sale of its shareholding in the company,

Merrill Lynch maintained a contractual relationship with Phatra under Business Service and Research Co-operation agreements.

PHATRA'S BUSINESS OPERATIONS

Phatra is licensed by the Ministry of Finance to carry out five types of securities businesses—namely, securities brokerage, securities dealing, underwriting, investment advisory, and securities lending and borrowing businesses. It has also obtained approval from the Securities and Exchange Commission of Thailand (SEC) to act as a financial advisor and unit trust sales supporting agent. At present, Phatra operates three core businesses:

- securities brokerage;
- investment banking; and
- investment.

In addition to these core businesses, Phatra also has a number of support departments, including the Research Group, the Office of General Counsel and Internal Audit (OGC), and the Technology Department.

THE ALLIANCE PARTNERSHIP

Although Merrill Lynch is no longer a shareholder of Phatra, the two companies maintain a strong relationship and exclusive cooperation in connection with their businesses, as described below.

Business Cooperation

Phatra and Merrill Lynch International Incorporated (Merrill Lynch Inter) entered into a Business Services Agreement dated December 1, 2003, in which they agreed to cooperate with each other in their business, and Merrill Lynch Inter agreed to provide certain advice to Phatra. In return for Merrill Lynch Inter's services, Phatra agreed to pay a fee, the amount of which is decided by both companies from time to time.

This extremely successful alliance partnership covers the following services:

- equity securities brokerage services;
- investment banking services;

- private client services;
- derivatives services;
- other services; and
- local and international research.

The Brand Personality Fit—Professional Friendship

From the outset, Phatra and Merrill Lynch have enjoyed a very warm relationship. Phatra found that Merrill Lynch wasn't typical of US brands in its culture and strategy. Merrill Lynch wanted to come in on a local, not regional, basis and so respected the different Asian cultural norms and practices. Phatra found that Merrill Lynch had a genuine desire to understand, work through difficulties, and transfer knowledge. For example, there were exchanges of people between the Thai and US companies, such as the creation of joint CEOs and COOs.

For its part, Phatra had always espoused globalization, and was the first securities company in Thailand to open an independent research institute. It was also very open to learning from Merrill Lynch and wasn't concerned about being "Merrillized." There were no egos in this relationship. The business and cultural fit was good.

In terms of the perceived brand personality of Merrill Lynch by Phatra, the company was (and still is) seen overall as "a good friend," with the following characteristics:

- understanding;
- kind;
- open;
- patient;
- consistent;
- helpful;
- strict; and
- professional.

Phatra was ambitious and matched the Merrill Lynch personality in many ways. Since the change of structure of the business relationship—from joint venture to alliance partnership—the friendship has remained. Merrill Lynch's strategy has changed and its people have changed, whereas those of Phatra have tended to stay the same, but the spirit between the two brands is still strong.

This long-term business relationship, admired and envied by many other local companies, has noticeably strengthened the Phatra brand and rewarded Merrill Lynch with a firm foothold in the Thailand market.

PHATRA'S COMPETITIVE STRENGTHS

Phatra has a number of competitive business strengths that it has developed over its relatively short life span.

A diversified range of financial services both in securities brokerage and investment banking

Phatra is now one of the leading securities companies in Thailand, providing a broad range of financial services both in securities brokerage and investment banking to its corporate, international, and local institutional customers and high-net-worth individuals. It secured an approximately 10% market share of institutional customers during 2004 and acted as underwriter in a number of large high offering value transactions.

Phatra's distribution platform provides it with the ability to secure international and local institutional customers and high-net-worth individuals for companies that approach it with investment banking business. In addition, its investment banking relationship with leading Thai companies enables Phatra to provide its domestic and international institutional clients with unique access to primary and secondary Thai equity. Phatra is also able to offer such institutional clients exposure to top Thai corporations, through its award-winning research and institutional road shows and investor forums. Only a limited number of securities firms can provide comparable services.

One of the leaders in underwriting Thai equity offerings

Phatra is recognized by its clients, both domestically and internationally, as one of the top underwriters of equity offerings by leading Thai companies. It has lead-managed eleven out of twelve largest ever initial public offerings in Thailand, and in the past five years has assisted many prominent Thai corporate and state enterprise raised fund over Baht 170,000 million.

This market dominance, experience, and expertise help Phatra to secure new underwriting mandates. It also helps it to secure brokerage clients who seek to gain access to such offerings.

International business practices and an international
investor network combined with local experience,
knowledge, and expertise

In the past 18 years, the company has had relationships, either through equity or contractual arrangements, with international financial institutions, including SG Warburg, Goldman Sachs, and most recently with Merrill Lynch. These relationships have provided Phatra with considerable knowledge and benefits, including access to international distribution networks, credibility with international investment institutions, and the ability to learn from their own established international standards of business practices.

Phatra has been able to combine such international knowledge, standards of business practice, and distribution networks with its local securities experience, knowledge, and expertise. This has enabled the company to develop its leading market position in securities business domestically.

Internationally recognized research

Phatra's research publications in both the economic and equity research fields have been acknowledged by both international and local investors, as evidenced by the various awards it has received from *Asiamoney, Institutional Investor Magazine,* and the SET. At present, Phatra offers macroeconomic and equity research covering 64 Thai companies listed on the SET, which represent a total value exceeding 70% of the SET's market capitalization. Such credible and recognized research, which it either produces by itself or co-authors with Merrill Lynch, provides valuable support to both Phatra's investment banking and brokerage businesses. In addition, Phatra distributes Merrill Lynch non-Thai research on global economic and regional industrial conditions so as to give its clients a full understanding of all relevant information.

An experienced management team and high-quality staff

The management team of Phatra has on average more than 20 years' experience in the securities field, and many of them have worked with the company since they entered the securities business. This has been vital in securing and maintaining long-term relationships with its clients, both in the public and private sectors, and establishing

Phatra's dominant position in securing underwriting business. The management team is supported by high-quality staff, and this has been key to providing the company with suitable financial products to satisfy clients' needs and to maintain quality and international-standard services.

FUTURE GOALS AND BUSINESS STRATEGIES

Looking to the future, Phatra's principal objective is to be the leader in Thailand in all the core businesses in which it operates and to be the first choice of customers in those businesses. Phatra intends to achieve these objectives by focusing on the following:

- providing investment banking services for large-size, high-value transactions;
- retaining flexibility when providing its services in order to consider revenue opportunities across business lines;
- seeking to expand its private client business;
- developing its direct investment business;
- continuing to identify complementary business lines; and
- continuing to attract and retain a qualified workforce.

Following its successful listing in May 2005, Phatra looks to be heading for further brand success with its partner Merrill Lynch. However, it is not complacent and will continue to strengthen its brand. As Khun Banyong Pongpanich, chairman of Phatra Securities Public Company Limited, says: "At Phatra, we strongly believe that a powerful brand image contributes heavily to business success. Over the last few years we have leveraged on the quality of the talents of Merrill Lynch and ourselves. The two companies have complemented each other in providing a very strong value proposition in terms of image and results for our clients. However, we recognize that brand building is an ongoing process. We are not complacent about our image and are working hard to further improve."

Brand strengths

- The tremendous knowledge and loyalty of staff.
- Research capability.
- The Merrill Lynch alliance partnership.

Brand weaknesses

- The prospect of a future "brain-drain," as key staff are now very wealthy and highly sought—after since Phatra's listing in May 2005.
- Great expectations from its clients.
- Doubts about the research division's capability to reach out to the market and develop relationships and not just churn out reports.
- Somewhat high pride or its success to date.

Source

Phatra Securities Public Company Limited.

CONCLUSION

The complexity of branded businesses such as those mentioned in this chapter isn't confined to the private sector. The public sector is now applying branding techniques, as illustrated in the next chapter.

CHAPTER 12

DESTINATION BRANDS

INTRODUCTION

The first question to be asked here is: Why should the public sector—countries, destinations, and so on—be concerned with branding activities, when branding has traditionally been confined to the corporate world?

The public sector has now realized how success via branding can be replicated, particularly in the way that brand planning can generate differentiation in the face of global competition. Destination branding is now in full swing. Cities and countries from all over the world have realized how important the branding of destinations can be in developing their national image and building wealth.

Why Asian Countries Should Concern Themselves with "Brand Image"

Reason no. 1

The problems they face are the same—parity and the need to differentiate in the face of increasing competition. Just like companies in Asia, countries have to attract various customer groups and must market and sell their products, ideas, and services to people in other countries. And again just like companies, countries are beginning to find that the best way of doing this isn't usually by offering the lowest price, but by building perceived value. There is a dawning recognition that a nation's image is made up of "perceived value," and that value can consist of intangible as well as tangible elements. Countries have entered the world of branding.

Reason no. 2

Relying on past reputation won't ensure success in the future. To survive in a changing world, countries must also change, as what may have been good perceptions of them in the past may not be so good now. For example, New Zealand wants to update its image from being a country famous for its sheep and rugby to include its medical science expertise and transparency; Canada wants to be seen as a high-tech global player, in addition to being thought of as a good place to go for a holiday or an education; and Britain wants to be seen as more innovative, friendly, trendy, and "with it," rather than as solid, conservative, reliable, and "past it."

Reason no. 3

Brands are strategic assets in their own right, and can bring both power and financial rewards. They can help countries by replacing the "push" factor with the "pull" factor. Strong brands differentiate, and attract people to them, rather than having to chase after them.

Reason no. 4

Countries need to manage perceptions and control their image in order to manage particular issues of national concern. This has specific relevance to Asian countries, where differentiation is lacking, images are very unclear, and the country-of-origin factor is often detrimental to exports and domestic sales.

Many Western countries have already established their identity and strengths in certain areas. Germany's reputation for precision engineering, Italy's association with fashion, and the romantic associations of Paris are examples. Indeed, countries such as Spain, Ireland, and others have carried out deliberate branding programs to help them make a global impact. Asian countries have yet to do this.

But what do Asian countries stand for? Japan has closely linked itself to consumer electronics through its brands, but other countries don't have such strong positive images or associations. On the contrary, they often have negative images. For example, China is perceived as a producer of cheap, poor-quality products. What Asian countries have failed to do is manage their brand image well by managing market perceptions, promoting their strengths, and eliminating their perceived weaknesses. However, throughout the world, despite geo-politics and national and foreign policy agendas still dominating government thinking in the race for power and influence, these factors are being eroded by the attention that decision-makers are giving to image and the benefits it can bring to the table.

THE BENEFITS OF BRANDING FOR THE PUBLIC SECTOR

The public sector stands to gain a great deal from branding destinations, including:

- development of international credibility and investor confidence;
- attraction of global capital;
- an increase in international political influence;
- export growth of branded products and services;
- increases in inbound tourism and foreign direct investment;
- development of stronger international partnerships;
- enhancement of nation building (confidence, pride, harmony, ambition, national resolve);
- attraction and retention of talent—the human resource and global knowledge; and
- greater access to global markets.

Many of these issues revolve around how much confidence, positive mental associations, and misconceptions various target audiences have in or about particular countries. But most Asian countries have a perception gap between what they *want* to be seen as (their identity) and how they *are* seen (their image). Like companies, they have brand strengths and weaknesses. For example, Singapore has a very pro-business image, but also a reputation for excessive bureaucratic controls. And while Hong Kong wants to be seen as the "gateway to China," many investors don't consider this to be the case.

Importantly, countries in Asia are also competing with each other to gain a favorable "share of mind." For example, when Global Japan president Nancy Lee was asked about the decision where to base her company's headquarters for the rest of Asia, she replied: "We are constantly pulled between Hong Kong and Singapore." (For further information on branding in the public sector, see my book *Public Sector Branding in Asia* (Marshall Cavendish International (Asia) Pte. Ltd., 2004).)

In Asia, there is now considerable effort being put into destination branding, and the competition is becoming very fierce. Singapore, Malaysia, Hong Kong, India, China, Vietnam, Indonesia, Thailand, Taiwan, South Korea, and other countries are all currently on the campaign trail to capture the business and tourist dollars.

In this chapter I have chosen two of the most important rising stars of destination branding. These two cases demonstrate the seriousness and determination of how brands are being built in the public sector. You will read first about the sheer pace of development in Shanghai, and then about the huge brand plan for Dubai. There appears to be no doubt in anyone's mind that both of these destinations are well on track for global brand status.

CASE STUDY 24—SHANGHAI

China's Cheerleader

★ ★ ★ ★ ★

Shanghai has always been a fusion of Western and Chinese cultures. As a city it is only 150 years old, but it has always been a center of cross-cultural excitement and adventure. It has 5,000 years of Chinese culture behind it and yet it still maintains global relevance.

Following the Opium War of 1843, Shanghai was run by foreigners, although it wasn't properly colonized. It wasn't ruled by China, but most of its residents were Chinese. In 1845, Britain set up its concession, followed by the United States in 1848 and France in · 1849. In 1863, the British and American concessions amalgamated into the Chinese Section, the International Settlement, and the French Concession.

By the early decades of the 20th century, Shanghai was one of the hottest spots for having a great time in business and in pleasure. Chinese, British, Russian, Indian, Austrian, Dutch, French, and many other nationalities traded and lived an exotic and frantically entertaining lifestyle. Shanghai was a Western trading port built on the east coast of China, and virtually anything was up for sale. Dancing, the latest music, fine food, opium, and a breathtaking nightlife awaited those who were adventurous enough to come to this melting pot of the Orient.

It was referred to as the "Whore of Asia" by some, and the "Paris of the East" by others. Westerners saw a very Western city, but in Old Shanghai the Chinese lived in their own world. It had the best and worst of everything. Being "Shanghai-ed" was an expression that came from this city, whereby sea captains had so much difficulty getting crew they would drug people, who would wake up as sailors.

While warlords fought and bombs fell in the early decades of the last century, Shanghai just got on with business and partied. It was a society that lived to excess in every way—that lived life to the full. Shanghai has always demonstrated a "can do" attitude that has never deserted it. It did disappear for a time when communism took over in the late 1940s, but the politically correct terminology of "communism" has evolved into what is commonly described now as "socialist capitalism," once again ensuring that Shanghai is the city where it all happens.

Shanghai is a hugely successful city once again, attracting people from all over the world. It is also attracting back some of the families that made a rapid exit when the 1949 crackdown came, especially tycoons from Hong Kong and Taiwan, such as Vincent Lo who has built the Xintiandi entertainment district. People like Lo are bringing back to Shanghai the business skills they have honed so well elsewhere and are transforming the city.

THE TRANSFORMATION

I have never seen a city change so rapidly in such a short time—from poverty and pessimism in the early 1990s to riches and optimism today. Shanghai has regained its brand identity of progressiveness, excitement, optimism, allure, and sheer audacity. Shanghai has face and isn't worried about strutting it.

Between 1998 and 2002, the city pulled down 15 million square meters of old living areas and developed more than 80 million square meters of new residential land. There are three million migrant workers applying themselves to the task of changing the city, with villas, Tudor-style cottages, and complexes that sound nothing like a Chinese location, such as Merlin Champagne town and Versailles de Shanghai. (Apparently, in an effort to curtail this trend, a new regulation governing the property development industry stipulates that all real estate names that are "feudal, aristocratic, foreign and immoral" must be changed to names that promote "national dignity.") Shanghai is planning to build 11 satellite cities by 2010, with over a million people in each to cater for the continued expansion and boom times.

In recent years, a number of modern buildings have been added to the city, such as the Oriental Pearl TV Tower, Shanghai Museum, Shanghai Library, Shanghai Stadium, Shanghai Grand Theatre, Shanghai Circus City, Shanghai City-Planning Exhibition Hall, Shanghai Science and Technology Museum, and Jin Mao Tower. Muddy streets and one tall building have given way to fashionable and elegant plazas and over 300 skyscrapers. A 430 kph US$1.2 billion magnetic levitation train travels from the airport to the city in eight minutes, symbolizing the energy of Shanghai. Thousands of foreign companies have flooded in.

But Shanghai has also been careful to retain some of the older districts where the expatriates used to live in the 1920s and 1930s. Many old buildings once inhabited by the British and French are being designated as "heritage buildings" by the Shanghai urban-planning authority. The Bund was, and arguably still is, the most famous street in Asia and it was the financial center of Shanghai. Many foreign firms still have their offices there. The fusion of East and West remains as the architectural landscape changes.

CHINA'S WINDOW TO THE WEST

Shanghai is China's window to the West—its branded showpiece. It has already overtaken Hong Kong as the place where East meets West, and will soon be its successor as the financial capital of Asia. Formula One and other motor sports are there; the NBA is there (the famous NBA player Yao Ming comes from Shanghai); the 2008 Olympic Games will be held in Beijing, and Shanghai is expecting a huge amount of tourism and business exposure as millions visit the country in the run-up to and during the actual Games.

All the Western brands are resident in Shanghai to cater for the nouveau riche of China. Armani has a 1,000-square-meter flagship store, and sales of Rolls-Royce cars are booming. It seems that nothing is impossible for Shanghai. As an example of this new-found wealth, the *Financial Times* (January 12, 2005) wrote that at the Shanghai Museum, despite all the beautiful artifacts from bygone centuries, including from the Roman Age, the most popular special exhibition consisted of 300 pieces of contemporary branded jewelry, such as pieces by Cartier, which sponsored the exhibition. Evidently, 400,000 people visited the exhibition during its two-month run.

Shanghai will be the venue for the World Expo in 2010. The number of visitors attending this event is expected to top 100 million. It is estimated that 17,500 families and more than 270 businesses and institutions will have to be relocated to make room for the five-square-kilometer site at a cost of 20 billion RMB. Chen Xianjin, president of the Shanghai World Expo Group, says: "In terms of technology, we will try to make it possible that whatever one could think of in a dream, can be seen at that Expo." He maintains that culture will play a big role in the event's success and that World Expo 2010 will provide a stage for many different cultures and appeal to people of all ages.

Shanghai is also trying to attract more foreign investment, especially in the service sector. In February 2005, the Shanghai Municipal Economic Relations and Trade Commission (SMERTC) and Shanghai Foreign Investment Commission (SFIC) said the city would aim for an increase in foreign trade of 15% this year, while the average actual investment growth rate of 10% would be maintained. The director of the two commissions, Pan Longqing, said: "Shanghai has pledged to improve the quality of foreign investment this year. Quality is more important than the amount."

The local government is to focus on getting more foreign investment in six key areas, namely:

- transportation;
- financial services;
- exhibition and travel services;
- information services;
- professional services; and
- entertainment.

The goal of the plan is to avoid direct competition with surrounding areas while strengthening Shanghai's existing competitive advantages.

Targeting foreign direct investment in manufacturing would compete with other provinces of China. An equally important goal is to bring Shanghai up to the level of services provided in leading developed countries.

TOURISM CITY

Shanghai is fast becoming a tourist destination as well as a business hub for China. New tourist drawcards include the Shanghai Tourism Festival and Shanghai China International Arts Festival. The needs of tourists can be met at all levels. For example, there are over 1,000 restaurants serving the 16 different styles of Chinese food, as well as any international food a visitor could want. There are over 40 Chinese and foreign airlines operating on over 300 routes out of Shanghai. The combined passenger traffic of the two airports at Pudong and Hongqiao is around 30 million people annually.

But all this hasn't just happened by chance. There has been a deliberate effort by the Chinese government to build this city of the future. Shanghai is a sub-brand of China that has been developed to promote both itself and the master brand. Former president Jiang Zemin, a former mayor of the city, was instrumental in the Shanghai brand's development by giving back to Shanghai the freedom it was deprived of for several decades.

Shanghai has developed its tourist industry by creating "city scenery", "city culture," and "city commerce." The itinerary for city tours, business, and shopping is organized around the People's Square and both sides of the Huangpu River. The itinerary for cultural tours around the city incorporates the public entertainment places and communities. The itinerary for recreation and holidays in the outer suburbs is organized around Mount She, Dian Shan Lake, the deep-water port, and Chong Ming Island.

GLOBAL CITY, GOLDEN BRAND

The Chinese government has great ambitions for the country and its brand ambassadors, and Shanghai is certainly a brand champion for China. It isn't in the Chinese culture to brag and shout about success—the culture is more about doing things that matter, than talking about them. Actions speak louder than words, and while the government retains and projects its cautious perspective to the out-side world, it encourages and lets its destination and corporate brands do the talking and create the new image of China.

Shanghai is a global city and a golden brand, with undeniable charisma. It could claim to be the world's "City of the Future." No other city in Asia is likely to be able to claim that position or deliver on that promise.

Brand strengths

- China is determined to play a full part in the World Trade Organization. With this in mind, the Chinese government is willing to put in as much as it takes to showcase China to the world.
- The Shanghai authorities have so far shown that if they make a promise, they will deliver on it.
- The carefully crafted blend of modernity and old-world charm makes Shanghai a destination of interest.
- Chinese culture is high on the "must see" list for travelers to Asia.
- China is the place to be for business now and for the foreseeable future, and Shanghai is leading the way in the development of business and commerce.

Brand weaknesses

- In terms of tourism, Shanghai faces stiff competition from other Asian destinations, and will have to work hard on "selling" Chinese culture as well as the cosmopolitan aspects of urban tourism.
- As a financial and business center, regulatory matters need improvement—for example, with respect to intellectual property infringements.
- Some say the expansion has been too fast and that there is a real estate "bubble" that will burst.

Brand architecture

Shanghai is a sub-brand of China. Although it adopts a corporate approach, it relies on the fact that it belongs to and is a part of China. It adopts a shared branding approach with its master brand and its own products and services (example: the Shanghai China International Arts Festival).

CASE STUDY 25—DUBAI

The Jewel in the Desert

★ ★ ★ ★ ★

With a total population of just 1.5 million (only 10% of whom are local people from Dubai itself), and occupying only 1,506 square miles (3,900 square kilometers), one of the seven emirates that make up the United Arab Emirates has shown the power of focused branding, strategic alignment, and service quality. If you haven't been to Dubai, it is difficult to imagine what astonishing sights there are there. In this case, I will attempt to explain the rapid development of this small nation and how well it is branding itself.

BACKGROUND

Archeological findings in the Jimma Valley have led scientists to estimate that Dubai was first settled in the third century BC. It started its life as a small fishing settlement, until the Al-Maktoum family assumed leadership in 1830. By the beginning of the 20th century, despite its small size, Dubai was making quite a reputation in the trading world through its liberal attitudes. It was a British protectorate until 1971 when it joined with Abu Dhabi, Sharjah, Ajman, Umm Al Quwain, Fujairah, and (in 1972) Ras Al Khaiman to create the Federation of the United Arab Emirates (UAE). Within this small group of sultanates, Dubai has proved to be the brand leader.

The catalyst for rapid growth and development was the discovery of oil in 1966, but liberal attitudes have still remained. Dubai has a remarkable leader in His Highness General Sheikh Mohammed bin Rashid Al Maktoum, Crown Prince of Dubai and UAE Minister of Defense. He is a true visionary leader who has consistently adopted a pro-Western and very commercial approach to the development of the sultanate. In contrast to some of the other oil-based economies of the region, Dubai is investing heavily in industry, infrastructure, and tourism. With a vision to turn Dubai into a world-class tourist destination, this approach has established a state-of-the-art transportation, information, communications technology, and utilities infrastructure.

Dubai is now a powerhouse luxury-branded destination offering tourism, logistics, event management, financial services, and more, to the world. Skyscrapers and construction abound, but the real goal is to establish a global brand.

Its strategy has been to establish a brand identity that has associations of political stability, safety, comfort, luxury, and efficiency. The result has been that, although Dubai is situated in the oil-rich Middle East, more than 60% of its revenue comes from non-oil businesses. Even throughout the Iraq crisis and war, Dubai remained focused on its international business strategy and was not deflected or distracted by what it considered were short-term issues.

In fact, in the first quarter of 2003, when the US–Iraq war was under way, Dubai tourism increased by more than 5% compared to the same period in 2002. And profits of Emirates' for the year-end (March 31, 2003) increased by a whopping 95%! Both of these amazing feats were accomplished as the two global industries they belonged to—tourism and air travel—were being hit very badly. (For more details on the airport and the airline, see the Emirates case on pages 89–95.)

Dubai's success in remaining afloat in the wake of debilitating developments such as 9/11 and SARS was a lesson in crisis management. Indeed, in April 2003, the World Travel and Tourism Council (WTTC) used Dubai's success story and crisis management strategy as a specific case study and benchmark in a White Paper for a US government domestic tourism recovery plan.

THE DUBAI BRAND IDENTITY: "BIG THINKER"

Dubai has enormous ambitions for a tiny destination, but they are all based on one single element: vision. There doesn't seem to be any small ideas emanating from Dubai; Dubai thinks big. For example, it is fast becoming a global financial services center. In September 2003, it played host to over 14,000 visitors at the World Bank/IMF annual meeting. This was a big branding event for Dubai, enhancing its image enormously.

Tourism is the fastest-growing part of the Dubai economy, and huge commitments have been made; in fact, 11.6% of Dubai's GDP is invested in this sector. The government's ambition is to increase the number of visitors in terms of hotel guests from a 2004 figure of 5.4 million to 15 million by 2010. In 2004 alone, 23 million visitors used Dubai's airport, so this figure could well be delivered.

Dubai is often called "the shopping capital of the Middle East," with traditional souks (markets) offering an endless array of Eastern goods and crafts exist side-by-side with world-class shopping malls. Traditional bargaining is alive and well in the souks, providing an interesting experience and the opportunity for spectacular deals.

Established only in 1983, Dubai Duty Free (DDF) at the Dubai International Airport, is ranked number three in turnover in the category of global airport retailers. Every day over 1,000 staff complete an average of 21,000 transactions, and yet still give customers a fantastic experience. Want a pair of sunglasses? In DDF you can choose from over 35 brands and 1,500 pairs. DDF has become a very established and famous sub-brand of Dubai already.

The Department of Tourism and Commerce Marketing (DTCM) is the principal authority for the planning, supervision, and development of the tourism and commerce sectors, and its innovative campaigns have greatly increased Dubai's popularity as a year-round destination.

Underlining the importance attached to tourism and commerce development at the highest level, the DTCM's chairman is His Highness General Sheikh Mohammed bin Rashid Al Maktoum. Its director-general is Khalid A. bin Sulayem.

The substantial expertise in DTCM used to promote and market Dubai has helped create global awareness about the Dubai brand. Its commitment to quality and customer satisfaction has made the department synonymous with Dubai tourism and a catalyst for its growth. Its activities have been so well regarded that many other destinations are copying Dubai's way of doing things, and it continues to inspire academic and professional studies. It is evident, after talking to the DTCM director of operations and marketing division, Mohammed K. bin Hareb Al Muhairy, that there is a clear understanding of the difference between building a brand and running a series of campaigns, a fact that many other tourism authorities would do well to take on board.

SELLING DREAMS

Dubai acts just like a consumer luxury brand—it sells dreams and concepts. It is aspirational in its approach to market development. Everything in Dubai is spectacular and consumer-centric. The evolution of Dubai into a destination that offers the best of lifestyle and leisure options has been attracting celebrities from the world of sports, film, and business. Dubai's innovative infrastructure and real estate projects continue to attract unfaltering global interest.

Here are a couple of examples of how Dubai is targeting the rich, the famous, and those who want to be both. These projects are being developed by the private sector in conjunction with the government, and are just two of many projects either planned or already in the process of being built.

"The World"

One Dubai project, called "The World," intends to create 300 new offshore islands set in the shape of a world map. One of the promotional advertisements for "The World" uses the wording, "Introducing the World. 300 private islands. 300 big dreams."

"The World" is a US$4 billion project, due for completion in 2008. The properties will be named after real places, such as "Ireland" and "Thailand." "Utah" island, covering 2.8 acres, will go for US$10 million. Fifteen properties have evidently been sold for a total of US$500 million. The Australian shaped island was sold for US$200 million and it hasn't even been built. Rumor has it that pop star Rod Stewart has bought "Great Britain" for US$30 million, and that Donald Trump has the project in his sights. Don King has already taken a look and no doubt is considering Dubai as a place to stage a global boxing promotion, and possibly to buy an island. All the rich and famous come to Dubai to invest in spectacular and unique projects.

Dubai is very brand-conscious and wants to involve big brand names with its big ideas. Another interesting project is the massive Dubailand, an incredible feat of innovative thinking, designed for both tourism and commerce.

Dubailand

Dubailand is positioned as a one-of-a-kind tourist, entertainment, and leisure project in the region. It has been planned and designed using leading-edge expertise across a spectrum of disciplines. A unique multi-faceted development of pure family entertainment and education, with universal appeal, Dubailand will incorporate a mix of day and night activities, and a variety of accommodations to encourage longer visits and overnight stays. Dubailand projects anticipate becoming landmark projects within the tourism and leisure industry. These landmark projects will be responsive to world tourism trends.

Dubai hopes to attract 15 million tourists by the year 2010. Dubailand is a massive complex, based around the entertainment industry, that will act as a major boost in achieving this goal. The launch phase is already under way and will continue to 2006. This phase will include initial infrastructure such as major roadworks and the enabling of the provision of utilities and other services. Further infrastructure development will be carried out from 2007 to 2010 as more parts of this giant project come on line.

Dubailand will span two billion square feet and feature 45 major attractions. They will include theme parks, a zoo, a water world, a film world, a space center, luxury hotels, a rainforest, dinosaur land, Olympic-sized stadiums, a Formula One racetrack, an equestrian center, and a ski world. When operational, the "Mall of Arabia" in Dubailand will be the world's largest shopping mall.

These attractions, and more, will be zoned into the following categories:

- *Attractions and Experience World:* a family world of theme and water parks, roller-coasters, and adventure using the latest technology for thrills and safety. There are 14 projects in this section of Dubailand alone, occupying 145 million square feet, including:
  - Pharoah's Theme Park;
  - Giants World;
  - Kids World;
  - Global Village;
  - Space and Science World;
  - Space Hotel;
  - Tourism Park;
  - Film World;
  - Desert World Theme Park;
  - Snow World;
  - Aviation World;

- ◆ Water Park;
- ◆ The Castles; and
- ◆ Arabian Theme Park.
- ◆ All the other planned zones of Dubailand described below also have their own list of projects, the zones being:
  - ◆ *Retail and Entertainment World:* retail facilities, including a wide variety of global brands, boutiques, and discount stores—a shopper's paradise;
  - ◆ *Themed Leisure and Vacation World:* a relaxing world of spas, health and well-being;
  - ◆ *Eco Tourism World:* a natural world focused on the beauty of Planet Earth, including desert-based attractions and cultural activities;
  - ◆ *Sports and Outdoor World:* a high-energy world of heroes and champions, featuring a wide variety of sporting facilities; and
  - ◆ *Downtown:* a world of retail, dining, and entertainment facilities for day and night.

And more...

More projects are also under way such as the "Lost City" development with villas, townhouses, and an 18-hole, Greg Norman-designed golf course. (Now, *there's* an interesting brand!) Two palm-shaped islands costing US$3 billion will have Fairmont Hotels & Resorts and Hilton International among the resorts. The first palm-island is under construction and all properties which are sold are either built or under development.

All in all, the scale and speed with which Dubai is gearing up in order to be a global tourism-branded destination is colossal, but Dubai has not lost sight of the fact that attracting businesses into the sultanate is equally important to its future survival, and so it is also catering for the commercial sector.

DUBAI MEANS BUSINESS

Attracting business and foreign direct investment is also a focus for Dubai, and several initiatives to stimulate this have been implemented. For example, Dubai has an Internet City, launched in 2000—the world's first free-trade zone for e-business. It has many other free zones targeted at various segments, including low-volume, high-value commercial and industrial companies. The prospective customer gets all the assistance required, including permission for 100% foreign ownership and zero taxation. Internet City is sold out, attracting over 700 multi-nationals, 25,000 employees from 200 nationalities. IBM, Microsoft, and Oracle, and all the well-known brand names are already there. Another initiative is Media City catering to media firms such as Reuters, CNN, and Associated Press.

The bottom line to Dubai is a boost to GDP in the form of shopping, dining, and property, which help to offset the declining revenues of oil, now only 5% of GDP compared to 35% in 1990.

With the success of Internet City, Dubai has now set its sights on a new target audience—business outsourcers—with the announcement of DOZ (Dubai Outsource Zone). This will be a 70-acre commercial park with a 50-year tax-free status for companies who set up there. Additional key selling points are cheap labor and state-of-the-art infrastructure. Dubai has moved in to fill the gap created by India's rising wage costs and Ireland's lack of available human resources, As usual, companies can expect all their needs to be attended to, including:

- incorporation of foreign subsidiaries within 48 hours;
- visas issued within 24 hours;
- call centers;
- financial research houses; and
- managed and furnished buildings and offices.

THE BRAND EXPERIENCE

Innovation and customer delight are norms for Dubai. It is always evolving its brand in line with customer needs. Importantly, it never ceases to gain inclusivity. Everyone and every organization seem to be behind the brand; there is apparently no intra-brand competition, and each different activity and initiative is on strategy. Dubai constantly seeks to give a great brand experience.

Dubai offers everything a tourist visitor could want, from safaris to sports, cruises to camel racing, arts to beaches, dancing to dune bathing, a vibrant nightlife, and the Dubai Shopping Festival. It also hosts prime sporting and other events, including horse-racing (the Dubai World Cup is the world's richest horse-race), international powerboat racing, the Dubai Air Show, the Dubai Desert Golf

Tournament, the Dubai Tennis Championships, the Dubai Desert Classic (the world's richest golf tournament), and the Dubai Rugby Sevens. It is seen as warm, safe (the crime rate is below 3%), and exotic. Its facilities are among the best in the world.

To businesses it offers speed, flexibility, and an understanding of how to facilitate bottom-line improvement. It is an open market with no exchange controls, quotas, or trade barriers. The perception of Dubai by investors and businesses is similar to that of the tourism sector; it is seen as innovative, friendly, and empathetic. This consistency of Dubai's image across major market segments that matches its intended brand identity has been achieved by design and not by accident, as is the case with all powerful global brands.

Because Dubai has thought through carefully what it needs to do to safeguard its future when the oil runs out, it looks set to become a global destination brand for tourism and commerce—a small destination, but one with big, actionable ideas that delivers on its promises.

SUMMARY

Through its visionary leadership, Dubai has become:

- ◆ one of the world's fastest-growing economies;
- ◆ a regional business hub—a nexus between West and East— with world-class infrastructure and facilities;
- ◆ an accessible market served by more than 170 shipping lines and 86 airlines; and a huge and growing tourist destination with the highest hospitality standards.

From beaches to business to boutiques, Dubai has it all. Dubai shows that small can not only be beautiful, but powerful and rewarding, too—for the nation and its customers.

The main driver of the Dubai brand is undoubtedly DTCM. It has remained at the forefront in branding Dubai in line with the expectations of the industry and the desire to be a big-league destination for business and leisure. As Mohammed K. bin Hareb Al Muhairy says:

> "Branding is at the top of the agenda in terms of strategic importance to the future success of Dubai. Image is everything. Of course, we have to deliver on what we promise, and we will continue to strive to do this—managing the brand is a tough job but absolutely critical. We will endeavor to prove

that our small nation can be a truly global brand for tourism and commerce despite the intense competition from all corners of the world."

Brand strengths

- The government's aim and determination to promote Dubai as a tourist destination.
- Dubai is strategically located between Europe and Asia-Pacific and is just a short flying time from both.
- Aggressive investment in R&D to reach the vision.
- Core competencies in digital technology. Dubai has proved its competencies in different market segments, including aviation, tourism, port management, and free trade zones.
- Substantial expertise in the Department of Tourism and Commerce Marketing. It has embraced almost every technology and medium in order to broaden the appeal and image of Dubai, and thereby maintain brand awareness.

Brand weaknesses

The sheer scale of all the projects, especially Dubailand, is phenomenal, and after all the pre-publicity there is a danger of not meeting investor and consumer expectations. There have been fears and concerns expressed in the recent past by certain sections of society, especially the speculative realtors, about some projects not meeting expectations with respect to returns and completion deadlines.

Like all great brands, Dubai will have to keep its eye firmly on the big picture while also managing the brand meticulously in terms of its operational aspects.

Brand architecture

Dubai is a national brand employing more than one method of architecture. It is trying to control as many aspects of the brand as possible. Clearly, the main similarity with the private sector is its use of "corporate" branding with linked branding (example: Dubailand) and shared branding (example: Dubai International Airport). Dubai is a good example of how a nation can build its brand in a corporate manner.

The national brand is already a powerful regional brand that appears to many to be bigger than the Arabian Gulf. Perception can, indeed, be fact or fiction.

Source

Department of Tourism and Commerce Marketing, the Government of Dubai.www.dubaitourism.co.ae

CONCLUSION

Brand management is tough for any organization or destination. The above cases show determination in this respect. The next chapter examines more closely what brand management is and how it can be achieved.

CHAPTER 13

BRAND MANAGEMENT

INTRODUCTION

So far, this book has focused on brand strategy, but good strategies are relatively ineffective unless they are managed well, both internally and externally across markets.

The really smart companies in the world of branding accept the fact that powerful brands are the only route to survival and differentiation. They occasionally have massive worldwide defining moments of truth in the form of a major crisis, but they also recognize that they face moments of truth every day in terms of the brand–consumer relationship and experience.

As brands exist only in consumers' minds, every contact with consumers can potentially be a moment of truth. This philosophy is similar to that described by the former CEO of Scandinavian Airline System (SAS), Jan Carlsson, who simply and effectively told his entire workforce that with 12 million customers a year and an average contact rate per customer of five SAS people on a single journey, this translated into 60 million moments of truth—60 million moments to get the brand experience right or wrong. His message was that *all* touch points with *all* consumers count, and companies have to look meticulously at how they can manage these. That's brand management thinking.

BRAND MANAGEMENT ISN'T EASY

"If only it was that easy," say many people with responsibility for turning around a company's or (re)building a brand's image. But if we study what Carlsson said and did, it wasn't just rhetoric—he changed structure, systems, technology, and many other things, and—importantly—empowered staff at the frontline to take decisions that impacted immediately on the consumer's brand experience. He succeeded in bringing the SAS brand to life by motivating and empowering employees so that they saw their contribution to the value of the brand and the business. In short, he created a massive organizational change project based around the brand–customer relationship and involving every function in the company. It was no easy task.

The big challenge for CEOs such as Carlsson, and for brand managers in charge of major corporate and/or product brands, is to bring the brand(s) to life through strategy and change, and to motivate people to deliver on the brand promise. This is particularly important for those involved in any business that uses a corporate or house/endorsed branding approach.

Great brands are built on consistency, and this necessitates consistent and appropriate behavior in all areas of operation. But consistency depends on clearly defined brand strategy. This is where the skills and influence of brand managers need to be at their peak. Ask yourself and your colleagues the following questions:

- Is the brand vision and platform clearly articulated in written statements?
- What is currently happening in each area of the organization to manage the brand consistently?
- What needs to be done to improve management of the brand in each area?
- Are you making the right brand architecture decisions; decisions that will impact on the customer experience?

What the above really boils down to is the need for companies to build a strong brand culture.

Living the Brand: Developing a Strong Corporate Brand Behavior and Culture

Companies are judged by their behavior. Everything they say or do affects their image and reputation. In order to build a powerful corporate brand with a corresponding image, the behavior of the company has to be controlled and shaped in such a fashion that people's perceptions of it are always favorable. This also makes for good customer relationships; corporate behavior perceived in a negative way will give rise to poor relationships.

One of the roles of brand guardianship is to manage corporate behavior, and this role is both vital and wide-ranging. However, to develop a powerful corporate brand image, where the company is the center of attention and where customers interact frequently with the company's representatives, a whole brand culture has to be built around the brand and what it stands for.

Corporate Image, Branding, and Culture

Corporate culture is a much-discussed topic these days, as companies try to accommodate modern work practices and to change management styles. Many sophisticated training and organization development initiatives are implemented by internal and external specialists to suit current corporate cultures, and to help promote efficiency and effectiveness for the future. Corporate culture, in its crudest form, is described as "the way we do things around here." Essentially, it is the sum of a complex blend of employee attitudes, beliefs, values, rituals, and behaviors that permeate a company and give it a unique style and feel.

Corporate culture can have a profound effect on both staff and customers. For staff, it can provide an invigorating, stimulating, and exciting place to work, or it can make going to work a dismal daily experience. It can empower people or enslave them. Because culture is ubiquitous, it inevitably has an impact not just inside, but also outside the organization. Customers who come into contact with staff can feel it through the morale, attitudes, and expressions of the staff, and see it in the staff's comments and service standards. Corporate culture impacts considerably on corporate image in both negative and positive ways, and has to be controlled.

When a company tries to develop and maintain a good brand image, it has to create a suitable culture. If the company is creating and maintaining a corporate brand, a service brand, or whatever, then the culture has to be appropriate to the essence of the brand. Branding is a very positive and well-received way of changing the culture of an organization.

When building a new corporate culture or changing the existing one, companies often do this by establishing what their brand really stands for and creating values as a behavioral guide for people to follow.

BRAND MANAGEMENT AND REPOSITIONING

Finally, brand management is concerned with evolving the brand in order to keep it relevant to its customers, as their needs and wants change over time. Sometimes the dynamics of the markets change, too, and a company finds itself with more businesses and a somewhat outdated image. Brand architecture issues come into play as more business activities and brands emerge internally as the company grows. For all these and other reasons, brand managers sometimes have to reposition their brands to ensure modernity, relevance, and attractiveness. The Wipro case is a good example of a company that has repositioned itself and managed the brand across several businesses.

PETRONAS is highlighted for various reasons, but especially because the company is trying to manage all aspects of the brand, and has realized that if internal branding isn't done well, then the external brand image will never be what is expected. Petronas is trying hard to build a strong brand culture that will be capable of giving a great customer experience at all touch points.

Raffles International has been chosen as the third case study, as it is known for its constant quest to provide a better customer experience. It is also a good example of how a company has had to expand via acquisition without endangering the separate brand identities, yet linking them via a carefully thought-through brand architecture. In this case, the company brought together two separate brands that enjoyed different corporate cultures that gave customers very different experiences. The skillful Raffles International team has managed to keep the cultures, join the brands, and enhance the experience of two customer bases.

Brand management is tough. These three cases provide examples of management teams that are determined to manage their brand well, and of the benefits that can result from strong and thoughtful brand management.

CASE STUDY 26—WIPRO

Repositioning and Managing the Brand across Different Businesses

★ ★ ★ ★ ★

Brand management sometimes has to deal with the growth of the business and how the brand can effectively cover all situations. In some cases, it is about managing the perceptions of consumers to present a different image that is more relevant and attractive to the markets that the brand currently targets. The case of Wipro is a good one to illustrate this. Not only did it have to manage its brand image as it changed its business direction, but it also had to create a brand architecture that would be capable of covering a multi-business structure. This case shows that branding for technology companies is an imperative, and also demonstrates the tremendous impact of Indian brands in technology markets.

WIPRO: "APPLYING THOUGHT" AND DIVERSIFYING SUCCESSFULLY

The Indian giant, Wipro is the world's first PCMM Level 5 and SEI CMM Level 5 IT services company. Wipro provides comprehensive IT solutions and services, including systems integration, information systems outsourcing, package implementation, software application development and maintenance, and R&D services to corporations globally. In the Indian market, Wipro is a leader in providing IT solutions and services for the corporate segment; it also has a profitable presence in niche market segments of consumer products and lighting. In the Asia-Pacific and Middle East markets, Wipro provides IT solutions and services for global corporations.

THE BRAND STORY: THE ROAD TO SUCCESS

Wipro had its beginnings in 1945 when Western India Vegetable Products Limited was incorporated in India. The company was started as an oil-crushing unit making hydrogenated cooking oil. Later, in the 1970s, Wipro embarked on an ambitious phase of expansion.

The vegetable products factory gradually grew into a consumer products group, manufacturing soaps, and then entered the infotech area. Successful diversification, restructuring, and transformation from being a consumer products minor to an IT major has been Wipro's unique strength in its 60-odd years of existence. Its turnover went from Rs 40.82 million in 1965/66 to Rs 104.09 million in 1970/71. The first diversification came about in 1975, in the form of hydraulic cylinders and fluid power components.

In the early 1980s, when India was on the threshold of an IT boom, Wipro entered the infotech area and tasted early success through its R&D efforts. With the success of R&D in India, it was natural for Wipro to look at the global market to grow the business. That was the beginning of its most profitable business, Wipro Technologies.

Today, Wipro has over 30 offices across North America, Europe, and Asia, with annualized revenue of US$1.6 billion in combined IT businesses and a market capitalization in the region of US$10 billion. Wipro was ranked fifth in the world in *Business Week*'s rating of the "Most Profitable Global IT Services Companies." Azim H. Premji, the company's chairman, was declared the richest man in India and ranked among the top 50 billionaires in the world in the *Financial Times*' top billionaires rating for 2004.

Wipro currently has the following businesses:

- *Wipro Technologies:* the global IT services business.
- *Wipro Infotech:* provides customers with high-value IT solutions, infrastructure service, and platforms in India, Asia-Pacific, and the Middle East markets.
- *Wipro Consumer Care and Lighting:* the FMCG arm of Wipro Limited, which continuously introduces innovative products and adds value to existing brands.

◆ *Wipro Fluid Power Limited:* addresses the hydraulic equipment requirements of mobile original equipment manufacturers in India.
◆ *Wipro GE Medical Systems Limited:* the market leader, with unmatched distribution and service reach in South Asia, and India's largest exporter of medical systems.
◆ *WEP Limited:* a leading IT peripherals solutions and services company in India.

Wipro's clients include Microsoft, Sony, Toshiba, ABN Amro, City of Toronto, Dubai Government, General Motors, and Nokia.

THE BRAND PROMISE

The brand name Wipro was devised by Azim Premji in 1979 as an acronym for Western India Products. Fortunately for him, the name was unique and gave the feel of an international company. By the early 1990s, Wipro had spread its wings by expanding into various products and services. The Wipro product portfolio had soaps such as Wipro Shikakai, baby products under Wipro Baby Soft, hydraulic cylinders branded Wipro, a PC business under the brand name Wipro, a joint venture company with GE named Wipro GE, and software services under the Wipro brand. The Wipro logo was an alphabetical "W," but there were no clear guidelines for using the logo in a uniform way.

In my opinion, Wipro was late in realizing that the organization wasn't leveraging its brand name across the various businesses. The main issue at hand was the possibility of using a uniform identity and personality for a diverse organization such as Wipro. More importantly, could the Wipro brand reflect similar values to its customers, who could be businesses or even families? It was only in 1996 that Wipro undertook a branding initiative. Research at this point showed that Wipro as a corporate gave an impression of being:

◆ ambiguous and small;
◆ not integrated—there was no strong linkage between the different businesses;
◆ not easy to do business with and lacking in warmth;
◆ not associated with any visual mnemonic; and
◆ not dynamic—seen as a "me too" organization.

However, the negative associations were an outcome of no corporate brand philosophy being communicated internally or externally.

The only positive side was that Wipro was seen as a company that was trying, and making or providing fairly good-quality products and services. At this time, Wipro started its brand-building journey. The corporate brand name was to be made the pivot, and it was decided to research the use of an umbrella brand strategy. This strategy was advantageous because it synergized the strengths of the different business units under a single brand name, helped to reduce the cost of maintaining multiple brands, and gave consistency to the brand image.

Wipro conducted a large-scale research study among consumers in order to find the right emotional connection. The research included over 50 focus groups for testing four positioning statements and five logos. Everyone from housewives to heads of IT departments was included in the sample set. The research was a breakthrough, and what emerged out of it adorns every Wipro office, product, and employee today.

In 1998, the new brand promise and tagline "Applying thought" was unveiled. A rainbow flower was the new visual identity of the brand. The flower was seen as warm, caring, and flamboyant, with a tagline that appealed to the right (emotional) side of the brain. The new brand represented three things about Wipro:

- It was thinking for the customer.
- It was providing innovative solutions.
- It was a solid company looking for continuous solutions.

But going one step further, this rather rational-looking brand was enhanced by a more balanced rational–emotional personality.

The entire process of brand building, and the Wipro brand promise of "Applying thought," carved out a unique personality for the brand. The Wipro brand personality has the following traits:

- trustworthy;
- humane;
- competent;
- warm;
- having integrity; and
- innovative.

Wipro leverages on its vast experience and hands-on technology expertise to offer not just IT solutions, but solutions for an IT-centric business environment. This implies that it understands not just technology, but businesses where it will be employed.

THE WIPRO BRAND TODAY

Wipro has experienced exponential growth over the last five years. It has been aggressive in acquisitions and is making giant strides. In 2004, Wipro landed what was regarded as a breakthrough deal with Sony Corp.: a US$5 million contract to write IT applications for its TV and computer assembly plants in the United States. The deal ensured future partnership, too. Proving itself to giants such as Sony, Compaq, Nokia, and Home Depot is vital to the Indian company's strategy. Wipro also ranks as one of the world's largest R&D contractors, with 4,000 engineers designing chips and telecom equipment for top US electronics companies. Since 1997, Wipro's software exports have leaped nearly fivefold. In the recent past, it has won contracts from Lehman Brothers and Delta Air Lines, along with a US$70 million deal from National Grid Transco PLC, a British power and telecom utility company. Wipro broadened its services with its recent acquisition of India's top call center, Spectramind, which handles everything from computer help-desk support to airline reservations.

In 1999, Premji hired Vivek Paul from GE, in the United States, to put the company at the forefront of the global race. The Indian-born maverick has taken Wipro to stratospheric levels, and Wipro has contributed heavily in making India an IT superpower. Paul says, "Clients used to tell us to drop down and do 100 push-ups. Now they say, 'We want you to lead.'" If Wipro can keep clients happy, there is nothing stopping it from becoming a lord of the IT ring.

Brand strengths

- ◆ Global recognition.
- ◆ Strong top management.
- ◆ Customer-oriented.
- ◆ Aggressive.

Brand weakness

Imagery is only IT-focused (keeping in mind the consumer products business).

Brand architecture

Corporate branding for all IT services, with shared sub-brands (example: Wipro Technologies) and product branding for consumer products (example: Santoor Soap). Wipro tends to keep its corporate name when the brands are close to its core businesses.

Sources

- ◆ Corporate website, www.wiprocorporate.com.
- ◆ *Business Week*, November 25, 2002.
- ◆ Various articles from www.domain-b.com.

CASE STUDY 27—PETRONAS

Malaysia's Global Brand Ambassador

BACKGROUND

PETRONAS, the acronym for Petroliam Nasional Berhad, was incorporated on August 17, 1974 and is wholly owned by the Malaysian government. The *Petroleum Development Act 1974* vested in PETRONAS the entire ownership and control of petroleum resources in Malaysia. Ranked among the Fortune global 500 companies, PETRONAS is an integrated international oil and gas company with business interests in more than 30 countries.

The group is engaged in a wide range of activities, including upstream exploration and production of oil and gas to downstream oil refining; marketing and distribution of petroleum products; trading; LNG, gas processing, and transmission pipeline network operations; petrochemical manufacturing and marketing; shipping; and property investment.

PETRONAS recognizes the significance of balancing economic, environmental, and social objectives in all its business undertakings without compromising the needs of the present and future generations. The group is therefore committed to sustainable development, giving utmost priority to protecting the safety and health of its employees, and the local communities, as well as preserving the environment and its biodiversity. Various community projects in the fields of education and health, among others, have been and will continue to be undertaken, some of which are referred to later in this case study.

During its growing years, PETRONAS developed a mission statement to provide clarity of purpose, a strong set of shared values that remain at the core of its corporate culture, and a vision statement that defined its future direction. All of these elements were the foundation upon which PETRONAS' unique identity began to take shape in the minds of its domestic and global stakeholders.

THE CORPORATE VISION

The vision statement is much like that of many other corporations, fairly general; in this case, it is: "To be a leading oil and gas multinational of choice."

THE CORPORATE MISSION

The mission of the company articulates four statements:

- We are a business entity.
- Petroleum is our core business.
- Our primary responsibility is to develop and add value to the natural resources.
- Our objective is to contribute to the well-being of the people and the nation.

CORPORATE SHARED VALUES

Petronas has four shared values, which are defined as:

- *Loyalty:* Loyalty to nation and corporation.
- *Professionalism:* Committed, innovative, and proactive, and always striving for excellence.
- *Integrity:* Honest and upright.
- *Cohesiveness:* United in purpose and fellowship.

THE DEVELOPMENT OF THE BRAND

In the late 1990s, in line with its vision and aspirations, PETRONAS moved increasingly into the highly competitive and volatile global arena. It began to compete with major multinationals with long histories that were already household names with established corporate identities, such as BP, Shell, and Exxon-Mobil.

By this time, too, PETRONAS was fully involved in the broad spectrum of the industry, as well as in areas outside of its core business. Its growing and diverse portfolio of companies included some that didn't even bear the Petronas name. Its workforce had swelled by several thousands, embracing people of diverse nationalities from around the globe.

Against this background, it became increasingly critical to create a clear and consistent understanding of what PETRONAS stood for as an organization among all of its global stakeholders, not least of all its employees. In order to compete effectively in the global arena, it would need to proactively manage the development of a strong, consistent identity for the PETRONAS group as a whole. PETRONAS thus embarked on a brand-building exercise aimed at articulating and ensuring the successful delivery of its business promise consistently throughout all significant touch points within the group.

The brand journey began in 1999 with an analysis of stakeholder perceptions, giving a clear picture of the brand strengths and weaknesses. This effort culminated in the crafting of a brand essence, which encapsulated the founding philosophy and values of the organization and linked the mission, vision, and shared values into a single statement.

PETRONAS felt it reaffirmed what the organization stood for and was capable of connecting emotionally with the outside world. Internally, it would create a new impetus for the development of a strong and brand-led business culture. To reinforce and provide clarity for its day-to-day stakeholder interactions, a set of corporate brand values was created, enabling PETRONAS to forge enduring stakeholder relationships and build distinctive value for the brand.

From the time of its inception, PETRONAS has aspired to advance humanity through business by returning the value that it creates to its stakeholders in a meaningful and sustainable manner through the sharing of benefits, experience, knowledge, and wealth. At the very heart of this philosophy is the company's aspiration to excel in its business performance, thus enabling it to share its success with the nations and communities wherever it operates.

PETRONAS has always been very particular about doing things right; professionally, ethically, and morally. It has an impeccable reputation.

DRIVING PETRONAS TO GLOBAL BRAND STATUS

PETRONAS uses a variety of means to promote and manage its brand globally. The next section of this case study provides a brief overview of a number of key methods it employs in this respect. Before that, however, we will first take a look at its early entry into the global brand world through the platform of Formula One.

Formula One as a Global Branding Platform

PETRONAS first entered the highly competitive and prestigious world of Formula One motor racing in 1995 with the deliberate aim of positioning itself as a global brand. Since then, Formula One has not only catapulted PETRONAS' image on to the international stage, but has also fast-tracked its experience in high-tech fields, advancing both the company and the nation to the brink of a new technological frontier.

The PETRONAS partnership with Team Sauber provided IT with an ideal test-bed for its products and has since made significant advancements in various aspects of automotive engineering. Most significant are the breakthroughs in fuel and lubricant development achieved by Malaysian engineers who developed the advanced, fully synthetic PETRONAS Syntium engine lubricant and the Primax Formula One fuel, both powering the Sauber PETRONAS Formula One cars.

The glamor and high profile of motor racing aside, there is a deeper underlying and more socially conscientious motivation at the heart of PETRONAS' pursuance of automotive and racing technology. The technological expertise and insight acquired by PETRONAS through the various technology transfer projects is ultimately reinjected into the very pulse of the nation, thus providing impetus to the company's ambition of helping Malaysia to reach the status of being a fully industrialized nation.

Using the concept of partnership for growth, PETRONAS, through the Sauber Petronas Engineering team (SPE), has shown its determination to develop its human capital. Perceived as national heroes for their significant contribution to the local engineering industry, the Malaysian SPE engineers have achieved numerous successes over the years.

PETRONAS' serious involvement in an array of motor sports activities, inclusive of Formula One, is driven by its desire to harness a deep reservoir of technological expertise. It is envisaged that this powerhouse will have the potential of advancing national growth and instilling the seeds of interest in high-end technology among future generations.

Managing the Consistent Development of the Corporate Brand Globally

We saw in the previous section how PETRONAS has successfully leveraged its strategic involvement in Formula One to build its global profile. Today, its association with powerful brand icons such as Formula One and the PETRONAS Twin Towers greatly facilitates its entry into new markets while reaffirming its standing among existing stakeholders.

Since it launched its corporate branding efforts at the turn of this millennium, it has introduced a number of branding initiatives aimed at further building and enhancing the PETRONAS corporate brand across the span of its global operations. This section provides some insights into how the company manages its employee brand communication programs, as well as the various methods it engages to ensure the consistent development of the corporate brand group-wide.

Employee Brand Engagement

PETRONAS understands that key to the success of any branding initiative is the company's employees, who ultimately represent the brand. At the outset of its branding efforts, therefore, a conscious decision was taken to focus on engendering internal buy-in of the staff, so that any subsequent efforts to communicate the brand externally would be clearly supported by their actions and behaviors.

With this in mind, the company held an internal launch of its brand essence and values to senior executives from across the group. An internal brand communication program was carefully planned and executed to create meaningful engagement with the brand that would, ultimately, inspire desired behaviors. An employee brand communication package was designed to articulate the brand messages in a manner that would win the hearts and minds of employees, and also, just as importantly, guide them through what it means in their day-to-day interactions with stakeholders.

Subsequently, a comprehensive series of road shows was undertaken throughout the group's operations worldwide to promote global consistency. Today, every new employee is initiated into the brand at entry point so that nothing is left to chance.

Brand Integration Programs

To promote a more brand-led business culture within the group, brand workshops were held with several key units in the corporate center that play a key role in shaping and defining the organizational culture. It was recognized that PETRONAS' systems and processes needed to be aligned with the brand in order to support brand delivery.

Subsequently, a pilot was undertaken to institutionalize branding into a key business unit interfacing with domestic stakeholders—Petronas Dagangan, which operates its retail business. An important part of organizational learning to be built upon, this pilot forms a springboard for other subsidiaries operating within the PETRONAS group to leverage the corporate brand strengths while growing their respective global businesses.

Strategic Brand Direction

Building a great brand, as we know, takes many years and an awful lot of hard work, commitment, and discipline. It also requires rigorous planning, execution, and monitoring. Underpinning its seriousness in this respect, PETRONAS' management established a Corporate Brand Unit to spearhead, direct, and manage its corporate branding exercise. Today, the unit provides strategic brand direction and guidance to units within the PETRONAS group of companies on matters impacting the corporate brand. Among other things, it works in close collaboration with key business units within the group, as well as with PETRONAS' regional and global representative offices worldwide, to formulate brand positioning strategies for PETRONAS' entry into new markets and to ensure that any brand promotion or development programs are aligned with the aspirations of the corporate brand.

Corporate Brand Website

To further promote consistent understanding of the PETRONAS brand among employees, a corporate brand intranet website was created. Aside from information about the brand essence and values, it contains guidelines for the development of any printed communications such as reports, brochures, and newsletters undertaken by members of the group and a user-friendly guide on execution of the company's corporate identity/logo. The website also contains an interactive section on the principles that drive the planning and design of the company's corporate environments to ensure experiential consistency throughout its global offices.

Corporate Brand Architecture

It is easy to become overwhelmed by the sheer magnitude of this challenge, but the trick lies in maintaining simplicity in the core brand platform across the broad spectrum of the business. Anchored in very universal human values, PETRONAS' brand essence and values have broad appeal across all cultures and peoples, and are therefore capable of creating meaning in many different contexts.

At the same time, the corporate brand essence and values are capable of being interpreted at many different levels throughout the business. The corporate brand architecture, by determining that the many sub-brands and product range brands of the group reflect off the mother brand, helps to maintain clarity and consistency in approach across the group. At a corporate brand level, the brand essence and values provide an over-arching meaning to all of PETRONAS' diverse investments, while at the business level they can be translated into differentiated product or service offerings that are meaningful in the context of those businesses.

Brand Audits

One of the key challenges for PETRONAS in working toward global brand consistency is to maintain a constant watch on how its brand is surfacing and performing in the various aspects of its diverse portfolio across the breadth of its global operations. An important part of this exercise involves a brand audit. Commencing with an overview of the visual identity of the company, the exercise aims to promote greater consistency in the visual manifestation of the brand, including through its corporate identity, stationery, livery, uniforms, and corporate gifts or merchandise. Subsequently, this effort will necessarily encompass all other activities undertaken by the group that impact upon the corporate brand, including its stakeholder engagement programs.

PETRONAS AS A GLOBAL BRAND AMBASSADOR

All aspiring nation brands need good corporate ambassadors. The ambassadors of a nation's brand are not just government agencies—they are every company that ventures into foreign markets, and everyone a tourist meets. National and corporate brands have a symbiotic relationship that can work very favorably for all. For example, the United States, with its associations of freedom and success, has been a catalyst for the development of brands such as Levi's, Nike, Timberland, and others. Conversely, Coca-Cola, MTV, and Intel have helped to boost the image of the nation via their sheer global presence.

Italy is associated with fashion and style, and this perception has been driven by brands such as Armani, Versace, Prada, and Gucci. Brands like Ferrari have also put Italy on the brand-shopping list. So strong is the influence of these mental associations that some Asian brands have escaped their country-of-origin negatives by using Italian-sounding names (for example, the Hong Kong clothing company Giordano). Germany is associated with precision engineering, and feeds off brands such as Mercedes-Benz and BMW, just as the brands themselves do with the "Made in Germany" label. France is the home of chic, with Chanel, Dior, L'Oreal, and other brands.

By contrast, there is little surprise that Canada isn't seen as a high-tech country (a perception it wants to encourage) when it has few technological flagship brands or brands that publicize their country of origin. Suffice to say that brands that move around the world help to improve a nation's image, not to mention its "bottom line." They are national brand ambassadors.

PETRONAS falls into the brand ambassador category. Malaysia desperately needs to strengthen its brand image. As a nation, it has accomplished a great deal, but few people in the world are aware of its successes and talents. PETRONAS is helping Malaysia globally with its image. Not only is it highly respected by the global business fraternity, but it is helping to put Malaysia on the radar screen of ordinary people around the world. When international research was carried out on Malaysia as a tourist destination in the late 1990s, the country was an unknown to many travelers. The global reach and brand communications of PETRONAS have aided the awareness of the national brand and enhanced the image. The only problem Malaysia has now is to find more companies like PETRONAS.

THE FUTURE DEPENDS ON STRONG BRAND MANAGEMENT

PETRONAS has realized that having a brand strategy is one thing, and implementing it is another. The world's best brands have the skills to keep their eye on the big picture, the vision, but also meticulously manage the everyday detail needed to build a strong brand culture.

PETRONAS is clearly trying very hard to manage the brand properly; no easy task inside a giant corporation. No doubt mistakes will be made and lessons learnt, but this relatively young and fast-growing company has made a great start.

Brand strengths

- Determination to create a global brand.
- Creation of a corporate brand management unit.
- Perseverance in developing a brand culture.
- Willingness to invest in the brand as a strategic asset in its own right.

Brand weaknesses

- The brand isn't yet globally recognized and accepted—this will take time.
- If the brand mentality is to permeate throughout the group, more resources may be required, and more specialized training and development of brand champions needed.
- With reference to the above point, a major challenge will be managing the brand experience across different cultures and countries where the business operates.

◆ Greater consistency across brand architecture would help the corporate brand.

Brand architecture

Corporate branding (example: PETRONAS), shared branding for some subsidiaries but not all (example: PETRONAS Carigali), and some endorsed product branding (example: PETRONAS Syntium).

Source

PETRONAS Brand Management Unit.

CASE STUDY 28—RAFFLES INTERNATIONAL LIMITED

The Lifestyle Creator

★ ★ ★ ★ ★

In 1989, Raffles International Limited was formed as the hotel management arm of Raffles Holdings. Since then, Raffles International has quickly become very well respected in the hospitality industry for its standards of excellent service quality, innovations in hotel management, and award-winning concepts. Raffles International markets its hotels and resorts under two main brands: Raffles Hotels & Resorts and Swissotel Hotels & Resorts. It also has a sub-brand called Raffles Amrita Spa, and it appears to be creating another brand with its customer relationship management program called Raffles Capital.

Brand architecture has been a source of much debate for many brands in Asia as they try to expand and cater for more market segments. Raffles has also had to take some tough decisions in this area of brand management. This issue is discussed below.

An Award-winning Lifestyle Master Brand

Raffles International has often been described as a leader in the hospitality industry with a proven record in creating lifestyle experiences that define the highest standards of service excellence. Owning the title as a creator of lifestyles, Raffles International has extended its master brand to include signature food and beverage concepts, luxury Amrita Spas, its private-label Raffles Shops, and Raffles International-branded lifestyle events. These signature quality lifestyle concepts and products are innovative extensions to the Raffles International branding.

Raffles International has been given a huge number of awards for its hotels and resorts over the years, and the flagship hotel—Raffles Hotel, Singapore—received yet another on September 16, 2004 (aptly chosen, as this was the 117th anniversary of this famous hotel). In the *Condé Nast Traveller* readers' survey 2004, it was voted "Favorite Hotel in Asia" and number two in the world, ranked according to excellence in service/staff, food/restaurants, ambience, facilities, and location.

Raffles International is now a huge group and owns and manages a large number of properties globally. What is probably most surprising is that it has done this in a relatively short space of time, as brand-building goes. Jennie Chua, chairman and CEO of Raffles International, says of the brand:

> From one legendary hotel in 1989, we are now a global group with hotels across Asia, Australia, Europe, North America, and South America. However, we believe that building our brand equity is not a numbers game. We believe that for a brand to be successful, in addition to an integrated approach in our marketing and communications of our brand, we must consistently deliver what customers have come to expect of that brand.

This type of comment is heard infrequently, and only from chief executives who combine the skills of business development with a passion for branding. In any business you have to deliver the numbers, but large numbers don't necessarily equate with powerful brands that stand the test of time. Sometimes it is tempting to go for the "quick buck," and many sales-driven companies do. They are usually the ones that run out of steam (and customers) in the long term and compete to a large extent on price. The enduring brands that provide sustainable profits and asset growth over time are managed by that rare breed of people who can deliver the numbers while building customer satisfaction, emotional associations, and brand loyalty.

Raffles must at one stage have had a dilemma to deal with: how to grow a business hotel chain quickly, when the luxury hotel and resort business takes time to develop. The answer was for Raffles International to buy a hotel chain, but while this took care of some of the numbers, the luxury fit wasn't there, and thus there was a brand architecture issue to deal with. Let's look at this in a little more detail.

THE RAFFLES BRAND ARCHITECTURE ISSUE

Luxury hotels and resorts are hard to buy and expensive to build. From one hotel in 1989, how could Raffles achieve its global brand ambitions? Successful luxury hotels are rarely for sale. Well, Raffles International did buy luxury hotels and gained management contracts that enabled it to put its name on others, and still does so, but this is a limited business strategy. Raffles acquired the Swissôtel Hotels & Resorts group. The acquisition enabled Raffles to achieve volume—essential to success in the hospitality sector, where the old maxim still remains: "Get people into bed as often as possible"! The problem was that these weren't luxury chains, and so decisions had to be taken about whether or not to link brand names.

Master Brand Endorsement Challenge

Bearing in mind that Raffles was and is the master brand, the question was: should Raffles put its brand name on Swissôtel and its other acquisitions? Raffles management had to decide how to keep the brand equity of all the famous brand names in the portfolio, and yet build up the equity of the Raffles International master brand.

Two scenarios spring to mind: (1) linking the two might damage the Raffles luxury brand; and (2) a linkage of some form might lift the image of the acquired brand.

Basically, the Raffles brand is in the business of selling lifestyle. The Raffles-branded hotels and resorts are positioned to attract affluent leisure and business travelers, while Swissôtel hotels aspire to offer quality and comfort to modern business travelers.

Both successful branded hotels and resorts have different target audiences and brand images, and this poses important questions. For example, linking the Raffles exclusivity and luxury to the lower-tier brands may dilute the high-end Raffles-branded hotels and resorts' image, as the affluent rich and famous guests might not take kindly to losing the exclusivity of the Raffles brand name if attached to Swissôtel. On the other hand, Swissôtel business guests may be attracted by the fame and service of hotels that bear the Raffles name.

It appears that Raffles International chose to keep the two brands separate, and link them via endorsed branding. The separation isn't absolute, and is accomplished by keeping the endorsement "A Raffles International Hotel" below the hotel or resort name in taglines for corporate identity and communications. The "Traveler's Palm" (a brand design device), which is a part of the Raffles International logo, is only used for the Raffles-branded hotels and resorts, while Swissôtel has a totally different representation.

The resulting decision for Raffles, then, was to keep two distinct stand-alone brands, Raffles Hotels & Resorts and Swissôtel Hotels & Resorts, with minimal linkage via website and a management name endorsement. The parent company says in its literature that "Raffles International markets its hotels and resorts under two brands."

THE TWO BRAND OFFERS

Raffles Hotels & Resorts is a collection of luxury hotels located in major cities around the globe and distinguishes itself by the highest standards of products and services. Each hotel is a landmark in its respective city, and most are positioned at the top of their local markets.

Swissôtel Hotels & Resorts is a distinctive group of deluxe hotels for today's discerning modern business and leisure traveler. It combines individual, modern, and functional design with local character and renowned standards of Swiss hospitality, service efficiency, and product quality. Located in gateway destinations and city centers, the hotels offer convenient access to business and shopping districts and local attractions.

Below is a brief description of how the two brands differentiate their offerings based on the wants and needs of separate targeted customer groups.

The Raffles Lifestyle for Luxury-seeking Travelers

Flexible check-in and checkout

Raffles Hotels & Resorts has taken quality service standards to new heights by introducing flexible check-in and check-out.

Spa facilities

Apart from excellent quality services, Raffles International has created a spa facility that combines the legendary Raffles name with the Sanskrit word "Amrita," and will help to position the spas to leverage on the strength of the Raffles name. Originally just called "Amrita Spa," and looking like a stand-alone brand, the name has been changed to "Raffles Amrita Spa," which clearly positions it as a sub-brand of Raffles. Managing director of Raffles Hotels & Resorts, Markland Blaiklock, says: "This name change is geared to brand the spas with the hotels they are associated with—namely, Raffles hotels." Raffles Amrita's own private-label aromatherapy products will be available at its spas and Raffles Amrita Spa boutiques. At the end of 2004 there were eight spas worldwide, and this number is expected to increase.

Raffles shops

Underpinning the company's objective to present guests and clients with an opportunity to enjoy yet another lifestyle experience, Raffles International also operates Raffles Shops in its hotels and resorts. The merchandise carried in the stores ranges from essential sundries to exclusive and specially commissioned merchandise.

Raffles International-branded events

In keeping with its philosophy of creating lifestyle products for its guests, Raffles International also hosts and organizes various elite social and sporting events. They include the Raffles International Wine & Food Festival, the Raffles International Polo Championship, the Raffles International Cup, and the Raffles Gala Christmas Tree

Auction & Dinner. These annual events provide a platform for Raffles International to further enhance its master brand while at the same time showcasing its expertise in lifestyle creation.

Raffles Capital: Recognizing and rewarding customers

A recent development is the introduction of Raffles Capital, a customer relationship management program that offers to the most frequent residents both experiential and aspirational rewards and privileges that are "customized, once-in-a-lifetime experiences, premium merchandises and lifestyle-themed rewards." Membership is by invitation only, with pre-defined selection criteria. The design of the name and logo is distinctive and makes the rewards program appear like another Raffles product or sub-brand. Raffles Capital even has its own tagline: "Recognising Raffles residents."

The Swissôtel-brand Approach

Swissôtel is offering service in the tradition of its brand values—warm, reliable, and efficient. This brand targets mostly casual business travelers who are seeking convenience and one-stop accommodation integrated with business solutions. The attributes of Swiss precision and reliability, normally linked to the country of Switzerland, are not usually accompanied by warmth, and it is most likely that this brand value has been added to strengthen that area, which is a "must have" in the hospitality industry.

With its distinctive global collection of hotels and resorts, the Swissôtel brand name is now quite well known by world business travelers. Fundamentally, the hotel is aimed at providing extraordinary product quality and renowned standards of Swiss hospitality, along with individual style, design, and local character.

The warm, reliable, and efficient hotel

Swissôtel has a committed, dedicated team of professionals to coordinate meetings and functions with precision and efficiency—typically Swiss. The team coordinator takes care of all requests by customers and liaises closely with them, and all departments within the hotel, to ensure that everything goes smoothly and according to plan.

The hotel also provides venues for formal and casual gatherings. The banqueting teams at Swissôtel can create and customize unique menus to suit special occasions or to satisfy health-conscious or other lifestyle tastes. For memorable and festive events, the hotel can coordinate complete themed events, including planning and catering services, at a Swissôtel venue or off-site.

Passionate service and the finest tradition of Swiss hospitality

The global sales team of Swissôtel provides integrated sales assistance for all hotels worldwide. The sales team is dedicated to responding to all enquiries promptly within 24 hours to ensure that all details are addressed. Together with the "Travel Incentive" programs in place, Swissôtel has developed some powerful motivator programs to help inspire business travelers with a wide collection of destinations throughout the Americas, Asia, Europe, the Middle East, and the Mediterranean. These programs are intended to assist and provide the right environment for business travelers to realize their business goals and encourage team productivity.

Swissôtel.com: A new look for a key customer touch point

The website for this brand has been enhanced to provide visitors with easy access to information on properties, services, and promotions. It also allows for quick reservations. In 2004 the number of visitors and online reservations made on the Swissôtel website increased by over 80% and 50%, respectively. According to the managing director of Swissôtel Hotels & Resorts, Meinhard Huck, "This clearly indicates that the Internet is an important touch point for us to maintain and enhance relationships with our existing and new customers."

SUMMARY

Raffles International has become a global brand in a relatively short time. It has expanded its empire rapidly without losing sight of the customer, and has an unrelenting pursuit of quality. Its future is already assured as one of the most admired hotel and resort chains in the world.

Brand strengths

- ◆ Depth of branding expertise.
- ◆ Top management commitment.
- ◆ Dedication to quality.

Brand weaknesses

◆ Difficulty in acquiring more really top-class hotels around the world.
◆ A small brand management team that will need to increase as the business grows further.

Brand architecture

Corporate and endorsed branding—two principal sub-brands (Raffles Hotels & Resorts and Swissôtel Hotels & Resorts) endorsed by the parent company (Raffles International). Under the Raffles sub-brand is shared branding (Raffles Amrita Spa and Raffles Capital).

Sources

◆ Corporate websites, www.raffles.com and www.swissotel.com/homepage.asp.
◆ *Raffles World,* December 2004–February 2005.

POSTSCRIPT

An announcement made on July 18, and reported on July 19, 2005 in the *Wall Street Journal,* told the world that Raffles Holdings Ltd. had sold its entire business to Colony Capital LLC from the United States for a whopping US$859.1 million.

According to the chief executive of Raffles Holdings, Jennie Chua, if the business was to be competitive, it needed to operate on a global scale, and the investment and cash calls needed to do that were just too onerous. Although year-on-year revenues were increasing, it appears that the decision was made by shareholders (in particular, CapitaLand, which owned 59.7%) to unlock the value of the business and place the funds elsewhere, most likely in its core business of real estate development.

What will Happen to the Brands?

The buying and selling of brands is of concern to many stakeholders, including customers, but the new owner, Colony Capital, stated that it will retain the Raffles and Swissôtel brands and expand both chains, especially in Asia. When brands are successful, as Raffles' brands were, it is advisable not to tamper with them except to evolve them over time in line with customer expectations. Colony Capital is clearly cognizant of that fact.

It is somewhat surprising that the jewel in the Raffles crown—the world-famous Raffles Hotel—has been sold, but both sides say that things won't change. The hotel is designated as a national monument in Singapore. The Singapore government will continue to have control of future renovations, and Raffles Holdings will still own the memorabilia, which will be on loan to the new owner. There is also reported to be an option for Raffles Holdings to buy back the hotel at the market price in 2087.

Raffles Holdings will be left with a 45% stake in the Raffles City development owned by another company that has two hotels, a shopping mall, and a convention center. As for the shareholders, the price gives a premium of 64% over the company's net tangible assets. Brands are valuable strategic investments and assets.

CONCLUSION

Holistic brand management is usually the chosen route for companies that put the brand first; they believe that branding is total and continuous organizational change. The next chapter examines how brands are built and managed in a holistic way.

CHAPTER 14

HOLISTIC BRANDING: TOTAL ORGANIZATIONAL CHANGE

INTRODUCTION

I have left this chapter to the end of the book, for I hope it will make a lasting impression on the reader.

To my mind, the most impactful reason why many Asian brands have not achieved global status is that they have not approached branding in a holistic manner. All too often we see the "cosmetics" of branding—the superficial glamor of advertising, promotion, events, logos, and so on—plenty of up-front, in-your-face brand communications, but a sad lack of delivery behind the easily made brand promises.

The top brands in the world manage to put brand strategy and management together in almost a magical way. But the truth is that there is no magic. It is hard work and involves meticulous management of all the activities in an organization.

Branding must be seen as a total organizational change concept. In the earlier sections of this book there has been mention of all the touch points that a brand can have with its customers; this applies to any organization, whether public or private sector, B2C or B2B. Great brands get to where they are by giving the customer a great brand experience in every possible way. And this doesn't mean merely training frontline staff to be nice to them; it means making sure that every possible contact there may be will be appreciated and valued.

The brand management wheel (see Figure 14.1) outlines just some of the areas that anyone managing or responsible for a brand needs to look at.

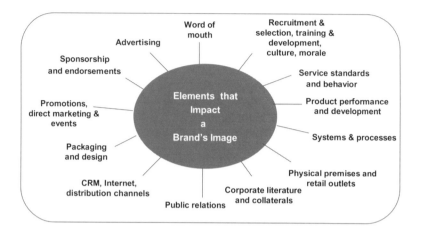

Figure 14.1   Brand management wheel

The point I want to make most strongly is that it is of little use having a brand strategy if it isn't executed properly and consistently over time. To do that, those responsible for the brand must keep an eye on and remain true to the brand's vision, values, and so on—the big picture of where they want the brand to go and what it stands for—but also they have to manage meticulously every aspect of the brand's interaction with customers. This is a difficult job.

The two brands that I have chosen for this chapter are both from Malaysia. In one sense, this choice at first sight makes little sense, in that Malaysia has few internationally successful brands, and neither of these companies features on global brand radar screens. But at second sight it makes a lot of sense, as Malaysian brand owners are now catching up rapidly with their Asian counterparts and competitors. The change in mindset in this country, spurred on by the government, is bringing major repercussions to the captains of industry.

Neither of these companies are famous brands. Nor for that matter are they well-known brand names outside their industries, but they deserve such recognition for what they are attempting to do and the manner in which they are doing it. They will no doubt receive accolades in the future.

I admire both companies, because the top management teams have decided that the brand should run the business and not the other way round. They are using brand as a vehicle for corporate strategy and are changing their respective organizations in every way to make this happen.

I have chosen these two companies because of their bravery in biting the bullet and embracing real holistic branding; a decision that has made them completely change the way their companies and brands have been managed in order to achieve future international brand success. Both are taking considerable risks in the face of orthodoxy, but they both have top managers who understand what it takes to create a major regional and/or international brand.

The first case is Opus International Group plc (formerly known as Kinta Kellas plc), which is a B2B professional services brand; the second is Pensonic Holdings, a B2B and consumer electronics brand. Neither company has completed the total organizational change programs that they are undertaking, and thus some information concerning ongoing brand strategy execution is excluded for reasons of confidentiality. Both firms are fundamentally changing everything in every part of their organizations in order to build a powerful brand, and so far the results are looking very good.

Opus is a government-related project management consultancy company that is part of a huge conglomerate with wholly owned subsidiaries overseas. The Pensonic Group is a private-sector, family-based listed company specializing in consumer household electronics that has influenced government to support Malaysian corporate branding efforts, working closely with MATRADE, an export promotion division of the Ministry of Trade and Industry.

CASE STUDY 29—OPUS INTERNATIONAL GROUP PLC

Where Branding Means Commitment to Total Change

★ ★ ★ ★ ★

This case starts with a description of the company using its former name (Kinta Kellas plc). The change of name of the brand, to Opus International Group plc, was just one important part of a huge re-branding and repositioning exercise to create a powerful international brand.

Kinta Kellas plc is an industry leader in project management of large-scale transportation infrastructure and infrastructure development projects. Originally a tin mining company when it began in 1926, Kinta Kellas has a rich corporate history. Today, it extends beyond project management into facilities management services for expressways, infrastructure, and built environment.

Kinta Kellas is an asset management and development company—"assets" meaning property and construction, not financial assets. It is a professional and specialized consultancy, and is a part of the huge U.E.M. World Group of companies. As a Malaysian company, it has been the proud manager of most of the huge infrastructure projects that have put its country on the world map, such as the North-South Highway, the 1998 Commonwealth Games Stadium, and many others.

But the heady days of huge projects required by government have virtually gone in Malaysia, and Kinta Kellas, in its endeavor to move forward in a continually changing and sometimes turbulent operating environment, had to make urgent decisions about its future strategic direction in the face of the more challenging economic environment ahead, coupled with international liberalization and competition.

The group managing director, Suhaimi Halim, realized that the route to success in an ever-changing world, where parity rules, is branding. He understood that only a strong brand can provide the means of differentiation necessary for long-term survival and profitability, and that a strong brand name can actually be worth multiples more—in dollar terms—than the other tangible assets of the company.

Suhaimi explained:

> Like many companies, we are faced with challenges that arise from shifting trends in the domestic market, the need to expand internationally, and a need to change our business accordingly. Whilst considering our response to these challenges, the opportunity arose to re-name our main company in Malaysia and link it with our fully owned subsidiary in New Zealand.
>
> We decided to take full advantage of this situation to change our whole business, but there had to be a focus for this, and we decided that the catalyst for change should be the brand. By this I mean we needed to develop a brand strategy that would drive all the changes necessary for us to be successful in the future.

We knew that a brand-driven business means holistic change and that it would be no easy task. We have been working hard at this now for over a year, and are in the midst of changing mindsets, systems, processes, procedures, services and communications. Nothing is to be excluded.

It is a challenging and exciting time, but the brand implementation is already bringing benefits to us. We are determined that Opus International Group plc will become a global brand name.

Kinta Kellas thus decided to seek out new strategies to retain its position as a leading provider of project management services domestically, and a leading supplier of road asset management services in New Zealand, where it has a 100% fully owned subsidiary called Opus International Consultants Ltd., formerly a part of the government public works department. This meant that the company needed to be more efficient in its services and to accelerate its growth and performance, including introducing new and improved quality and added-value services.

However, several challenges were ahead that needed urgent attention, identified as follows.

THE BRAND IMAGE AND ARCHITECTURE CHALLENGES

Kinta Kellas has an image challenge to overcome if it is to forge greater growth and brand preference. The name is still perceived, to some extent, as being that of a mining company, although it has achieved some degree of new brand awareness. There is a perception gap—internally and externally—as to what Kinta Kellas was and now is becoming. There is also another heritage factor—that of parent company U.E.M Group (see below). Kinta Kellas has very specific targets and not the mass market, but the need still exists to develop trust in the company and an image driven more by emotional associations and less by rational factors.

There is also the issue of brand architecture. The parental image has some previous negative imagery, which has to be carefully handled. Additionally, a subsidiary company has achieved more awareness as compared to the parent company. Consequently, there are brand architecture challenges to overcome, such as should Kinta Kellas grow via stand-alone brands or should it try to lift its image through association with them? Would a Kinta Kellas endorsement add to or dilute other brand images, and what would be the financial consequences of the strategic alternatives?

The architectural strategy for managing such a combination of brands within the company, at this moment, is still unclear, and so these and other questions need to be resolved urgently within the context of the international business strategy.

THE NAME ISSUE

Kinta Kellas had to make a very important decision in 2004—whether to change its name to support the intended corporate and brand strategies. Not only did it have to face a domestic market that was moving away from large infrastructure projects and so shift its business focus to managing assets as well as developing them; it also had to move more into international markets. Its wholly owned New Zealand subsidiary, Opus International Consultants Ltd., had already got a broad business balance and a solid brand name in and out of New Zealand.

It was decided that the Kinta Kellas brand name would not travel well across markets and cultures, but that "Opus" would, and so the new organizational name of Opus International Group plc was adopted to replace Kinta Kellas. This decision was to have many implications for all aspects of the business, not the least brand communications. However, first the new entity needed a brand platform to move forward on that tied in a master brand to the New Zealand brand.

THE BRAND PLATFORM ISSUE

The Kinta Kellas brand had no clear brand vision, but management realized that a powerful brand vision that connects the future of the brand emotionally with consumers across all markets and segments is vital; that true value lies in the emotional power of the brand itself, which leads consumers to pay price premiums and gives companies higher margins.

But the brand platform wasn't clear, and needed to be reviewed. A brand personality (set of brand values) would be needed to support the new brand vision, and these two brand elements would be used to develop a strong brand culture. In a service organization, these elements are essential for differentiation and building strong relationships with clients, suppliers, investors, and others.

Brand positioning statements would also be required to help create a communications strategy that would pull all messages together consistently across all international markets, and develop brand awareness for the new brand name.

THE NEED FOR A COMPREHENSIVE BRANDING STRATEGY

In sum, Kinta Kellas needed a comprehensive brand strategy in order to defend and improve its business, market share, and profitability, and to expand internationally. It was agreed that this strategy should be driven by a powerful vision, supported by relevant brand values and a clear differentiation path via positioning statements.

The top management of the company also saw the need to undertake a clear review of the systems, processes, and culture that would enable the new brand promises to be delivered. The company's philosophy was that power brands drive everything in successful businesses, and that this approach should be adopted by Kinta Kellas, under its new name of Opus International Group plc.

THE MAKING OF THE NEW OPUS BRAND

If a company doesn't know where it stands with respect to its brand image, then it is difficult to move forward, and so Opus began its brand journey with a brand audit to assess its strengths and weaknesses.

The Brand Audit

As a part of the brand audit, a selection of people from inside the organization were interviewed as well as a substantial number of external third parties, such as government officers, contractors, suppliers, clients, and others. The results were in some ways expected and in some ways a bit of a shock. Positives and negatives were clearly identified in terms of the brand's current image as perceived by various audiences. Interestingly, the company also received valuable feedback as to where everyone's future expectations lay, and how the image could be improved.

The Brand Vision, Personality, and Positioning Process

All powerful brands have a brand vision that drives their business strategy. Brand vision defines what the brand stands for emotionally in the minds of consumers; it is really the brand's dream. It is the brand's guiding insight into its world.

After analysis of interview research findings and two top management workshops in Malaysia and New Zealand, a brand vision statement for Opus was agreed and written. The next step was to agree a set of brand values that would support that vision by constructing a brand personality.

The Brand Personality

Many successful companies use closely defined brand values to attract and retain customers. The aim of defining brand values in terms of a personality and its characteristic traits is to take the focus away from ordinary attributes and features, and move toward the kind of relationship companies want to establish with consumers, and consumers wish to have with them.

The brand personality characteristics for Opus were agreed as follows (with the meanings of the words defined in brackets). The brand personality contained both rational and emotional elements.

- ◆ **Rational**
  - —*Innovative* (Creative, Resourceful, Entrepreneurial)
  - —*Professional* (Commitment, Knowledgeable, Expert)
- ◆ **Emotional**
  - —*Caring* (Warm, Approachable, Friendly, Helpful)
  - —*Trustworthy* (Reliable, "Can Do," Timely)
  - —*Versatile* (Responsible, Flexible, Fast, Active, Open-minded)
  - —*Energetic* (Fun, Passionate, Proactive)

The more rational personality traits tended to be brand strengths of the company, but it was seen to be weaker on the emotional side, which isn't surprising for a professional technical consulting business. The strategy, therefore, was to maintain the strengths and eliminate the weaknesses. However, the characteristic of "Innovative" was regarded as essential to transform the business and the brand image, so this was one of the personality traits that attracted more focus when the brand implementation started.

BRAND MANAGEMENT STRUCTURE

The development of the brand, as described above, had to be inclusive, with commitment from both the Malaysian and New Zealand sides. To this end, the vision, values, and positioning statements were subject to a process of iteration, with involvement from both sides via management workshops. But importantly, a structure was put into place to ensure that everything to do with brand implementation was agreed, synchronized, and implemented in all geographical areas of the business.

Early on in the strategic thinking process, a brand management committee (BMC) was set up to facilitate this process and in anticipation of the tasks to be determined under the implementation program to follow. This is essentially a top management team, chaired by the chief executive, that takes all important decisions regarding brand implementation, and gains support from the board of directors where necessary.

As soon as the brand strategy elements were agreed across the companies, then a brand working committee (BWC) was created to look at all the details of the brand transformation and implementation over the next two years, to 2006. The BWC reports to and receives direction from the BMC regarding focus, priorities, and high-level decisions for brand execution.

BRAND IMPLEMENTATION

The task of implementing the new Opus brand is ongoing, but certain activities have already taken place. The critical issue to enable the repositioning of the brand is described well by the general manager, group human resources and administration, Tunku Siti Raudzoh Tunku Ibrahim, who said:

> Human capital is the key to any professional services brand, and at Opus we are focusing very hard on training, development and performance management systems that are linked directly to the brand.
>
> We have trained a pool of trainers so that everyone can understand not just what the brand means, but how they can

impact on it in their everyday work. After all, everyone is a brand ambassador for the company, and they will be recognized and rewarded for performing well in this role. To help them, every employee, from the top management to the receptionists, has undergone training to represent the brand in a way that is relevant to their work, but consistent with our desired image.

Talking of receptionists, we have also renovated our reception area and staff working spaces to reflect the new brand personality. A new corporate visual identity is in place and the website has been revamped. We have a detailed public relations program in place and each department has submitted plans for how they will bring the brand to life. We believe that a strong brand is the only route to sustainable success, and it is our people that will make it happen.

Below are a few of the activities the general manager is referring to.

Brand Action Planning

The first phase of brand implementation was to get senior management groups to work out plans for action in executing the brand strategically across all business units. This involved a series of workshops with prioritized short- and long-term goals as the outputs.

These workshops were then taken down to departmental level, with a similar process and outputs at a more functional and specific level. While these were going on, a Training-of-Trainers program was designed and developed so that the brand could be rolled out to all staff, to explain to them what the brand was, and to help them think through how they could contribute in their jobs both individually and in their teams.

Brand training handbooks

For the brand training programs, a brand handbook was produced for all staff, to be used as a vehicle for training as well as for information purposes. A trainer's guide was written for the trainers. Both of these booklets were used by the trainers in their practice sessions.

The trainers' programs have now been completed for both Malaysia and New Zealand, and the roll-out to all employees started in the second half of 2005 following the launch of the new brand name in May.

Induction and Orientation

The brand has now been incorporated into the orientation and induction programs, so that all new employees are told about the importance of the brand and why they should reinforce it within their job scope.

Human Capital

Opus understands that people must be recognized and rewarded for performing well on the brand values, just as they are with other important aspects of their work. This will reinforce the training initiatives, and make employees realize that the company is taking its brand image seriously. This motivation is important in building the brand culture with speed.

- *Recognition:* The recognition of people who help make the brand come to life is important and can be achieved in many ways. Opus has already embarked on a scheme to recognize employees who have performed well on one or more of the brand values, which includes possibilities such as:
  - role model recognition;
  - nominations for awards;
  - values performance certificates;
  - an Opus annual award for outstanding all-round brand performance; and
  - team awards for certain important areas, such as innovation.
- *Rewards:* Rewarding people in monetary terms by incorporating values performance into annual performance appraisal schemes has proved to be very effective, and it shows the seriousness with which the company is taking its brand-building task. People should be rewarded for their good performance on the brand values.

Linking pay, increments, and promotions to the brand values via the annual appraisal scheme does this. It entails the analysis of jobs at various levels, and possibly role model analysis, to determine what constitutes good and not so good performance on each value. While it isn't easy to do, it certainly motivates employees and lets them know that the issue of branding is of high importance to the company's future.

With this in mind, Opus has begun to devise ways in which it can incorporate the brand into its performance management scheme, in conjunction with other aspects of individual scorecards.

Corporate Communications

With the introduction of a new brand name, inevitably there has to be a carefully designed and managed corporate communications strategy. This was the responsibility of the BWC with the final green light given from the BMC, and it consisted of mainly corporate identity changes and a public relations plan.

Corporate identity manual

Opus decided not to change its logo and to base its corporate identity on that of the New Zealand subsidiary, but there were many changes to make. A new corporate identity manual emerged that produced consistency across the companies and guidelines for all aspects of communications.

Public relations plan

An agency was selected and briefed to work with the BWC to produce an appropriate 12-month plan to take the company up to and beyond the brand name change. This included looking at all the target audiences that needed to be informed about the new brand and what it stood for, and why the re-branding had been done. As Opus is an international group, the public relations plan had to take into account careful timing of announcements across markets, as well as events and media placement.

Brand strengths

- Top management commitment to holistic branding.
- Support from all associated companies and subsidiaries.
- Genuine desire of employees to embrace change.

Brand weaknesses

Currently under-resourced in brand management and marketing.

Brand architecture

Corporate.

Source

Opus International group plc.

CASE STUDY 30—PENSONIC HOLDINGS BHD

Building a Regional Brand Holistically

★ ★ ★ ★ ★

BACKGROUND

Pensonic was founded by Dato' Seri Chew Weng Khak in Penang in 1965. It was first known as Keat Radio & Electrical Co., but in 1977 the business was incorporated into a private limited company under the name of Keat Radio Company Sdn. Bhd. (KRC). In 1994, Pensonic Holdings Berhad (PHB) was incorporated as an investment holding company to consolidate the various companies under the Pensonic group and as the vehicle for its listing exercise. PHB was listed on the Second Board of the Kuala Lumpur Stock Exchange in 1995.

Initially the company was appointed as the distribution agent of Japanese products, but Dato' Seri Chew realized the threat of depending solely on Japanese products, which are relatively more expensive, and the possibility of the principal withdrawing the distributorship. The name "Pensonic," which means "sound from Penang," was conceived in 1982 by Dato' Seri Chew. PHB is based in Penang (an island in northern Malaysia, also known as "Pearl of the Orient"), with its manufacturing plant located at the Prai Industrial Estate (on the mainland of Malaysia).

Pensonic was conceived with a vision to provide local consumers with locally made audio appliances at more affordable prices. Various branches were set up, and as business subsequently improved, audio and visual products from Original-Equipment Manufacturers (OEM) were imported in 1982 and marketed under the "Pensonic" brand name. In 1988, the Pensonic group began to manufacture its own products under the "Pensonic" brand. The group now manufactures and distributes a full range of electrical home appliances under the "Pensonic" brand.

In August 2004, Pensonic announced that its new assembly plant located in Bukit Minyak Industrial Estate in Prai was due for completion and would soon begin operations. When it is completed, the new assembly plant is said to be able to produce up to two million fans and 70,000 washing machines annually. On December 18, 2004, Daffodil Computers Ltd., an information, communications, and technology (ICT) company in Bangladesh, signed a partnership agreement with Pensonic. Under the accord, Pensonic, in collaboration with Daffodil Computers, will develop the market for its electrical home appliances in Bangladesh within one to two years, and will then look into the viability of setting up a manufacturing plant in Bangladesh.

THE PENSONIC CHALLENGE

Pensonic is not a great brand—yet. It has many challenges to overcome, but it is determined to use brand strategy as the vehicle for growth and development. The main challenges it faces are:

- the B2B2C connection;
- indifferent consumer perceptions of the brand, and non-emotional associations;
- the lack of a prestigious brand image; and
- the threat of in-bound competition, especially from China, at the lower end of the market.

A brief analysis of these issues follows.

The B2B2C Connection

Although Pensonic produces domestic consumer goods, it distributes them through a network of over 800 distributors and agents, from hypermarkets to tiny one-man stores. So, although it communicates with its customers through advertising and promotion, it doesn't really come face-to-face with most of them. It relies on a scattered dealership to represent the brand. Relationships with the distributors have been good overall, and this was how the founder built the business. But as the demographic and psychographic profile changes, motivating and supporting them becomes an increasing and vital factor in Pensonic's success.

On the B2C front, it has used event management to its advantage but has only communicated with mass consumers by newspaper advertising. Pensonic realizes that it needs to get much closer to consumers if it is to establish an emotional bond with them. It has plans to do so, as you will see later in the case.

Indifference and Lack of Emotion from Consumers

Pensonic has operated at the high end of the lower, and the lower end of the middle, income segments and until recently has dominated a field of mainly local competitors. It has avoided competing with the Japanese middle to higher brands, such as Panasonic and Sharp. It has therefore placed itself in the commodity area of the market, where the traditional fighting ground has been price and, to some extent, quality. Nevertheless, it has done well in this area and is the number one in its local Malaysian market.

Because of the "value for money" approach to marketing, brand loyalty hasn't been good and consumers at this level don't have much emotional attachment to the brand. Past years of quality problems, common to all the producers in this category and segment, have not helped and there is a somewhat indifferent consumer attitude to the brand.

The Lack of a Prestigious Brand Image

All in all, the above issues have meant that Pensonic has a very high level of brand awareness, but a relatively low level of brand esteem. As if this wasn't enough, over the last few years, cheap copies of similar products are flowing into the market from China, eroding the lower end of the customer base.

The Threat from China

Pensonic products are targeted to lower- and middle-income groups, with about 15% of total products manufactured exported to Thailand, Indonesia, Hong Kong, the Middle East, Sri Lanka, and Vietnam.

The group imports about 40% of its raw materials and components, with a substantial part from China. It now faces its own low-cost competitors, as Chinese companies that have tired of supplying the world with cheap parts now want to reap richer profit margins by turning themselves into global players. With the flood of cheap Chinese products, prices for Pensonic products have been under pressure. Brand building is seen as the key to moving back up the value chain and into sustainable profitability with the ability to raise prices rather than lower them.

China's exports to Southeast Asia grew 27% to US$23.57 billion in 2002 over 2001, and Chinese companies have seized a 30% share of Malaysia's 29-inch TV market, up from just 9% in 2001. Their share of Malaysia's DVD market soared to 25% in May from 7.8% in 2001.

Solutions to the threat from China

Pensonic bought equipment to churn out electronic products, but when the Chinese products start to trickle in and multinational companies that were engaged in a price war in China itself were starting to export their own lower-priced products, Pensonic wrote off that investment and instead began to buy entire units made in China. It also used China-made products instead of locally made parts to cut costs, and managed to lower the costs by 40%. Pensonic revenue grew by 25.6% for the 12 months until May 2004.

The products that carry Pensonic are targeted at the lower- to middle-income groups, but it is expanding its brand portfolio to move into other segments. On top of that, the company is also expanding the regional reach by scaling up distribution in Vietnam, Thailand, and Sri Lanka. Pensonic has also engaged in production for other labels of well-known Japanese and international companies under Original-Equipment Manufacturing (OEM) and Own-Design Manufacturing (ODM) contracts. By undertaking OEM/ODM contracts, Pensonic is on a fast learning curve to world-class quality, but it must not rely on the OEM/ODM business for its future if it is going to build a strong brand.

Pensonic is also signing contracts with neighboring countries' manufacturers to help distribute its appliances in their countries. It has signed contracts with HIFI Orient from Thailand and Daffodil Computers from Bangladesh. Pensonic has plans to expand its regional market to China, India, Laos, and Cambodia.

Pensonic's products are designed specifically to cater for Southeast Asian preferences—for example, blenders with stronger blades, and fans with sturdier motors and better circulation.

THE SURVIVAL GUIDE FOR PENSONIC

Pensonic took a good, hard look at its position and the changing market dynamics, realized that it couldn't compete on price alone, and that it must create a distinct difference between itself and its competitors. The main way to achieve that point of differentiation was seen to be the strengthening of its brand name.

While the brand work was going on over a couple of years, Pensonic had to survive and grow. Basically, its survival guide included working on the following areas of the business.

- importing components and finished goods from China;
- making appliances for other major companies;
- selling abroad;
- getting government aid;
- choosing partners with care;
- nurturing relationships;
- starting to build a brand name; and
- overhauling financial management.

The rest of this case is concerned with the branding element.

BRANDING PENSONIC

Pensonic has now created its first ever brand strategy, defining how it wants to be seen externally, and what it needs to do to achieve its desired brand image. The first step it took in developing this strategy was to carry out a brand audit.

Brand Audit and Vision

The process of developing the brand strategy began with an audit of what people from both inside and outside the company thought about the brand currently and where they saw opportunities for improvement of its image in the future. Included in the one-to-one, in-depth research interviews were suppliers, distributors, and retailers of Pensonic products.

As this research was carried out by an independent brand consultancy, the data provided was very honest, objective, and clear.

A top management workshop followed that took into account all the data from the brand research audit, and used this as the basis to create a vision, personality, and positioning statements for the Pensonic brand that would clearly differentiate it from the competition.

At the heart of Pensonic's brand strategy is a brand vision statement, which is focused around the key emotional trigger of "enjoyment" and the quality of life of its customers. After the vision statement was written, a brand personality (set of brand values) was agreed that would form the driving force for changing everything in the company that would help the vision to become reality.

The Brand Personality

Pensonic chose four personality traits (brand values) to help deliver its vision:

- innovative;
- trustworthy;
- caring; and
- a leader.

These four traits were carefully defined. If the vision and values were consistently brought to life, Pensonic management felt that the customers would get a great brand experience. The top management team realized that building a brand isn't just limited to communications, but that it also involves delivering on the brand personality traits across all departments inside the company.

As Dixon Chew, group managing director, said:

> We want all ranks in the organization to live the brand—from the cleaner to the CEO. Specific brand training and workshops are conducted to instill the Pensonic brand vision and values into everyone. We are now planting the seeds of the Pensonic brand in the entire organization to build a strong brand culture. We want all employees to carry and display the brand values in their daily work. The whole organization will be the future driving force to elevate Pensonic into a powerful brand.

It is very refreshing to hear words such as these from a chief executive. Branding is a top-down process and has to have total commitment from those who are responsible for strategy and results. Of course, these must not just be rhetoric, but have real substance in action. Dixon Chew started to put these words into action by creating a total organizational change program to align everything to the brand strategy and change the mindset of all employees and business partners.

ORGANIZATIONAL CHANGE

Pensonic's branding initiatives were broadly classified to focus on seven categories, namely:

- innovation, product design, and development;
- quality;
- customer relationship management and customer service;
- public relations and events;
- advertising and promotions;
- corporate support; and
- governmental support and recognition.

Innovation, Product Design, and Development

At the soft launch of the brand in late 2004, Chew said:

> . . . on innovation, product design and development, we have put in place our infrastructure for this critical function by establishing Product Design & Development teams in China, Hong Kong and in our Headquarters at Penang, Malaysia. For Pensonic, quality is a key pillar for its branding endeavor. Continual quality improvement through reinforcement of Pensonic's quality assurance processes and procedures for in-house manufacturing is a daily event.
>
> We have also established a Quality Assurance Team in Zhuhai, China to ensure that Pensonic's outsourced manufacturing is also subject to the same exacting standards and quality that we have defined for Pensonic products. The design and R&D team in Zhuhai, China has been expanded, and is also carrying out R&D on new material for heating elements for application on to electrical home appliances. (*Note*: A heating element is a core-component for electrical home appliances besides the motor-element.)

To further leverage our quality assurance capabilities, cross-training and expertise-sharing programs between the team at our HQ and the China and Hong Kong team are also in place.

Customer Relationship Management (CRM)

Customer relationship management and customer service are areas which we are now building up to support the Pensonic brand. Major activities that we have embarked on are:

- Our toll-free call center facility is already in place.
- Flagship showrooms cum customer-care centers were built in Petaling Jaya, and at the Penang and Prai headquarters.
- A customer-care team is now established to handle customer complaints and service needs, to provide guidance to customers, etc.
- We have established better communication channels with our business partners through:
  — dealer visits, particularly by the senior management of Pensonic;
  — conferences;
  — a quarterly newsletter to provide updates of the various brand-building activities that we have carried out for Pensonic; and
  — the Pensonic website, which has been recently revamped, to provide easy and user-friendly access by both our business partners as well as end-consumers.

In addition to this, Pensonic is developing a CRM-based loyalty program that recognizes and rewards high-value, medium-value, and other dealers. The main idea is to tier the dealers, and encourage them to support the Pensonic brand and in turn support them with greater levels of service, promotions, and even sales training. Pensonic recognizes that its dealers are the lifeblood of the business, and that if it helps them to build their businesses then they will reciprocate, resulting in a win-win situation.

Public Relations and Events

Pensonic is placing greater focus on public relations activities and events due to successful past experiences in elevating the image of the Pensonic brand in both the domestic as well as export markets. Some notable public relations activities that the company organized in 2004 included:

- the signing ceremony of the distributorship agreement with Pensonic's Thai business partner, Hifi Orient (Thai) Co., Ltd. in Bangkok, which was witnessed by Y. B. Dato' Seri Rafidah Aziz, Malaysia's minister for international trade and industry, together with other Thai ministers and officials;
- a media-tour by seven Hong Kong media groups to cover the event and Pensonic in Thailand and Penang; and
- in July 2004, the grand opening of the Pensonic Hong Kong office, which was again officiated over by Y. B. Dato' Seri Rafidah Aziz.

Advertising and Promotions

Other than the regular advertisements in the press media, printed media, and the like, Pensonic has also put more resources into the following promotional activities to enhance the awareness and image of the Pensonic brand:

- local and overseas trade fairs and exhibitions;
- road-shows and promotional circuits in various states in Malaysia; and
- redesigning of Pensonic billboards throughout Malaysia, which started in 2005.

Corporate Support

As Pensonic continues to grow with the support of its business partners, the company has acquired a new warehouse facility adjacent to its existing office in Petaling Jaya so as to better serve the central and southern regions of Malaysia. It has also completed the construction of a new plant at Bukit Minyak Industrial Park that will add 83,000 square feet of production area to the now 160,000 square feet in two existing plants to expand production capacity.

Pensonic's business model is basically to bring production back into Malaysia once economies of scale in terms of sales and quantity have been reached for a particular category of product. Due to tariff preferences under the ASEAN Free Trade Agreement, and the focus of Pensonic in ASEAN countries, the company is able to achieve cost-competitiveness to compete even with China's products. This is also in line with Pensonic's aspiration to be a regional brand in Asia. This move is contrary to what many companies are now doing—outsourcing their production to China—and this has clearly impressed the Malaysian government.

Government Support and Recognition

To build Pensonic into a powerful Malaysian brand in the region, governmental recognition, support, and assistance are of paramount importance. As Chew says:

> We are glad to record that, from Pensonic's experience, our government has been very receptive to and supportive of Malaysian-owned brands and in promoting deserving Malaysian brands into regional and global brands. Pensonic is thankful to the Malaysian government, in particular MITI and its agencies—MATRADE and MIDA, for giving the Pensonic brand its due recognition.

Among the governmental recognitions Pensonic has obtained are the following:

- the only electrical home appliances brand selected as one of the 20 leading and prominent Malaysian brands for Showcase Malaysia 2003 during the NAM (Non-Aligned Movement) 13 Summit;
- the first company to obtain approval from MATRADE for the Brand Promotion Grant for the export market; and
- approval by MATRADE to use the logo "MADE IN MALAYSIA FOR THE WORLD."

Top Management Brand Ambassadors

CEO Dixon Chew, and group executive director Vincent Chew, talk constantly about the Pensonic brand wherever they go, and to every audience they can.

Pensonic held events to mark the inaugural Pensonic brand launch in Malaysia, Hong Kong, and Bangkok in late 2004, with the branding consultancy that helped them to develop the strategy showing guests how the Pensonic brand had been developed. The two top executives explained where the brand was going in the future and said to the assembled guests:

> We trust that with this event you are able to see that Pensonic is putting its full commitment into building the Pensonic brand into a powerful Malaysian brand in Asia.
>
> We are very thankful to each and every one of you who are present here today to spend valuable time with us in understanding the vision, aspiration, and values for the Pensonic brand. I am very confident that with your continual support, the Pensonic brand would be able to achieve its aspiration of "Pensonic for Asia." Many more branding events and activities for Pensonic are already being planned for the next two years to ensure that the brand identity and image of Pensonic is elevated to the status as we have envisioned it to be. It is Pensonic's commitment to work closely with all our business partners to reap sustainable growth and profitability for the long term together. Pensonic will be a true friend to all of you, now and into the future.

BRAND MANAGEMENT

Pensonic is continuing its organizational change process. No part of the organization is to be left untouched by the brand. The management of the company recognize that, despite having a strong strategy for future brand development, it will take time and everyone in the organization will need to contribute.

Lee Yew Weng, the group financial controller, summarizes the Pensonic commitment and philosophy when he says:

> The way we manage the brand is of prime importance. We need to formulate brand initiatives for all touch points with the customers to support the brand vision and values that we have defined. These initiatives, if carried out with focus and diligence, will transform into core competencies within the organization. These core competencies will form the pillars of the Pensonic brand. They are the differentiating factors for the Pensonic brand and would be difficult for competing brands to imitate.

Summary

Pensonic is a brand on the move, having developed from a small family firm into a regional enterprise. Top management has realized that the only way to survive in a commoditized market is to develop a powerful brand image. Although much has been done, there are still many initiatives to take. Pensonic has to reposition itself as quickly as it can to combat increasing levels of competition, but with a determined top management team there is no reason why it cannot reach its desired regional brand status.

Brand strengths

- A founder willing to give succession managers backing and commitment.
- A dedicated team of brand believers at the top.
- Proactive change management.
- Willingness to invest in brand building at all levels.

Brand weaknesses

- Some quality issues to resolve in some product areas.
- Not enough brand management and marketing expertise as yet.
- Still some OEM dependency.
- The need to get consistent and better brand management and communications across all countries and markets.

Brand architecture

Corporate, with product descriptors (examples: blenders: PB – 323, PB 501, PB – 330G).

Sources

- Pensonic corporate headquarters.
- Pensonic Holdings Berhad website, www.pensonic.com.
- Yahoo search engine, http://search.yahoo.com/search?fr= slv1-&p=pensonic.
- "Sink or Swim," *CFO Asia*, October 2, 2004, www.cfoasia.com/archives/200410-02.htm.

- "Manufacturing: Low Intensity Export Wars," *Far Eastern Economic Review*, August 28, 2003, www.fsa.ulaval.ca/personnel/vernag/eh/F/cause/lectures/Low-Intensity%20Export%20Wars.htm.
- Business Bangladesh website, http://businessbangladesh.info/all_file/bizbreeze.htm.
- "Pensonic to Open Indian Assembly Plant," *Appliance Magazine*, August 13, 2004, www.appliancemagazine.com/news.php?article=7283&zone=0&first=1.
- Bursa Malaysia website, www.klse.com.my/website/listing/lc_old/pensoni.htm.
- Matrade website, www.matrade.gov.my/matrade_virtual_exhibition/mbn/electrical-and-electronic/pen.htm.

CHAPTER 15

CONCLUSIONS

As I mentioned in the introduction to this book, it is impossible to showcase every brand in Asia that is doing well and improving, or even hitting the global stage. The brands you have read about here have been chosen to illustrate certain elements of the branding process. From these cases we can determine some lessons for branding in Asia.

THE LESSONS TO BE LEARNT

As with any study of any business activities, there are lessons we can learn from history, even recent history. The following are key points that the brands featured in this book have brought to light.

1. Anything can be branded. It doesn't matter whether you are branding a business-to-consumer company, a business-to-business company, a consumer or commodity product, a service organization, a destination—or anything else, for that matter. The principles of branding still apply
2. Although innovation is absolutely a "must have" in today's world of branding, it does not, on its own, guarantee success. In fact, consumers *demand* innovation in this century, as their lifestyles are changing very rapidly. The clever brands are carrying out research and development, of course, but they are quick to seize new technologies developed by other

companies, and to utilize speed to market in product development, to gain the competitive advantage.

3. Technology is a vital component when seeking to provide
consumers with value added and innovative products. Brand
evolution is becoming faster as technology changes more
quickly. Technology also provides the means of access for a
company to cross over into many different categories and
industries. On its own, though, as with innovation, it doesn't
guarantee a great brand.

4. A brand's country of origin can be hidden to a great extent,
but not its quality. It is very clear that no company can develop
a strong brand name outside its own country without possessing
top-class quality in products and services.

   For those companies that have brand images associated
with negatives such as poor quality and country of origin, it
may be necessary to bite the bullet and change both name
and identity, as long as this is accompanied by putting right
the weaknesses that exist in people's perceptions.

5. It is also clear that many companies in Asia are speeding up
the growth process by acquiring businesses that have both
brand and international marketing experience. Organic growth
sometimes takes too long, and market dynamics push companies
into developing branded alliances, mergers, and acquisitions.
One of the issues to watch out for here is the matching of organizational cultures to ensure a successful fit, and that effort is
put into keeping existing customer bases happy.

6. There are signs of a completely different mindset about branding in Asia, as companies realize that spending large sums on
advertising, promotion, and logo design doesn't in any way
guarantee anything more than brand awareness. And brand
awareness doesn't necessarily equal or lead to brand acceptance,
preference, repeat purchase, and loyalty.

7. Asian brands are beginning to accept that a strong brand is the
focal point for corporate and business strategy, and in many
cases is the driver for these activities. Branding is now to be seen
as building an asset and an investment, as opposed to a cost.

8. In connection with the above two points, many Asian companies are now focusing on brand as a matter for organizational
change. As brand becomes the major weapon in the world of
parity, so all aspects and activities concerned with the branded

customer experience have to change, in support services as well as front-line essentials. Branding is holistic.

9. Finally, it appears that Asian brands, which have been behind in many areas of business, are rapidly catching up. To my mind the next few decades will see Asian brands dominating the global "brandscape." It is even conceivable that the heavy-weight countries of the West might have to adopt niche player strategies as the mass consumer audiences are taken from them by speedier and more cost-effective, quality counter-parts from Asia. If this scenario turns out to be true, the his-toric global business scene will be turned on its head.

INDEX